JOB ANALYSIS:
Methods and Applications

JOB ANALYSIS: Methods and Applications

Ernest J. McCormick

amacom

A Division of American Management Associations

Library of Congress Cataloging in Publication Data

McCormick, Ernest James.
  Job analysis: methods and applications.

  Includes index.
  1. Job analysis.   I. Title.
HF5549.5.J6M22   658.3'06   79-7334
ISBN 0-8144-5504-2

Second Printing

Preface

HUMAN life has always involved some type of work. In the dim ages past, and even in some parts of the world today, such work has been primarily concerned with eking out a bare, subsistence living. In primitive cultures the major concerns of people have been getting food (hunting, fishing, or simple agriculture) and providing shelter.

Somewhere along the line people started to *make* things (simple tools, utensils, and clothing), to *build* things (thatch huts, stone houses, and igloos), and even to engage in the *arts* (decorating pottery, painting the walls of caves, and creating dances). Mankind's accumulated experience, education, science, and technology have in relatively recent centuries produced the pyramids of Egypt, the cathedrals and castles of Europe, and the skyscrapers of Milan and New York; the means to move across the surface of the oceans and the land, to fly through the air, and to reach even the moon; an array of products that our ancestors simply could not have imagined, such as TV, automobiles, and telephones; and health care that includes the so-called miracle drugs, X rays, and surgery by laser beam. As the unplanned by-products of some of these accomplishments, we have also succeeded in polluting our environment and undermining our own well-being.

These developments, which have had a major impact on the nature of human work, can be viewed within either of two frames of reference. In the first place, we can consider the changes in the ways of carrying out certain types of activities that have been a part of human life for a long time. For example, many aspects of agri-

v

culture are now mechanized, cloth is now woven by machines instead of by hand, and (at least in some places in the world) medical care is under the aegis of trained physicians instead of witch doctors or the voodoo practitioners.

In the second place, we can consider the tremendous array of new products and services that have been made possible, for better or for worse, by modern technology—for example, machine tools, computers, household appliances, helicopters, pinball and slot machines, newspapers, moving pictures, and roller coasters. Such developments have of course resulted in the creation of entirely new types of jobs.

Because of the changes that have occurred, at least in the more developed countries, any current inventory of jobs would be markedly different from an inventory made a couple of centuries ago, or even at the beginning of this century.

There are two reasons for being concerned about people's jobs—that is, about the nature of their involvement in the production of the goods and services of the economy. Such human involvement should contribute to efficiency in the production of such goods and services but it must be so structured that it enhances, or at least maintains, such values as safety, health, and possibly job satisfaction. Because of the importance of both these goals, the domain of human work should be viewed as a legitimate subject for systematic study and analysis.

In the past, the study of human work has tended to be more descriptive than analytical. It has not benefited from the systematic, scientific approach that has characterized, for example, the physical and biological sciences, or even the behavioral sciences such as psychology. However, in more recent years there have been certain developments that provide for the measurement and quantification of human work. This suggests that the field is becoming more systematic and scientific. In fact, various labels have been proposed to cover the study of human work. For example, Dr. James Teller suggested the term *ergology,* from the Greek word, *erg,* a unit of measure of work energy, and the suffix *ology,* meaning *study of.* And Dr. William J. Cunningham suggested the term *ergometrics* to refer to the measurement of work.

This book deals with at least some aspects of the study of human work (or what we will call job analysis, for the sake of simplicity). In particular it covers various methods of job analysis (including both conventional methods and some of the more recently developed systematic, or structured, methods), and deals with the application of the data obtained by such methods to certain practical objectives.

I would like to express my gratitude to the many individuals and organizations whose material is referred to in this book; these sources are included in the references at the ends of the chapters. I am grateful to Prentice-Hall for permission to reprint certain portions of Chapter 15 of *Industrial Psychology* (McCormick, E.J., and Tiffin, J., Englewood Cliffs, N.J.: Prentice-Hall, 1974), which appear in Chapter 12 of this book. In particular I would like to express my appreciation to Dr. H. G. Heneman, Jr., Dr. Dale Yoder, and the Bureau of National Affairs for permission to draw freely from "Job Information; Its Development and Application," which I prepared for the *ASPA Handbook of Personnel and Industrial Relations,* edited by D. Yoder and H. G. Heneman, Jr. (Washington, D.C.: Bureau of National Affairs, Inc., 1979). Extracts from that source are scattered throughout this book.

Ernest J. McCormick

Contents

PART ONE

Prologue

1

Introduction

Jobs are primarily for the purpose of producing the goods and services of the economy. On the basis of this *raison d'être* of jobs, it has been argued that there are two related objectives in planning the involvement of people in producing such goods and services, namely, efficiency in the use of human talent and the maintenance or enhancement of certain human values (health, safety, job satisfaction, and the like).

Over the years, those responsible for the creation of jobs have undoubtedly been more concerned with the first of these objectives (functional effectiveness in getting work done) than with the second (human welfare as related to human work). In more recent years, however, we have seen evidence of much greater concern for the welfare of people in their jobs, and it is probable that such concern will increase in the future.

Because of the importance of both these objectives, human work comprises a legitimate area of systematic study and analysis in its own right; the hope is that such inquiry might produce information of practical utility in achieving these two objectives. This book deals in large part with the study of human work and with certain practical applications of the possible results of such study. In a sense, the phrase *study of human work* is more descriptive of the intended content than *job analysis* in that it is somewhat broader and more encompassing. However, because it is more commonly used and because of its semantic simplicity, *job analysis* is the term generally used in this book.

Functional Effectiveness of Work

Job analysis methods, as related to the functional effectiveness of human work, have generally been tied in with two types of functions involved in the operation of at least some organizations. One of these is the function of methods analysis as typically carried out by industrial engineers or others who are concerned with the development of work methods. For our purposes we will consider what is sometimes called *human factors engineering*, or *human factors*, as a phase of methods analysis, since human factors are generally concerned with the design of equipment, facilities, and environments in terms of human considerations. In practice, method analysts frequently are involved in this area.

The second function concerned with achieving functional effectiveness is what is commonly thought of as the personnel function, including personnel selection, training, and remuneration. A major focus of this function is matching people to jobs in terms of their abilities, skills, knowledge, and other characteristics.

Human Welfare in Work

The human welfare of people in work covers a wide range of considerations: safety; health, including protection from occupational disease; avoidance of undue physical or psychological stress; human comfort; and job satisfaction and other possible subjective values that might accrue from work. Certain of these considerations frequently are taken into account in connection with the methods analysis and personnel functions mentioned above, especially safety and health. Thus the objectives of functional efficiency and of human welfare are—and have been for some years—at least somewhat related to each other.

Perhaps the aspects of human welfare that have received most attention in recent years are job satisfaction and the quality of working life. These and related aspects of work deal with the subjective reactions of people to their working life. The current concern for such matters is probably triggered by the evidence that many people take a pretty dim view of their jobs and by the gnawing notion that people should gain some type of positive psychological satisfaction from their work (in addition to earning their daily bread).

The attitudes and other subjective reactions of people to their jobs represent an admittedly mixed bag. We have all heard individuals describe their jobs in such varied terms as necessary evils, exciting, lousy, enthralling, tough, easy, grueling, challenging, rewarding, crummy, stinking, "for the birds," dull, deadly, and satisfying. Readers probably could add a few other cogent adjectives—positive and negative, printable and unprintable—to characterize jobs they have or have had. Such characterizations are not intrinsic to the jobs to which they refer. Rather, they reflect the perceptions of people about the jobs. A job that is one person's meat may very well be another person's poison. The expression "beauty is in the eye of the beholder" applies equally well to the many descriptions people give of their jobs.

A person's perspective about any given job, or jobs, may be influenced by his or her prevailing attitude toward work in general or by his current employment status. A person who has been among the unemployed for some time may well have a different attitude toward a given (possible) job than a person actually on that job.

Clearly the optimum employment situation would be one in which each individual had a job that provided some measure of positive satisfaction for him or her. Unfortunately this possibility is not in the cards, at least at the present time. However, through occupational research efforts over a period of time it may be possible at least to narrow the gap. Such an effort requires the development of data about the characteristics of jobs that different types of people like and the redesign of jobs to incorporate those characteristics.

Although it is unlikely at the present time that all workers are getting "a kick" from their jobs, there is, at least for many persons, another positive value from employment in the labor force (aside from the income derived therefrom), and that is the opportunity to "have something to do." Although there are many who would argue with this pronouncement, it is probably still generally true that, for most people, "having something to do" is better than the alternative of continuous indolence. With time hanging heavy on their hands, some people find themselves climbing the walls.

Discussion

We need to recognize that the problems associated with human work seldom can be "solved," although in many instances they can at least be minimized. A first step in dealing with such problems is to collect and interpret relevant data, and it is in this regard that data obtained by job analysis can be useful. In some circumstances, the raw data so obtained can serve the intended purposes. In other instances, such data may serve as input into a research effort that, with appropriate statistical analyses, can produce the basis for taking appropriate action.

Organization of This Book

This book deals with job analysis methods and applications. It is organized into the following parts.

Part One: Prologue. This section presents a brief overview of the world at work.

Part Two: Job Analysis Method. Chapter 3 deals with the uses and development of job-related information. Chapters 4, 5, and 6 cover different methods of job analysis.

Part Three: Job Interrelationships and Classifications. Chapter 7 discusses the bases and methods relating to the analysis of job interrelationships and to the establishment of job classification systems. Chapter 8 includes examples of such job interrelationships and job classification systems.

Part Four: Applications of Job-Related Information. Chapters 9, 10, 11, and 12 cover vocational choice and work adjustment, establishing job requirements, job design, and job evaluation.

2

The World of Work

THE basic nature of the jobs in the labor force of any country is largely determined by the activities that need to be carried out to produce the goods and to provide the services of the economy in question. The kinds of goods and services available in an economy are influenced, in turn, by such factors as cultural patterns, the level of technology, economic considerations, and political policy. In the so-called developed countries the nature of the jobs of the labor force is different from that in the so-called developing countries. One obvious difference, of course, is the degree of the dependence upon machines versus human labor as a source of energy.

Employed Labor Force in the United States

In the economy of the United States there have been changes in the nature of the jobs in the labor force over the years, and further changes will take place in the years to come with changes in technology and cultural patterns. Before we get into a discussion of job

7

analysis methods, it would be useful to take a quick overview of the world of work in the United States, including an impression of the relatively current employed labor force, an over-the-shoulder look at changes in the employed labor force over recent decades, and some reflections about the changes expected within the near future. Such an overview can be best presented in terms of the distribution of employed workers by major industry divisions and major occupational groups. The data are taken from the *Occupational Outlook Handbook* published by the Bureau of Labor Statistics of the Department of Labor in 1978.

Employment by Major Industry Category

In 1976, employment of American workers was distributed as follows. The figures are given in percent of total workforce.

Service Producing Industries		*Goods Producing Industries*	
Government	17%	Agriculture	4%
Services	18	Mining and petroleum	1
Finance, insurance,		Contract construction	4
and real estate	5	Manufacturing	23
Wholesale retail trade	22		
Transportation and			
public utilities	5		

Manufacturing, the largest category, accounts for about 18.9 million workers.

Over the last several decades, the service producing industries have expanded while employment in the goods producing industries has remained relatively constant. This pattern is shown in Figure 2-1. It should be noted that in 1950 employment figures in the service producing and goods producing industries were about equal (around 26 million in each), whereas more recently the service producing industries employ almost twice as many people as the goods producing industries. Since employment in the goods producing industries has remained relatively stable over this time span, the service producing industries have accounted for virtually all the additional jobs that have developed during that time period. Of the service producing industries, Government has increased most (primarily at the state and local level, and especially in agencies providing education, health, sanitation, welfare, and protective services). In addition, the Services category (which includes miscellaneous industries) has experienced substantial growth, especially in the areas of health services, maintenance and repair, and advertising. The fi-

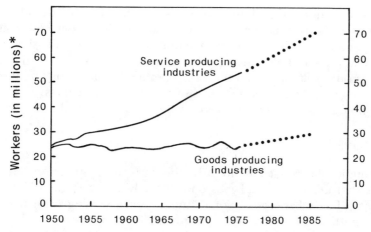

*Wage and salary workers except agriculture, which includes self-employed and family workers.

Figure 2-1. Employment in goods producing and service producing industries since 1960, with projected figures to 1985. (Source: *Occupational Outlook Handbook, p. 21*)

nance, insurance, and real estate category has also had very substantial growth.

Projected relative increases in employment are expected to be greatest in such categories as services, mining, contract construction, and finance, insurance and real estate. The relative growth in trade, manufacturing, and transportation and public utilities is expected to be limited, and agriculture is expected to decline.

Employment by Major Occupational Group

In 1976, employment by major occupational groups was as follows: The figures are in millions of workers.

Clerical workers	15.6
Operatives	13.4
Professional and technical	13.3
Craft workers	11.3
Service workers	12.0
Managers and administrators	9.3
Sales workers	5.5
Nonfarm laborers	4.3
Farm workers	2.8
Private household workers	1.1

The occupational distribution of workers over the past decades, as shown in Figure 2-2, indicates very clearly a shift from blue collar occupations to white collar occupations. The projection for the next few years is that the relative growth of the clerical group and the service group will be greatest. The operative, sales, and nonfarm laborer groups are expected to show slowest growth rates, and private household workers and farm workers are expected to decline.

Basic Job Functions

Although jobs vary tremendously, there are four operational functions that are basic to all jobs and virtually every form of human activity. These basic operational functions are sensing (information receiving), information storage, information processing and decision, and action functions. A simple diagram of the model is shown in Figure 2-3. Since information storage (our ability to remember things) interacts with all the other functions, it is shown above the others in the figure.

This model provides us with a logical framework in viewing job activities. In many typical job situations the job incumbents receive from the work environment stimuli that serve as information input to them. Such information — for example, from observing a machine in operation, the traffic on a street, or the instruments on an airplane panel, or from receiving a message over the telephone —

Figure 2-2. Employment in four major classes of occupations since 1947, with projected figures to 1985. (Source: *Occupational Outlook Handbook, p. 23)*

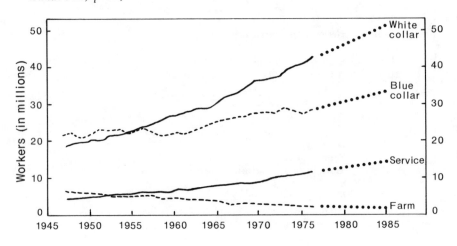

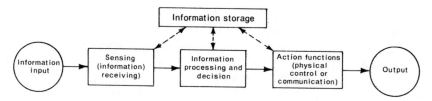

Figure 2-3. Four basic operational functions involved in all human work activities. (Source: McCormick, 1976, p. 9)

interacts with the information that is stored (that is, our memory), typically triggering some form of information processing that leads to a decision to take some type of action or make some type of response. The action may be a physical act of some type (such as putting on the door handle of an automobile on an assembly line, lifting bags from a conveyor, turning the steering wheel of a tractor, or operating a keyboard of a typewriter), or the action may be a communication act of some type (such as the instructions to aircraft from a control tower, a direct verbal response to a patron in a filling station, or a signal to a crane operator).

It should be pointed out, however, that the actions taken by people on many jobs stem from some form of mental activity on the part of the job incumbent rather than from some external stimulus. This is particularly the case with relatively unstructured jobs that involve considerable judgment and decision making, such as many management, professional, and technical jobs.

Although each of these operational functions is involved in virtually every job, the degree and nature of that involvement vary widely from job to job. In the case of highly repetitive jobs, for example—such as some machine operation or assembly-line jobs—the activities may approximate those of a conditioned response: with the presentation of a given stimulus (such as a part coming along a conveyor) the worker performs a predetermined action (such as picking it up, attaching another part to it, and placing it back on the conveyor). The information processing and decision between information input and the action functions is minimal, having been prescribed for the worker. By training he has become "programmed" to perform the same job activity every time a given stimulus (like the part on the conveyor) appears.

In some jobs the information input may be of major importance because of heavy dependence upon one or another of the sensory mechanisms (the eyes, ears, sense of touch or taste). In the navy, for example, sonar operators need to be able to detect very slight differences in sound signals. And certain types of visual inspectors need to be able to identify very minute flaws by sight.

In other types of jobs there is much greater involvement of information processing and decision, with heavy dependence on information that has been stored; such jobs may involve long periods of education, training, and/or previous experience.

In still other types of jobs there may be a premium on the use of psychomotor skills in executing physical actions that must be done very carefully (such as in engraving work), actions that are executed in exact sequence (as in key-punching), or actions that are executed with precise time control (as in playing a piano or transmitting Morse code).

Certain jobs place heavy demands upon communications as their output—oral or written as the case may be. Those involving oral communications may also require associated interpersonal skills.

We can see from the examples above that although all jobs involve the four basic operational functions in some degree, the mixture of these functions varies greatly from job to job. In turn, the various admixtures of these functions impose demands upon the incumbents of the jobs in question for corresponding abilities, skills, and knowledge. Such abilities, skills, and knowledge tend to fall into two major classes. One of these classes includes abilities which most people possess, in varying degree, such as sensory and perceptual skills, physical and psychomotor skills, various types of cognitive, or intellectual abilities, or personality characteristics. These are collectively the consequence of genetic and general environmental factors such as cultural, familial, social, and general educational exposures. The other class of abilities, skills, and knowledge includes those which tend to be job-related, that is, they are based on specialized education and training and on job-related experiences. Although these two classes of abilities, skills, and knowledge overlap each other somewhat, the distinction has some relevance as we consider the matter of job requirements.

References

McCormick, E. J. *Human Factors in Engineering and Design.* New York: McGraw-Hill, 1976.

Occupational Outlook Handbook. U.S. Department of Labor, Bureau of Labor Statistics. Washington, D.C.: U.S. Government Printing Office, 1978.

PART TWO

Job Analysis
Methods

3

The Uses
and Development
of Job-Related
Information

I N industrial and business organizations, in government organizations, in academia, in union organizations, in vocational counseling
offices, in the courts, and in private conversations one frequently
hears references that have something to do with the jobs people
perform. Such references may have direct or indirect implications
to personnel selection and training, vocational choice, com-
pensations, job design, job enlargement, jurisdictional disputes, job
satisfaction or dissatisfaction, promotions, transfer, and the like.
Such varied concerns about jobs can be viewed from the perspectives of employing organizations, of unions, of government
agencies (including courts), of individuals, and of research person-

nel. A partial listing of the possible uses of such information might include the following:

Uses by employing organizations
    Personnel recruitment
    Personnel selection and placement
    Personnel evaluation
    Job design
    Training and personnel development
    Personnel utilization
    Manpower planning
    Establishment of lines of responsibility
    Establishment of organizational relationships
    Union relationships (contract negotiations, grievances, etc.)

Uses by Unions
    Management relationships (contract negotiations, grievances, etc.)

Uses by government agencies
    Occupational standards, licensing, certification, etc.
    Equal employment opportunity matters
    Public employment service
    Public training and education programs
    Social security matters including unemployment compensation
    Working conditions, safety, etc.

Uses by individuals
    Vocational selection
    Vocational preparation

Uses for research
    Personnel and other behavioral research
    Sociological research
    Demographic (i.e., population) research
    Economic research

These and other possible uses of information relating to the involvement of people with their jobs argue for the systematic development of such information, to fulfill what might be considered to be society's legitimate needs as they crystallize. Although job-related information undoubtedly is used very extensively by many individuals and organizations, there seems to be relatively little comprehensive data on the extent to which it is used, by whom, and for what purpose.

The results of one survey, however, do reflect something about the uses of such data by private organizations. Such data come from a survey about jobs carried out by the Bureau of Business Research, California State College, Long Beach (Jones and DeCoths; *Summary of National Job Analysis Methods*). Questionnaires dealing with job analysis practices were sent to 1,805 firms. Of the 899 questionnaires returned (about half of those sent out), 76 percent indicated that the firms had job analysis programs. Of those with job analysis programs, 37 percent had such programs only for salaried personnel, 6 percent only for personnel on hourly rated jobs, and 57 percent for both. The uses of the job analysis information reported by the organizations with job analysis programs are given in Table 3-1. The major categories of use (in descending order of frequency) were as follows: job evaluation (including setting wage and salary levels); recruitment and placement; labor relations; manpower utilization; and training. (Note that the categories given in this table parallel somewhat those listed above for employing organizations, but in some instances are further subdivided. They do not include all of those listed above, and in some instances they are worded differently).

The development of job-related information (usually referred to as *job analysis*) typically involves a two-stage process. The first stage is to elicit the information from a source, for example by observing and interviewing a job incumbent or by having the worker report such information himself. The second stage is to organize and present the information thus obtained in the desired format. In the case of conventional job analysis procedures this format usually is a conventional job description. In the case of certain methods the format may consist of a computer output.

Terminology in Work Study

Terminology in the field of work study is far from precise and definitive, since certain terms have been used to convey various shades of meaning. Melching and Borcher, referring to the use of job analysis in curriculum development, express this state of confusion as follows: "While job analysis experts employ concepts such as task, function, responsibility, duty, etc. as though the distinctions among them were both obvious and fixed, this is simply not true. The curriculum designer should be warned that any attempt by him to place these terms into a reliable hierarchy may not turn out to be very rewarding."

TABLE 3–1. Frequency with which organizations with job analysis programs report various uses of job analysis results. (Source: *Summary of National Job Analysis Methods Survey*)

	Salaried n=638	Hourly n=430
Job evaluation	98	95
Setting wage and salary levels	92	88
Appraising personnel	59	44
Establishing incentives	11	14
Determining profit sharing	6	2
Other	2	1
Recruiting and placing	95	93
Making job specifications	74	75
Promoting, transferring and rotating	72	67
Constructing tests	14	18
Indicating sources of employees	18	16
Counseling (vocational)	25	26
Matching men with jobs	65	61
Placing the handicapped	17	25
Structuring jobs	58	54
Diluting jobs	19	19
Enriching jobs	26	25
Other	3	4
Conducting labor and personnel relations	83	79
Developing performance standards	48	42
Establishing responsibility	70	56
Establishing authority	64	44
Establishing accountability	66	46
Handling grievances	17	44
Conducting labor negotiations	8	34
Establishing channels of communication	32	24
Organizing personnel records	35	36
Other	1	1
Utilizing workers	72	67
Organizing and planning	56	47
Engineering jobs	17	16
Controlling costs	22	29
Controlling quality	14	16
Predicting changes	13	11
Avoiding excess task duplication	45	40
Other	1	1
Training	61	63
Developing courses	33	36
Selecting trainees	34	34
Orienting employees	36	36
Programming teaching machines	2	2
Other	1	1

Some Definitions

Recognizing these risks, we will nonetheless define a few terms, drawing in part from Melching and Borcher and the *Handbook for Analyzing Jobs* (issued by the United States Employment Service [USES]).

Occupation. The term *occupation* usually refers to jobs of a general class, on an across-the-board basis, without regard to organizational lines. Thus, one can refer to the occupation of accountant, machinist, or tightrope walker wherever people engage in these activities.

Job. A *job* is a group of positions which are identical with respect to their major or significant tasks and sufficiently alike to justify their being covered by a single analysis. There may be one or many persons employed in the same job.

Position. A *position* consists of the tasks and duties for any individual. A position exists, whether occupied or vacant.

Duty. The term *duty* is usually used rather loosely to refer to a large segment of work performed by an individual. It typically represents one of the distinct major activities involved in the work performed, and consists of several tasks that are or may be related. Some examples of duties are maintaining and repairing automatic transmissions, supervising data systems analysis and design, and performing mailroom activities.

Task. A *task* is usually considered to be a discrete unit of work performed by an individual. It usually comprises a logical and necessary step in the performance of a duty, and typically has an identifiable beginning and ending. Some sample tasks (Melching and Borcher) are: "solder minor leaks in radiator; type minutes of reports of meetings; replace brake and hose lines." Most typically a task statement consists of two basic elements, a specific action verb, and a brief indication of what is acted upon, such as: compute product moment correlation on a desk calculator. A task is more readily identified in the case of work activities that involve some specific physical activity than in the case of activities that are more mental in nature. (In mental tasks it is more difficult to identify the beginning and the ending of the activity, and, for that matter, the nature of whatever mental activity has actually taken place, without some overt indication by the individual in question.)

Element. The term *element* is sometimes considered to be the smallest step into which it is practical to subdivide any work activity without analyzing the separate motions, movements, and mental processes involved. However, this term (or its elaboration, *job ele-ment*) is used to refer to other types of job components as well, such as elemental motions, tasks, and even broader levels of work activity or behavior.

Elemental motion. An *elemental motion* (sometimes called an *element*) consists of very specific separate motions, or movements, as used in methods analysis procedures in the field of industrial engineering. Examples are "transport empty" (moving the hand from one place to another without transporting anything), and "position" (positioning a body member in a particular location).

Job description. *Job descriptions* typically consist of descriptions of the work activities that are performed in a job. They usually also include information about other job-related aspects such as working conditions and tools and equipment used. The descriptions can be very detailed or very brief. An *occupational description* is one which characterizes an occupation as the occupation typically is performed by incumbents.

Job specification. A *job specification* sets forth the personnel requirements or personal qualifications that are specified for those who might be candidates for the job in question. Depending on the job, a job specification might include statements of educational or work-experience requirements, skills required, age, sex, physical characteristics, vision, and other personal characteristics, and in some instances test-score standards that should be met by candidates.

Job analysis. *Job analysis* is the process of obtaining information about jobs. Although this is usually done by a job analyst who observes and interviews a job incumbent to elicit the desired information, there are other procedures as well that can be thought of as some form of job analysis.

Ergometrics. *Ergometrics* is a term that has been coined by J. W. Cunningham and defined by him as the application of psychometric principles and procedures to the study of human work. (The word is derived from the Greek word *ergon* meaning "work," and the *metrics* portion refers to the concept of measurement.) This field of investigation would draw from theories and principles of human behavior, as well as from established procedures in psychological measurement and job analysis. As characterized by Cunningham it would deal with the following four kinds of problems: (1) the definition, quantification, and classification of work variables; (2) the establishment of relationships between work variables and existing measures of human attributes (e.g., aptitude tests); (3) the development of measures of work-related human attributes or behavior potentials (such as vocational ability tests and interest scales); and (4) the study of the nature of the relationships among various work-related variables.

Aspects of Work Study Processes

The purpose or purposes of any work study program should be to serve as the basis for making decisions about specific aspects of the program. In making such decisions one should start with consideration of the type of information and format desired as an end product, and then plan the initial analysis procedures to insure the achievement of this objective. In planning the initial data collection stage, there are at least four aspects (adapted from McCormick) on which some determinations need to be made:

1. What *type* of information is to be obtained?
2. In what *form* is the information to be obtained (and usually presented)?
3. What *method* of analysis will be used?
4. What *agent* will be used? (Usually the "agent" is an individual, such as a job analyst, a supervisor, or the job incumbent himself; in special circumstances it may be a device such as a camera).

Each of these will be discussed separately, with reference to at least some of the alternatives of each.

Types of Job-Related Information

Following are some of the types of information that can be elicited by job analysis or work study procedures.

Work activities
   Job-oriented activities (description of the work activities performed, expressed in "job" terms, usually indicating what is accomplished such as painting, cleaning, cutting, etc.; sometimes such activity descriptions also indicate how, why, and when a worker performs an activity; usually the activities are those involving active human participation, but in certain approaches they may characterize machine or system functions)

Work activities/processes
  Procedures used
  Activity records (films, etc.)
  Personal accountability/responsibility
Worker-oriented activities
  Human behaviors (behaviors performed in work, such as sensing, decision making, performing physical actions, communicating, etc.)
  Elemental motions (such as used in methods analysis)
  Personal job demands (human expenditures involved in work, such as energy expenditure, etc.)

Machine, tools, equipment, and work aids (tangibles and intangibles)
  Materials processed
  Products made
  Knowledge dealt with or applied (such as law or chemistry)
  Services rendered (such as laundering or repairing)

Work performance
  Work measurement (i.e., time taken)
  Work standards
  Error analysis
  Other aspects

Job context
  Physical working conditions
  Work schedule
  Organizational context
  Social context
  Incentives (financial and non-financial)

Personnel requirements
  Job-related knowledge/skills (education, training, work experience, etc. required)
  Personal attributes (aptitudes, physical characteristics, personality, interests, etc. required)

Form of Job-Related Information

The "form" of job-related information refers to whether it is stated in qualitative or quantitative terms, or in terms that are partially qualitative and partially quantitative. Qualitative information is characterized by verbal, narrative descriptions of such aspects of jobs as their content, working conditions, social context, and personnel requirements. In turn, quantitative information typically is expressed in terms of "units" of information such as: job tasks; specific kinds of worker behavior such as using keyboard devices, coding, handling materials, and interviewing; production per unit of time; number of errors made; size of work group; heart rate during work; aptitude test standards; and ratings of job characteristics.

Method of Collection of Job-Related Information

The various methods of collecting job-related information are discussed below.

Observation. An observer (that is, a job analyst) observes the work activities of a job incumbent.

Individual interview. The job incumbent is interviewed by someone who is serving as a job analyst, usually at some location away from the job site. The interview usually is fairly structured. In some instances two or more incumbents of the same job may be interviewed, and the results consolidated into one job description.

Observation-interview. This is essentially a combination of the first two methods, although the "interview" aspect frequently is carried out at the work location.

Group interview. This method is similar to the individual interview except that two or more incumbents of the same job are interviewed by the job analyst at the same time. Under the guidance of the job analyst the job incumbents describe and discuss their various work activities. The job analyst then combines the information received from the various job incumbents into a single job description.

Technical conference. This method involves a few experts on the job in question, such as supervisors, trainers, or job incumbents with extensive experience. Under the direction of a job analyst they collaborate to provide information which forms the basis for a job description, prepared by the job analyst, that reflects their consensus.

Structured questionnaire. This method is based on the development and use of a questionnaire which consists of a listing (and sometimes a description) of various job-related items of information about the jobs of the individuals who are to use the questionnaire. The items typically include individual work activities (such as tasks), working conditions, etc. The respondents are usually job incumbents, but sometimes other persons (such as supervisors) are asked to complete the questionnaire as they relate to (other) job incumbents. Various types of responses may be provided for, such as whether the item does or does not apply to the job, time involved, judged relevance, and amount of supervision received.

Open-ended questionnaire. This type of questionnaire provides for job incumbents (or supervisors or others) to describe jobs in their own words, or to list the job activities involved in the job.

Diary. A diary is a record kept by individual job incumbents of their work activities over a period of one or more days. Diaries usually are unstructured, that is, the incumbent writes down what he does in his own words. In some instances diaries consist of prepared listings of work activities. The incumbent usually records the time spent on each activity. The entries should be made throughout the day as the incumbent changes from one activity to another, although sometimes they are completed at the end of each day's work. The entries made throughout the day are usually more accurate since they are not as dependent upon recall.

Critical incidents. Using this method an observer (typically the supervisor) records statements about those job behaviors of job incumbents which are considered to represent exceptionally "good" or "poor" job behavior. These statements are entered in record books at the time of observation or afterwards from recall. This method is actually more of a record of job performance of individuals than it is a method of job analysis. It does, however, help to identify what the critical aspects of individual jobs are.

Equipment design information. In the development of some items of equipment or systems to be used later by job incumbents, information from blueprints or other design data is used as the basis for inferring what work activities will ultimately be involved in the jobs which will be created when the equipment or system is actually produced. This method is used especially in human factors engineering processes for the dual purpose of identifying in advance any design features which are undesirable from the human factors point of view (and which should therefore be modified), and of planning selection and training of personnel who will ultimately use the equipment or system.

Recordings of job activities. Films and various mechanical recording devices are occasionally used as recordings of job activities.

Records. Occasionally various sets of records provide the basis for eliciting certain types of information that is job-related. Perhaps the best examples are equipment-maintenance records, which reflect the frequency with which various maintenance activities are performed.

Discussion of methods. Most individual methods have some special advantages in terms of the type, form, or adequacy of the information that can be elicited, the "agents" with which they can be used, or economy of time. Conversely, most methods also have certain constraints or limitations in terms of these or other considerations. Some of the advantages and disadvantages of certain methods will be touched on in subsequent discussions.

Agent Used in Collecting Job-Related Information

In most instances the *agent* is an individual, but in some circumstances a device of some sort is used. Possible agents include:

Individuals
   Job analyst
   Supervisor
   Incumbent
Devices
   Cameras
   Physiological recording devices
   "Force" platforms (for recording physical movements in three
      dimensions)
   Other devices

Discussion

One could contemplate other aspects of job information that might be added to the list above, such as, for example, the level of specificity of the information. (Work activity data, for example, can be characterized in terms of very minute detail such as elemental motions, or at a very gross level.)

Moreover, we can envision many combinations of the four aspects described above. For example, in the most common case, *job-oriented work activities* (type of information) may be recorded as *essay descriptions* (qualitative form), on the basis of *interview and observation* (method), by an *analyst* (agent). Needless to say, certain combinations are manifestly impossible; for example, an incumbent, as the agent, obviously cannot use the observation method on himself.

Air Force Study of Comparison of Job Analysis Methods

There have been very few systematic studies in which different methods of job analysis have been compared. The only such study of any consequence was one carried out some years ago in the United States Air Force by Rupe and his associates.

Methods Used in Study

The Air Force study consisted of a comparison of the effectiveness of five methods of developing conventional job descriptions. These methods are listed below:

Group interview
Individual interview
Observation interview
Technical conference
Questionnaire survey

These methods were described briefly above. However, a special note should be added about the questionnaire-survey method as used in this Air Force study. The questionnaire form used provided for the incumbents to report the same kinds of job information and the same amount of detail as provided for in the other four methods in which a job analyst was involved. The questionnaires were mailed to different Air Force bases with the request that one incumbent who performed all parts of each job in question and who was representative of the "average" journeyman skill level be assigned to complete the form for the job. He was permitted to obtain assistance and verification of his completed job schedule from his supervisor if he wished, but was not required to do so.

General Plan of the Study

Only the major features of this study and certain of the major results will be summarized here. In very general terms, analyses of 12 job types were carried out using the first four methods. In the case of the first three methods (the group interview, individual interview, and observation interview), the positions of three different incumbents at each base were analyzed and a single job schedule was prepared as if only one incumbent performed all the duties and tasks reported. In the case of the technical conference method, the three "expert" individuals of each base served as the committee with the analyst in accomplishing a single composite analysis of the job. In the case of the questionnaire-survey method the questionnaires were completed by incumbents themselves, as indicated above.

Since analysts were used in the first four methods, but not in the questionnaire-survey method, the primary analyses dealt with the first four methods. In the plans for the study with the first four methods, the 12 job types were divided into three groups of four jobs each. In the analysis of the jobs within each of the three groups, plans were made to analyze the jobs in such a manner as to randomize the possible influence of the individual analysts, of the Air Force bases, and of any possible training or practice effects on the part of the analysts. Thus, at each of four bases, an analyst analyzed each of the four jobs in the group by a different method, but the sequence in which he analyzed the jobs at the four bases was different. For any block of four jobs, 16 bases were used. No single base was visited by more than one analyst working on the same block of jobs.

Since the questionnaire-survey method involved no job analysts, it was not necessary to plan on such "controls" in the analysis process. For each of the 12 jobs, 10 Air Force bases were asked to arrange for one job incumbent to prepare a job schedule for his job.

Criteria Used

Three types of criteria were used in evaluating the five job analysis methods: (1) the number of job elements or "work performed" reported on the job schedules; (2) the discrete tools, equipment, and materials reported; and (3) time in man-hours involved in the analysis process. The second of these (tools, equipment, and materials) was found not to differentiate very much between the different methods and will not be discussed here.

Work performed criterion. The work performed criterion for any given job type was based on a listing of all the job elements (what we would consider tasks) included in any job analysis schedule prepared for a particular job by any method. (The investigators, with the aid of the analysts and the technical experts who worked on each job, developed each such list, initially working independently and then developing what was called a *trial criterion checklist* by committee agreement.)

The checklist for any given job, in turn, was reviewed by anywhere from 43 to 83 experts at from 10 to 16 Air Force bases to make a determination as to whether the individual job elements on the checklist were or were not performed by airmen in the job type on their bases. The percentage of experts who responded *yes* to each job element on the checklist was then computed. These percentages were then divided into 11 class intervals (0-4.9, 5-14.9, 15-24.9 . . . to 95-100), and these class intervals were then assigned weights ranging from zero through 10. The job elements in the trial criterion checklist, after being assigned these weights, comprised what was termed the *final criterion list*. In effect, the weight for any job element reflected the judged frequency of occurrence of the element at various air bases.

Each job schedule for a given job, as analyzed by any method, was then scored on the basis of the sum of the weights assigned to the job elements which were identified as being included in the schedule. The raw score for any job schedule was converted to a percentage of the total maximum criterion score that was theoretically possible. This maximum applied only if a job schedule included reference to each and every job element on the list. One would expect that because the job as actually performed by any given individual (or, in the case of a consolidated description, by any one of three individuals) would normally include only some, not most, of the job elements of any given job type. The percentage score for a particular job schedule usually would be relatively low; failure to include reference to job elements that actually are performed also would cause scores to be lower than they should be. In any event, the percentage score for a job schedule is a reflection of the relative amount of job information represented by the schedule, and thus provides a quantitative basis for comparing the amount of job information elicited by the various job analysis methods.

Man-hours of time. The man-hours of time involved in the preparation of each job schedule was recorded, including the time of the analyst, the incumbent, and the supervisor.

Results

The primary results relating to the work performed as reported on the schedules are summarized in Table 3-2. The table shows the mean percentage scores of individual job analysis schedules prepared by the various methods and the means of random combinations of four schedules (with common, or overlapping, job elements counted only once). Actually, combinations of various numbers of schedules were studied for combinations of two and three job schedules, as well as for four, but those for two or three reflected less consistent increases in the mean scores of single schedules as contrasted with combinations of four. In other aspects of the study, job schedules prepared by different methods were also combined, with the result that certain methods seemed to reveal more "unique" job elements than others. For each job, the combinations of methods were examined for two, three, or four methods, and

TABLE 3–2. Mean percentage scores of individual job analyses of combinations of four schedules produced by five methods of job analysis for 12 jobs. (Source: Rupe)

	Mean Percentage Score	
Method	*Individual Schedules*	*Combination of Four Schedules*
A Group interview	10.0	28.8
B Individual interview	16.1	45.8
C Observation interview	15.1	43.8
D Technical conference	14.9	44.2
Q Questionnaire-survey	05.5	

the highest and lowest means for any combinations of methods were derived.

Considering all 12 jobs, the highest and lowest means were as follows:

	Means Across 12 Jobs	
Number of Methods Combined	*Highest*	*Lowest*
2	70.3	49.6
3	90.1	71.4
4	97.3	87.0

The results of the analysis of man-hours of time required are given in Table 3-3.

Discussion

The conclusions reported by Rupe include the following (in somewhat modified form):

1. The individual interview is the most effective and most dependable because it is likely to yield scores above the means of the five methods. The cost in man-hours is about the average for the methods used.

2. The technical conference and observation interview are practically equal in producing information on work performed, but the technical conference is the most expensive in terms of man-hours and the observation interview is next most expensive.

3. The group interview and questionnaire-survey methods were generally the least satisfactory methods in reporting work activities. Although the mean scores derived by one group interview method tended to be somewhat higher than those derived by the questionnaire-survey method, the group interview was not as effective in

TABLE 3–3. Man-hour costs of five job analysis methods used in the analysis of 12 jobs. (Source: Rupe)

	Method	*Mean Time per Schedule*			
		Analyst	*Incumbent*	*Supervisor*	*Total*
A	Group interview	15:30	9:30	0:20	25:20
B	Individual interview	21:00	9:00	0:27	30:27
C	Observation interview	23:15	10:00	0:28	33:43
D	Technical conference	23:00	20:15	0:19	43:44
Q	Questionnaire-survey	0:00	5:00	0:20	5:20

producing "unique" items, and it was considered to be the least effective of all five methods. On the other hand, the questionnaire-survey method was less "dependable" since sometimes it yielded scores that were well above mean scores of the other methods, and just as frequently it yielded scores below. In terms of man-hour costs, the group interview method was the least costly of the four methods that involved job analysts, but the questionnaire-survey (which did not involve job analysts) was clearly the least costly in man-hours.

It is clear from Table 3-2 that combining job schedules derived from any given method increases the total amount of information obtained rather dramatically. This was also true when schedules derived from different methods were combined. However, it should be kept in mind that combining information from various job schedules (and those obtained by different methods) in part simply represents the consolidation of information about individual positions which may vary considerably in their individual assortments of job activities. Thus, the more schedules that are consolidated, the better the total pool of schedules would represent the total gamut of work activities carried out collectively by all the incumbents in the job type in question.

Aside from the implications discussed above, this study has made an additional important contribution through its focus on the use of checklists of job activities. Although the checklists were used primarily as the bases for deriving criterion scores, their use in this study probably was the primary basis for the subsequent development and use by the Air Force of task inventories as its major job analysis procedure. Task inventories, discussed further in Chapter 6, represent a significant stage in the development and use of job analysis methodologies.

Preparation for a Job Analysis Program

The ultimate success of a job analysis program in an organization depends in large part on the care that goes into the planning and preparation for the program. A few salient aspects of this phase will be discussed briefly.

Crystallizing the Program Objectives

A job analysis program should be considered by an organization only if there is some recognized need for the program. Although this recognized need might relate to one of the several possible objectives or uses of job-related information, the organization should carefully consider other possible legitimate uses of such data, and then set forth the specific objectives that it wishes to achieve with the program. It should be recognized, however, that although the information obtained from a given program might well serve several different purposes, there are limits to the purposes that can reasonably be fulfilled with any given program.

Developing Job Analysis Materials

Once the objectives of a job analysis program have been crystallized, the next stage is to develop the various materials that will be required. Paramount in this stage is the development of the job analysis format to be used and of the instructions to be followed in the actual analysis of jobs and in the preparation of final job descriptions, computer print-outs, or other end products. The job analysis format and instructions should provide for the collection of the *type* of information required to achieve the stated objectives, the *format* in which such information is to be obtained (and later presented), the *method* of analysis, and the *agents* (the individuals — or devices — to be used in the data collection phase).

In the case of a conventional job analysis program, the job analysis format would consist basically of a form that provides for the desired information. This form usually is used both for recording notes by the analyst and for preparing a final job description. (In the next chapter the format used by the United States Employment Service will be presented and discussed.) In the case of a structured job analysis procedure, appropriate questionnaires need to be selected or developed. (Some examples are given in Chapter 6.)

Instructions need to be prepared for all persons who will need them, such as for job analysts and for job incumbents (if the incumbents are to be asked to complete any questionnaires). The instructions should be as simple and straightforward as possible, and preferably they should be pretested with a sample of people before they are prepared in the final form.

Selecting and Training Analysts

When analysts are to be used, care should be taken in their selection. Generally, they should be persons with analytical ability, writing skill, and personal qualities that are useful in interviewing and dealing with others. Whenever possible the analysts should have some familiarity with the jobs that are to be analyzed. If the analysts are not already familiar with the jobs, one aspect of the training program should consist of reading relevant background material about the industry in question, the processes with which the jobs are involved, and the organizational structure in which the jobs exist.

The analysts should be trained in the job analysis procedures that are to be followed, and preferably they should do a few practice job analyses if they have never done any before.

Preparing Advance Information about the Program

When a job analysis program is to be inaugurated, there should be appropriate communications to all persons who will in one way or another be involved, such as department heads, supervisors, and job incumbents. It is usually good practice for management to prepare a letter or some other form of announcement that assures all interested persons of management support of the program.

When a job analyst is to analyze the jobs in a particular unit of the organization, arrangement should of course be made through the chain of command for conducting the analysis. Whoever makes such arrangements (the job analyst or anyone else) should make clear to the various officials (department heads, supervisors, etc.) the reasons for the analysis, and should indicate what will be involved, including the time required on the part of the job incumbents. In turn, the supervisor of the job incumbents should advise the incumbents themselves of the analyses, and should schedule the analyses at such times as are mutually convenient with the incumbents, the job analyst, and the work activities of the unit. Thus, the way should be completely paved for the job analyst, in order to allay any qualms on the part of the incumbents.

Observation and Interview in Job Analysis

Various job analysis methods involve the observation of incumbents performing their jobs, and/or the conduct of interviews with job incumbents, with their supervisors, or with others who are knowledgeable about the job in question. The interviews usually are with individuals, but variations of conventional interview techniques are also used with certain job analysis methods, for example in the group interview and technical conference, and sometimes interviews are used in obtaining data for developing structured questionnaires. The observation and interview processes adopted should elicit the particular type of information that is sought, but there are a couple of basic requirements that are common to observation and interview procedures as related to job analysis. One of these requirements concerns the reliability and validity of the information being elicited, and the other concerns the interviewing techniques that are used.

Reliability and Validity of Observation and Interview Data

Reliability of job-related data for any given job or jobs generally refers to the extent to which there is consistency in the information elicited by different analysts, or by the same analyst at different times.

When job-related data can be quantified in some fashion, the reliability of such data usually can be expressed as a coefficient of correlation. A correlation is a statistical index of the degree of relationship between two variables. It ranges from +1.00 (a perfect relationship) through intermediate values to .00 (which reflects no relationship at all) through intermediate negative values (showing varying degrees of negative relationships) to −1.00 (a perfect negative relationship.) Reliability correlations based on independent analyses of individual units of job information tend to vary quite a bit, with an average of about .70 (Morsh, 1964). With pooled data based on analyses from several analysts, reliability correlations sometimes may be .80 or higher. When job-related data cannot be quantified, the reliability (between two different analysts) admittedly has to be based on a subjective assessment rather than on statistical data.

The concept of validity refers to the essential correctness of the information obtained — that is, the extent to which the job-related data collected adequately represent the reality of the job. It should, of course, be the objective of the individual(s) who elicit job information by observation or interview to provide as reliable and valid job information as possible.

In these processes objectivity should be uppermost in the minds of those responsible for job analysis processes. As pointed out by Kuriloff et al. (1975), however, no hard line can be drawn between subjective and objective data. And some job-related data are predicated on some subjectivity on the part of the analyst in the observation and interview processes. Data obtained from two or more independent analyses may provide some inklings about the reliability of the basic data. It is sometimes difficult, or at least impractical, however, to determine the validity of job-related data, since such a determination would require some separate independent criterion against which to compare the data obtained by observation and/or interview. Since such criteria are difficult or impossible to obtain, it is usually necessary to infer the validity of such data from evidence of their reliability as based on results from two or more independent analysts.

In discussing reliability and validity, a side comment should be added regarding those circumstances in which subjective opinions, preferences, or judgments are to be obtained about jobs. For example, in some surveys respondents are asked to indicate their preferences for different jobs or job activities. Since people obviously can differ in such preferences, data on the reliability of such preferences can only be obtained by asking the same respondents a second time (what is sometimes referred to as test-retest reliability). The validity of such responses normally would have to be inferred from the reliability of their responses. For a discussion of reliability and validity as related to structured job analysis data, see Chapter 6.

Interviewing in Job Analysis Processes

Since interviewing is an integral part of various methods of job analysis, the individuals who serve as analysts need to develop interviewing skills which will enable them to get the most out of each interview.* Interviews are conversations aimed at obtaining or exchanging information. Although normally the interview involves an interviewer or an interviewee (or respondent), in some instances more persons may be involved in either or both roles.

---

*This discussion of the interview is based in part on material from Kuriloff et al. (1975) and from the *Handbook for Analyzing Jobs*.

The degree of structure in interviews can vary from unstructured interviews, to semistructured, to structured. In job analysis processes, semistructured interviews usually are most appropriate, especially if the interviewer uses a job schedule which provides for eliciting information on each of several aspects of a job. Such a schedule typically consists of a previously prepared list of questions or items about which information is to be obtained. The job schedule provides a basic structure around which the interview can be carried out, but the interviewer should adapt his interview approach to the circumstance, in particular to the interviewee and to the nature of the job about which information is being elicited.

Preparing for the interview. Kuriloff et al. make the point that the preparation for an interview should include three basic stages, namely, setting objectives, organizing the approach, and planning the methods to be used. Although the primary focus is on developing information for task inventories, these basic stages generally would be applicable in other job analysis contexts. The objectives affect the nature of the job analysis information to be obtained. For example, is the analyst obtaining data for a task inventory, or is he interviewing incumbents to obtain information about their jobs to use in a structured questionnaire of some sort? In obtaining data for a conventional job analysis, should he conduct a group interview, or should he develop further information about data to be entered on work diaries?

Deciding on the approach frequently involves carrying out some preliminary study of information gathered to provide the analyst with some background about the job in question. Such information sometimes can be picked up from training and instruction manuals, previous analyses of the job, organizational charts, or brief discussions with experts or supervisors. The analyst must also make decisions about whom to interview and how to schedule the times and places of interviews. When several or many jobs are to be analyzed, the scheduling should provide for coverage of all the jobs in question.

In planning the methods to be used, the analyst must also determine how the information should be recorded — for example, by manual note taking during the interview, by tape recorder for later transcription, or by recording the data from memory immediately after the interview.

Principles of good interviewing. There are three basic principles of good interviewing practices. First, the initiative should always be with the interviewer. However, the interviewer, although maintaining control of the interview, should not overpower the interviewee or cause the interviewee to become defensive. Second, the interviewer's manner and attitude should reflect sincere and genuine interest in the interviewee, in order to establish rapport. And third, the interviewer should guide and direct the interview toward obtaining the desired information but should not be overbearing.

Developing interviewing skills. Skill in interviewing is based in large part on asking the right questions at the right time in the right words. But in addition to asking the right questions, the interviewer must develop the ability to listen actively to the responses from the interviewee, that is, he should be sufficiently sensitive to understand what is being said and to be able to recall the important points to be recorded. Kuriloff et al. suggest that questions used by interviewers may be checked for their appropriateness against the following criteria:

☐ The question should be related to the purpose of the analysis.
☐ The wording should be clear and unambiguous.
☐ The question should not "lead" the respondent; that is, it should not imply that a specific answer is desired.
☐ The question should not be "loaded" in the sense that one form of response might be considered to be more socially desirable than another.
☐ The question should not ask for knowledge or information the interviewee doesn't have.
☐ There should be no personal or intimate material that the interviewee might resent.

Being a good listener. As indicated above, the interviewer should develop the skill of listening actively. The form of questions asked should encourage the interviewee to do most of the talking. Lack of clarity may be based on the interviewee's lack of understanding of the question, or on his use of language that is not familiar to the interviewer, or on lack of ability to express himself. In any event, the interviewer should probe further (with simple, diplomatic questions) until the point is clarified.

Kuriloff et al. suggest that while listening to the respondent the interviewer can engage in any of four mental activities, as follows:

☐ The listener thinks ahead of the speaker, trying to anticipate what the discourse is leading to and what conclusions will be drawn from the words spoken at the moment.

□ The listener weighs the evidence used by the speaker to support the points being made, asking mentally, "Is this point valid? Is the evidence complete?"

□ Throughout the conversation, the listener "listens between the lines" for meaning that is not necessarily spoken.

□ The listener pays close attention to nonverbal signs [such] as facial expressions, gestures, tone of voice, and emphasis to see if the meaning has been altered in any way.

General Guidelines in Job Analysis Interviewing

Although there are no simple cookbook rules for conducting good interviews, the general guidelines given below may be helpful to persons who will be serving as job analysts.*

PREPARING FOR THE INTERVIEW

1. Build the interviewee's interest in advance through well-prepared announcements, and be sure that each interviewee is advised in advance by his supervisor of the arrangements for the interview.
2. Select proper accommodations that ensure privacy for the interview.
3. Avoid or minimize the use of status symbols that earmark the interviewer as having a higher "status" than the interviewee.

OPENING THE INTERVIEW

1. Put the worker at ease by being at ease yourself. Learn his name in advance, introduce yourself, and discuss general and pleasant topics until you have established rapport.
2. Make the purpose of the interview clear. Explain why it was scheduled, what should be accomplished, and how the worker's cooperation can help produce the occupational analysis tools used for placement and counseling.
3. Encourage the worker to talk. Always be courteous and show a sincere interest in what he says.
4. Relate the interview to goals the worker holds important.

---

*Many of these suggestions are drawn from Kuriloff et al. (1975) and the *Handbook for Analyzing Jobs*. Certain portions of this material originally appeared in the *ASPA Handbook of Personnel and Industrial Relations*.

STEERING THE INTERVIEW

1. Help the worker to think and talk about topics according to the logical sequence of the duties performed. If duties are not performed in a regular order, have the worker describe the most important activity first, the second most important one next, and so forth. Also discuss the infrequent duties of the job, ones that are not part of the regular activities, such as the occasional setup of a machine, occasional repairs, or infrequent reports. (However, infrequently performed duties would not include periodic or emergency activities such as an annual inventory or the emergency unloading of a freight car.)

2. Keep the conversation alive during unscheduled portions of the interview by using probing techniques such as expectant pauses, brief assenting comments, unobtrusive neutral questions, or by summarizing what the respondent just said or repeating a question.

3. Allow the worker enough time to formulate and verbalize an answer to each question. He should be asked only one question at a time.

4. Phrase questions so that the answers will be more than simply "yes" or "no."

5. Avoid leading questions.

6. Use simple, easily understood language.

7. Show honest personal interest in the interviewee.

8. Do not be aloof, condescending, or authoritative.

9. Keep a steady, consistent pace.

10. Secure specific and complete information pertaining to all of the types of information required for a complete analysis of a job.

11. Consider the relationship of the job under analysis to other jobs in the department.

12. Control the interview with respect to the economic use of time and adherence to subject matter. For example, when the interviewee strays from the subject, a good technique for bringing him back to the point is to summarize the data collected up to that point.

13. The interview should be conducted patiently and with consideration for any nervousness or lack of ease on the part of the worker.

CLOSING THE INTERVIEW

1. Indicate that you are approaching the end of the interview by the kinds of questions you ask and by the inflection of your voice.
2. If relevant, summarize the worker's statements, indicating his major duties and the details concerning each of the duties.
3. Conclude by explaining the value of the information the respondent has given.
4. Close the interview on a friendly note.

MISCELLANEOUS DO'S AND DON'TS FOR INTERVIEWERS

1. Don't take issue with the worker's statements.
2. Don't take sides on issues concerning employer-employee grievances or conflicts.
3. Don't show any interest in the wage classification of the job.
4. Be polite and courteous throughout the interview.
5. Don't "talk down" to the worker.
6. Don't be influenced by your personal likes and dislikes.
7. Be impersonal. Don't criticize or suggest any changes or improvements in organization or methods of work.
8. Talk to the worker only with permission of his supervisor.
9. Verify job data, especially technical or trade terminology, with foreman or department head.
10. Verify completed analysis with proper official.

As he observes and interviews the worker, the analyst should make notes in as unobtrusive a manner as possible. Here are some specific suggestions for effective note taking:

1. Notes should be complete, legible, and should contain data necessary to prepare the job analysis schedule.
2. Notes should be organized according to the job tasks and the categories of information required for a complete analysis.
3. Notes should include only the facts about the job that emphasize the work performed and worker traits involved.

Following the observation and interview with the worker the analyst usually interviews the supervisor to obtain additional information on such topics as experience, training, and relationships to other jobs, and to clarify any points on which he is in doubt.

Job Analysis Writing

The end product of certain job analysis processes consists of some form of written material. The objective of the analyst in writing such material should be to convey the intended meaning in as reliable and valid a fashion as possible, consistent with the intended nature of the job analysis method in question. Some of the differences in the nature of job analysis material that are characteristic of different methods will be discussed and illustrated in later chapters. For our purposes here, however, we will touch on three aspects of job analysis writing which apply in various ways to different methods of job analysis: organization, sentence content and structure, and selection of words.

Organization

The preferable organization of job descriptive material depends very much upon the job analysis method used and on the nature of the job in question. In the case of most job descriptive material, however, the information is organized into related major job segments (such as duties) or in the sequence in which the job activities are carried out (if there is such sequence). If there are no logical or rational bases for organization, however, the descriptive information may be arranged by the judged importance of the various activities or the time devoted to them. In the case of certain structured job analysis procedures (such as task inventories that consist of listings of tasks) the tasks may be arranged alphabetically, in terms of the duties involved, or in terms of functional relationships.

Sentence Content and Structure

The content of sentences used in job description varies greatly with the method being used. In the case of some task and methods analysis procedures, for example, the sentences are very simple, consisting of only a verb (in the third person, present tense) and an object (possibly with an adjective modifying the object) such as "installs antennas" or "operates a power saw." In the case of conventional job descriptions, however, the sentence structures may be complex, compound, or compound-complex, as in the following examples (adapted in part from Kuriloff and Yoder):

Complex sentences (containing one main clause and one or more subordinate clauses): Replaces tube when test indicates that present tube is not good.

Compound sentence (containing two or more main clauses and no subordinate clauses): Removes tire from rim and inspects for defects.

Compound-complex sentence (containing two or more main clauses and at least one subordinate clause): At end of month, or when all accounts receivable and accounts payable records are received, prepares a listing of each and computes totals.

In connection with job descriptive material it should be noted that in some instances (as in some task inventories) the verb is in the first person, present tense form, as, "Solder minor leaks in radiator." In such instances a job incumbent can assume "I" as the subject. In some instances, statements are not complete sentences. This is especially the case with certain structured job analysis procedures in which items of equipment (such as "Blow torch") or descriptions of activities (such as "Use of keyboard devices") are used.

Selection of Words

According to Kuriloff and Yoder, in preparing job descriptive material, the analyst should be careful in the selection of words to minimize the possibility of ambiguity and yet be brief. A few general guidelines regarding the use of words are given below.

□ Prefer the simple word to the far-fetched.
□ Prefer the concrete word to the abstract.
□ Prefer the single word to the circumlocution.
□ Prefer the short word to the long.
□ Avoid technical words unless they have special significance for the intended audience and would be readily understood. Otherwise they should be explained.
□ Use adjectives sparingly and only if they add significant meaning.
□ Minimize the use of gerunds and participles. These are words derived from verbs and usually end in *-tion, -ion, -ing,* and *-ment.* A gerund is a verb used as a noun (as in the sentence, "The investigator's *findings* indicated that . . ."). A participle is a verb used as an adjective (as in the sentence, "While observing the bread *baking* . . ."). There are times, however, when gerunds and participles provide the most effective and efficient method of description.

☐ Limit the use of imprecise words such as *condition, situation, facilitate,* and *inadequacy.*

Discussion

There are various statistical indices of the reading level of written material, such as the Flesch count (Flesch), and the Fog index (Kuriloff and Yoder). These indices are based on such factors as average sentence length, average syllables per word, numbers of words with three or more syllables, various indexes of word difficulty and frequency of use, and so on. Certain readability indexes can be converted to a level of reading difficulty expressed in terms of average school grades. Although such indexes undoubtedly are quite appropriate in measuring the reading difficulty of conventional written material (such as in newspapers, magazines, and books), there is some question as to whether they can be used with at least some job description material because of the somewhat nontypical sentence structure and writing style used in describing human work activities, and because of the fact that some job description material includes a fair sprinkling of technical terms (which, although increasing the index of reading difficulty, are usually understandable to the typical users of such material).

Despite such arguments against the potential relevance of readability indexes to job description material, there are at least certain inklings that the application of certain "readability" principles that are suggested by various readability indexes may enhance the reliability of the use of task inventories (Murphy). In his study Murphy compared the reliability of an "original" task inventory (resulting from two administrations of the inventory) with that of a "revised" inventory in which the task statements had been rewritten in line with certain readability principles. Although only certain of the comparisons were statistically significant, the general pattern of the comparisons indicated that the rewritten task statements were somewhat more reliable in use than were the originally worded statements.

Such evidence—along with extensive experience—reinforces the point that careful, precise writing is essential in the preparation of good job description material.

Preparation and Review of Job Analysis Material

In many job analysis programs the persons who serve as the job analysts (the *agents* referred to earlier) prepare some descriptive material about the job(s) in question. Such material may be in the form of conventional job descriptions, listings of tasks that are (or might be) performed by job incumbents, or any of various types of forms listing the operations that are carried out. It is usually the practice to present drafts of such materials to supervisors, experts, or management personnel for review, possible modification, and ultimately (in some cases) formal approval. Structured job analysis questionnaires that are completed by job incumbents may also be reviewed by supervisors.

In the case of certain structured job analysis procedures, the final format of relevant information may consist of computer outputs. Examples of such outputs are given in Chapter 6.

Job Analysis: Past, Present, and Future

Job analysis is usually viewed in the frame of reference of conventional job analysis procedures which result in typical job descriptions. Such procedures have been used over decades, are being used now, and undoubtedly will continue to be used by some organizations. Their continued use—although far from universal—probably represents a form of testimony to the fact that they must serve some purposes well. However, there is a great deal of unease with such methods and this unease is reflected in some of the results in the *Summary of National Job Analysis Methods Survey* carried out by the Bureau of Business Research, California State College, Long Beach, as shown in Table 3-4. The table gives the percentages of responding organizations that rate their job analysis systems as "very satisfactory," "satisfactory," and "unsatisfactory." The dominant responses across the various rating factors were "satisfactory," the two major sources of dissatisfaction being currency of job information and the difficulty of keeping job information current.

In summarizing and discussing the results of this survey, Jones and DeCoths state that the reasons most commonly given by organizations for *not* having job analysis programs were (1) it would serve no useful purpose, (2) an acceptable system has not been found, (3) it is too expensive, and (4) it takes too much time. On the basis of the results of the survey they summarize the dissatisfactions of respondents regarding job analysis programs as follows:

The traditional methods of gathering job information are time consuming and difficult to perform with anything more than a modicum of consistency and currency. As a result, necessary updating of job information often proves costly and impractical. An additional shortcoming of traditional methods is that their subjective and narrative nature severely limits their adaptability to automation and the computer attributes of speed, mass data manipulation, and standardization.

The dissatisfaction with versatility of job analysis programs is related to the difficulty of adapting a common method of gathering job information for diverse purposes. It may be that some of the respondents' job analysis programs lack the necessary sophistication demanded by the more rigorous applications. Such applications are inherent in the construction of vocational tests, development of training courses, job dilution, and job restructuring.

Their conclusions are expressed as follows:

Three important conclusions may be drawn from information provided by this survey. First, there is widespread dissatisfaction with

TABLE 3-4. Ratings of job analysis systems by organizations with such systems. (Source: *Summary of National Job Analysis Methods Survey*)

Factor on which rated	Salaried			Hourly		
	VS	S	U	VS	S	U
Reliability (consistency)	25%	59%	2%	27%	54%	1%
Validity (accuracy)	22	60	4	23	55	3
Currency of job information	13	53	18	15	48	17
Developing job specifications	15	50	7	18	43	7
Costs	9	30	3	9	29	2
Employee production time	10	29	3	11	29	2
Supervision time	11	33	2	10	30	2
Clerical time	9	33	3	9	30	2
Analyst's time	10	32	4	10	28	4
Other	1	5	0	1	5	1
Simplicity	24	48	4	23	45	3
Employee attitude toward it	14	59	5	11	56	5
Broad use (multipurpose)	18	42	11	13	42	8
Ease of altering	21	45	9	16	43	8
Ease of keeping current	15	46	19	11	46	15
Flexibility	20	46	6	14	46	5
Overall rating	17	61	3	16	55	2
Other	0	3	1	0	3	1

LEGEND: VS = Very Satisfactory; S = Satisfactory; U = Unsatisfactory.

NOTE: The percentages do not add up to 100, presumably because of omitted responses.

present job analysis programs, particularly with respect to currency of job information and versatility for diverse purposes. The reasons for this dissatisfaction may be attributed to lack of standardized, quantifiable techniques for gathering, recording, and presenting job information, and limited use of EDP (electronic data processing). Second, most job analysis programs are characterized by relatively little emphasis on human relations type job variables. Third, due to the rapidly growing work force, the current emphasis on upgrading the unemployed and underemployed and the impact of technological change on the nature of work, the traditional techniques of job analysis may no longer be adequate to meet the needs of the economy.

These conclusions suggest the need for a two-pronged research effort in job analysis. One aspect of the research should attempt to develop a comprehensive model for improving the job analysis procedures. The objective of this research should center around quantifying job information, increasing its validity, eliminating its subjectiveness, and reducing the costs of its collection. In addition to standardizing job analysis methods, the successful implementation of such a model will greatly facilitate updating of job information. The other aspect of the research should examine ways to help job analysis practitioners define and measure psychological and sociological job related variables. Increased availability and validity of human relations type job data will enable manpower managers and planners to more effectively deal with the human aspects of technological change.

Such reflections, along with some of the comments in Chapter 1 about the present state of affairs in job analysis, give the impression that there has been something missing in the brew. This pervading sense of uneasiness leads to the conclusion that, with some notable exceptions, the study of human work has generally been more in the domain of the arts than of the sciences. Perhaps to express it differently, the study of human work (which occupies a major part of man's lifetime) probably has not generally benefited from the systematic, scientific approaches that have been characteristic of other domains of inquiry, such as the study of physical phenomena, biological phenomena, or of the behavior of man himself through psychological and sociological research. In this vein (and again granting that conventional job analysis procedures presumably do serve certain useful purposes despite their shortcomings) Jones and DeCoths make a strong case for the development and use of other, more standardized, quantifiable methods of job analysis that might better serve some purposes.

Recent Developments

The study of human work in the past has not been entirely unsystematic and lacking in the scientific approach. We could cite a number of examples to illustrate this, such as: some of the techniques of the industrial engineers; the measurement of the time of elemental motions; the measurement of physical effort by the work physiologists; numerous quantitative studies dealing with job evaluation methods (although these are more concerned with the use of the job analysis information than with its collection); and some of the work of the USES (Lewis).

Developments in recent years offer very encouraging prospects of pulling some phases of job analysis out of the doldrums. These developments are not panaceas for all purposes for which job information is used, but for certain uses they might be considered a breakthrough. Probably the common denominator of these new methods is the development and use of various types of structured job analysis procedures which provide for the identification and/or measurement of units of job-related information. The data resulting from such procedures typically lend themselves to more systematic analysis and application. These developments are typified by the task inventories of the Air Force Human Resources Laboratory (Christal; Morsh, 1969) and the Position Analysis Questionnaire (PAQ) that provides for the analysis of jobs in terms of worker-oriented job elements (McCormick et al.). Some of these are discussed in Chapter 6.

In the following chapters we will take an overview of various approaches to the study of human work, dwelling in particular on some of the more systematic, quantitatively oriented procedures. However, although the past several years perhaps have seen at least a small quantum step on the road toward the development of a science of human work, the millenium in this effort is by no means here or around the corner.

References

Christal, R. E. "Comments by the Chairman." In *Proceedings of Division of Military Psychology Symposium,* pp. 77–85, 77th annual convention of the American Psychological Association. USAF, AFPTRC, Personnel Research Division. Lackland AFB, Texas: 1969.

Cunningham, J. W. *"Ergometrics": A Systematic Approach to Some Education Problems,* Monograph No. 7, Raleigh, N.C.: North Carolina State University, Center for Occupational Education, 1971.

Flesch, R. *The Art of Readable Writing.* New York: Harper & Row, 1974.

Handbook for Analyzing Jobs. U.S. Department of Labor, Manpower Administration. Washington, D.C.: U.S. Government Printing Office (Stock No. 2900-0131), 1972.

Jones, J. J., Jr., and DeCoths, T. A. "Job Analysis: National Survey Findings." *Personnel Journal* 49(1969): pp. 805–809.

Kuriloff, A. H., and Yoder, D. *Communications in Task Analysis.* Evaluation of the Marine Corps task analysis program, Technical Report No. 8. Los Angeles: California State University, 1975.

Kuriloff, A. H.; Yoder, D.; and Stone, C. H. *Training Guide for Observing and Interviewing in Marine Corps Task Analysis.* Evaluation of the Marine Corps task analysis program, Technical Report No. 2. Los Angeles: California State University, 1975.

Lewis, L. "Job Analysis in the United States Training and Employment Service." In *Proceedings of Division of Military Psychology Symposium,* pp. 23–41, 77th annual convention of the American Psychological Association, USAF, AFPTRC, Personnel Research Division. Lackland AFB, Texas: 1969.

McCormick, E. J. "Job Analysis: An Overview." *Indian Journal of Industrial Relations,* July 1970, pp. 5–14.

McCormick, E. J.; Jeanneret, P. R.; and Mecham, R. C. "A Study of Job Characteristics and Job Dimensions as Based on the Position Analysis Questionnaire (PAQ)." *Journal of Applied Psychology* 56(1972): 347–367.

Melching, W. H., and Borcher, S. D. *Procedures for Constructing and Using Task Inventories.* Center for Vocational and Technical Education, Research and Development Series No. 91. Columbus, Ohio: The Ohio State University, 1973.

Morsh, J. E. "Job Analysis in the United States Air Force." *Personnel Psychology* 17(1964): 1–17.

Morsh, J. E. "Collecting, Analyzing, and Reporting Information Describing Jobs in the United States Air Force." In *Proceedings of Division of Military Psychology Symposium,* pp. 33–34, 77th annual convention of the American Psychological Association. USAF, AFPTRC, Personnel Research Division. Lackland AFB, Texas: 1969.

Murphy, W. F. "The Applicability of Readability Principles to the Writing of Task Statements." Unpublished Ph.D. thesis, Purdue University, 1966.

Rupe, J. C. *Research into Basic Methods and Techniques of Air Force Job Analysis,* IV. USAF, Air Research and Development Command, Air Force Personnel and Training Research Center, AFPTRC-TN-56-51. Chanute AFB, Ill.: 1956.

Summary of National Job Analysis Methods Survey. Long Beach: California State College, Bureau of Business Research, 1968.

Yoder, D., and Heneman, H. G., Jr., eds. ASPA Handbook of *Personnel and Industrial Relations.* Washington, D.C.: Bureau of National Affairs, 1979.

4

Conventional Job Analysis Procedures

THE conventional job analysis programs used in many organizations typically involve the collection of job-related information by observation of and/or interview with job incumbents, and the preparation of job descriptions that usually are written in essay form. The specific features of such programs as carried out by different organizations are quite varied in terms of the type of information obtained, the job analysis forms used, the procedures followed in the analysis process, and the format, organization, and writing style of the final descriptions or specifications. At the same time, the basic patterns used by different organizations have much in common.

Job Analysis Procedures of the USES

The United States Employment Service of the Training and Employment Administration (formerly the Manpower Administration) of the Department of Labor has had more experience in conventional job analysis activities than any other organization, public or private, so we will present as an example the format it uses (the job analysis schedule) along with a few of the points and guidelines covered in the *Handbook for Analyzing Jobs,* which is the basic manual used in its job analysis procedures.

Job Analysis Schedule

The job analysis schedule of the USES is shown in Figure 4–1, which presents a completed job description. The schedule provides for certain information that would not usually be relevant for most other organizations, for example, certain identification information and certain ratings that are to be entered on the schedule. The specific directions regarding the analysis process and the preparation of the schedule are given in the *Handbook for Analyzing Jobs* and are not repeated in detail here. However, we will briefly discuss a few sections of the schedule that typically would be provided for in most job analysis procedures. (Reference to these is by the item number on the schedule.) In addition, some supplementary observations and comments are made with respect to certain items, and in certain instances, relevant material from other sources is brought in.

In discussing the job analysis procedures of the USES we first illustrate and discuss the final product of typical job analysis processes in the form of a complete job description (as presented in Figure 4–1), and then back up to discuss certain aspects of the initial processes of obtaining the information ultimately presented in the form of a job description.

Establishment of job title (item 1). The title by which the job is commonly referred to is entered as the main title, in all capital letters. Under no circumstance should the analyst coin a title to use. If the title used is ambiguous a qualifying word or phrase can be entered in parentheses after the title. It is usually the practice to enter other alternate titles after the main title, but with initial capital and lower case letters.

Job summary (item 4). The job summary typically consists of a brief, yet comprehensive statement to describe the primary activities of the job and to characterize the role of the job in the organization. In this regard Bouchard, in discussing what he refers to as "defining the job," which is essentially the same thing as a job summary, urges that the analyst begin with a general statement of job objectives that should focus on general outcomes, or what a person who does the job well should be expected to accomplish. He goes on to make the point that even if there are multiple objectives (that make the formulation of such a statement difficult) it is still the job analyst's duty to create such a statement.

Figure 4-1. Job analysis schedule used by the USES in its job analysis program. (Source: *Handbook for Analyzing Jobs, pp. 42-45)*

JOB ANALYSIS SCHEDULE

1. Estab. Job Title   DOUGH MIXER

2. Ind. Assign.   (bake. prod.)

3. SIC Code(s) and Title(s)   2051 Bread and other bakery products

Code 520.782 WTA Group Oper. Control p. 435 DOT Title Ind. Desig.	

4. JOB SUMMARY:

Operates mixing machine to mix ingredients for straight and sponge (yeast) doughs according to established formulas, directs other workers in fermentation of dough, and cuts dough into pieces with hand cutter.

5. WORK PERFORMED RATINGS:

	D	P	(T)
Worker Functions	Data	People	Things
	5	6	2

Work Field   146 - Cooking, Food Preparing

M.P.S.M.S.   384 - Bakery Products

6. WORKER TRAITS RATINGS:

GED   1 (2) 3 4 5 6

SVP   1 2 3 (4) 5 6 7 8 9

Aptitudes   G 3 V 3 N 3 S 3 P 3 Q 4 K 3 F 3 M 3 E 4 C 4

Temperaments   D F I J (M) P R S (T) V

Interests   (1a) 1b 2a 2b 3a 3b 4a (4b) 5a (5b)

Phys. Demands   S L M (H) V   2 (3)(4) 5 (6)

Environ. Cond. (I) O B 2 3 4 (5) 6 7

7. General Education

    a. Elementary ___6___ High School _____ Courses _____

    b. College _None_ Courses _____

8. Vocational Preparation

    a. College _None_ Courses _____

    b. Vocational Education _None_ Courses _____

    c. Apprenticeship _None_ _____

    d. Inplant Training _None_ _____

    e. On-the-Job Training _six months_ _____

    f. Performance on Other Jobs _DOUGH-MIXER HELPER --- One year_

9. Experience _One year as DOUGH-MIXER HELPER_

10. Orientation _Four hours_

11. Licenses, etc. _Food Handlers Certificate issued by the Health Department_

12. Relation to Other Jobs and Workers

    Promotion: From _DOUGH-MIXER HELPER_ To _BAKER_

    Transfers: From _None_ To _None_

    Supervision Received _By BAKER_

    Supervision Given _DOUGH-MIXER HELPER_

13. Machines, Tools, Equipment, and Work Aids — Dough-mixing machine; balance scales; hand scoops; measuring vessels; portable dough troughs.

14. Materials and Products

    Bread dough

15. Description of Tasks:

    1. Dumps ingredients into mixing machine: Examines production schedule to determine type of bread to be produced, such as rye, whole wheat, or white. Refers to formula card for quantities and types of ingredients required, such as flour, water, milk, vitamin solutions, and shortening. Weighs out, measures, and dumps ingredients into mixing machine. (20%)

2. Operates mixing machine: Turns valves and other hand controls to set mixing time according to type of dough being mixed. Presses button to start agitator blades in machine. Observes gages and dials on equipment continuously to verify temperature of dough and mixing time. Feels dough for desired consistency. Adds water or flour to mix measuring vessels and adjusts mixing time and controls to obtain desired elasticity in mix. (55%)

3. Directs other workers in fermentation of dough: Prepares fermentation schedule according to type of dough being raised. Sprays portable dough Trough with lubricant to prevent adherence of mixed dough to trough. Directs DOUGH-MIXER HELPER in positioning trough beneath door of mixer to catch dough when mixing cycle is complete. Pushes or directs other workers to push troughs of dough into fermentation room. (10%)

4. Cuts dough: Dumps fermentated dough onto worktable. Manually kneads dough to eliminate gases formed by yeast. Cuts dough into pieces with hand cutter. Places cut dough on proofing rack and covers with cloth. (10%)

5. Performs miscellaneous duties: Records on work sheet number of batches mixed during work shift. Informs BAKE SHOP FOREMAN when repairs or major adjustments are required for machines and equipment. (5%)

---

16. Definition of Terms

Trough — A long, narrow, opened vessel used for kneading or washing ingredients.

17. General Comments

None

---

18. Analyst Jane Smith   Date 3/21/70   Editor John Rilley   Date 3/30/70

Reviewed By Alexandra Purcey   Title, Org. Foreman, Bake Shop

National Office Reviewer   Mary Moore

As a procedure for developing such a statement, Bouchard proposes that a number of qualified supervisors or their equivalent should be asked to specify what the objectives of the job are, indicating that such responses can be elicited with one or another of the following types of questions:

1. Please describe *in general terms* what objectives a person holding the position of ___(job title)___ should achieve in his/her job.
2. Please describe *in general terms* what the primary purpose of ___(activity)___ is.
3. What are the general aims that ___(job title)___ should strive for.

He suggests that respondents be allowed to answer such a question in as much detail as they wish, but that their responses should be followed by a request for a brief summary of the objectives, using a question such as this: "In a few words, or a sentence at most, how would you summarize the objectives (aims, primary purpose) of this job?"

Although the USES does not itself emphasize this point in its general job analyses procedures, it is argued here that an emphasis on the objectives of a job (or its role in the organization) would be very relevant in describing jobs or positions within specific individual organizations. This would be the case especially with higher level jobs or with jobs for which such objectives or roles are not otherwise clearly manifest.

A special aspect of the job description of the USES (especially of the job summaries) is the reflection of the level of involvement of the worker with *data, people,* and *things.* These three types of involvement are based on what are referred to as *worker functions,* which are discussed more extensively in Chapter 6 in connection with functional job analyses. The USES *Handbook* lists all the specific functions in each of the three categories. (See Figure 4–2.)

Each category is viewed as a hierarchy, with any given function subsuming all those below it. Examples of a few job summaries given in the USES *Handbook* are listed here, along with the respective level of involvement of each job with those worker functions that characterize the jobs.

- Shovels coal into mine cars for haulage (things relationship, nonmachine) (handling level).
- Examines structural aircraft assemblies to verify conformance to specifications (data and things relationships) (analyzing and handling levels).

Data	People	Things
0 Synthesizing	0 Mentoring	0 Setting Up
1 Coordinating	1 Negotiating	1 Precision Working
2 Analyzing	2 Instructing	2 Operating-Controlling*
3 Compiling	3 Supervising	3 Driving-Operating*
4 Computing	4 Diverting	4 Manipulating
5 Copying	5 Persuading	5 Tending
6 Comparing	6 Speaking-Signaling*	6 Feeding-Offbearing*
	7 Serving	7 Handling
	8 Taking Instructions-Helping*	

*Single functions.

Figure 4-2. Structure of worker functions used by the USES in its job analysis procedures. (Source: *Handbook for Analyzing Jobs*, p. 73)

□ Solves problems in higher mathematics in such fields as engineering, physics, and astronomy (data relationship) (synthesizing level).

□ Portrays role in dramatic production to interpret character to audience (data and people relationships) (synthesizing and diverting levels).

□ Polices premises of private business establishment (people relationship) (speaking-signaling level).

□ Sells ice to customers at ice house, cutting and weighing amount requested (people and things relationships) (speaking-signaling and handling levels)

□ Designs artistic interiors and sells decorating services (data, people, and things relationship) (synthesizing, persuading, and precision working levels).

□ Supervises and coordinates activities of carpenters on housebuilding project (data, people, and things relationships) (coordinating, supervising, and precision working levels).

Work performed ratings (item 5). In the procedures used by the USES, the worker function section of this item provides for recording the highest level of the worker's involvement in each of the three worker-function hierarchies (data, people, and things) as given in Figure 4–2. The work-field section as used by the USES provides for one or more entries from a specified list of work fields such as boring, knitting, researching, and teaching. An example of the description of a work field, that of Cooking–Food Preparing (applicable to the job of dough mixer as described in Figure 4–1) is given in Figure 4–3. Each such work field includes listings of "methods verbs," machines, tools, equipment, and work aids that are relevant to the work field, and examples of work activities that would be classified in that work field.

The section MPSMS as used by the USES refers to materials, products, subject matter, and services. Entries for this section are

Figure 4-3. Illustration of one of the work fields* used by the USES in its job analysis procedures. (Source: *Handbook for Analyzing Jobs,* pp. 121-122)

COOKING – FOOD PREPARING

Preparing foods for human or animal consumption, by any combination of methods which may include methods specific to other work fields, such as *Baking-Drying, Mixing, Shearing-Shaving, Stock Checking, and Weighing.*

Methods Verbs

Basting	Curing	Measuring	Roasting
Boiling	Flavoring	Pasteurizing	Rolling
Brewing	Frying	Pickling	Seasoning
Churning	Heating	Rendering	Spreading
	Kneading		Squeezing

Machines	Tools	Equipment	Work Aids
Continuous churn	Cleaver	Broilers	Charts
Pasteurizer	Cutters	Grills	Dishes
Vane churn	Forks	Ovens	Hoppers
	Ice Picks	Ranges	Kettles
	Knives	Roasters	Mixing bowls
	Paddles	Smoke chambers	Pans
	Sifters	Steam digesters	Pots
	Spatulas		Recipes
	Spoons		Storage bin
			Storage tank

Controls battery of smoke chambers in which such meat products as bacon, hams, meat loaf, sausage, shoulders, and weiners are cooked and cured.

Mixes and bakes ingredients, according to recipes, to produce breads, pastries, and other baked goods.

Mixes, cooks, and freezes ingredients to prepare frozen desserts such as sherbets, ice cream, and custards.

Operates ovens to roast dry breakfast cereals made from corn, rice, bran, and oats.

Plans menus and cooks meals in private home, according to recipes or tastes of employer.

---

*The work field for any given job is entered in the job analysis schedule (see Fig. 4-1) in a designated space labeled 5, Work Performed Ratings.

taken from a specific list, for example, clay (a material), bakery products (a product, the one applicable to the job of a dough mixer in Figure 4–1), horticulture (a subject), and retail trade (a service).

Although the USES procedures provide for ratings of these aspects of work performed, such ratings normally would not be involved in job analysis procedures used by individual organizations.

Worker traits ratings (item 6). Many job analysis procedures provide for the analyst to rate or make a judgment about the worker traits or attributes that are considered important to a job. Such ratings or judgments must be based on inferences from the job activities. (See Chapter 10 for further reference to this matter.) In the case of the USES procedures these ratings, as described in the *Handbook for Analyzing Jobs,* include the following:

- General Educational Development [GED]
- Specific Vocational Preparation [SVP]
- Aptitudes [G—Intelligence; V—Verbal; N—Numerical; S—Spatial; P—Form perception; Q—Clerical perception; K—Motor coordination; F—Finger dexterity; M—Manual dexterity; E—Eye-hand-foot coordination; and C—Color discrimination]
- Temperaments [10]
- Interests [5 bipolar interest factors]
- Physical Demands [ratings on a strength factor as expressed in terms of sedentary, light, medium, heavy, and very heavy, and on four other physical demand factors]
- Environmental Conditions [rating on seven environmental conditions]

For each of these worker traits there is provision in the USES procedure for rating any given job using specific rating scales that are included in the *Handbook for Analyzing Jobs.* Certain of these rating scales, and portions of others, are given in Appendix A. The job analysis procedures of other organizations (such as private organizations) frequently provide for the analyst to rate each job in terms of one or more human traits or attributes. The *Summary of National Job Analysis Survey Methods* includes provision for reporting the worker attributes for which ratings were obtained. The results of this part of the survey are summarized in Table 4–1. It can be seen that ratings of experience required, training and education, and mental skills were the attributes most commonly included. Such ratings typically are used as the basis for establishing the personnel specifications for the job in question.

Description of tasks (item 15). What is referred to in the USES job analysis schedule as the *description of tasks* is sometimes referred to as the *work performed*. Since this portion of a job description is generally the most important one, certain of the instructions relating to it in the *Handbook for Analyzing Jobs* are given below:

> Describe in concise form the tasks performed, following the concepts and procedures outlined in this handbook. Each description must designate the worker's actions and the results accomplished; the machines, tools, equipment, and/or work aids used; materials, products, subject matter, or services involved; and the requirements made of the worker.
>
> This description should provide a basis for and be compatible with the assignment of work performed and worker traits ratings.
>
> In order to provide the clearest presentation, divide the job into its major tasks. Number each task consecutively and introduce it with a flag statement. (The flag statement is a short summary of the task and should be followed by a description of the elements it encompasses. For many kinds of jobs the tasks should be described in the chronological order in which they are performed. However, in other types of jobs the tasks should be listed in order of importance.)
>
> Indicate in parenthesis at the end of each task description an estimate of the percentage of time required for its performance. The percentage should be on the basis of 100 percent for all of the tasks performed.

The description-of-tasks section should include the occasionally performed activities as well as those that are a more regular, ongo-

TABLE 4–1. Frequency with which organizations with job analysis programs require analyst ratings of various worker attributes. (Source: *Summary of National Job Analysis Methods Survey*)

Worker Attribute	Salaried	Hourly
Experience (job knowledge)	89%	86%
Training, education (level, type, time)	83	84
Physical (strength, coordination, senses)	32	64
Manual, manipulative skills (dexterity, accuracy)	40	71
Mental skills (adaptability, judgment, initiative, creativity, technical)	77	71
Aptitudes (type, level)	39	41
Interests, motivation, (activity preferences)	24	19
Personality (adjustment to job situations)	27	21
Social skills (human interactions)	38	21
Other	1	1

ing part of the job. In this regard, when activities are performed on a "now-and-then" basis it usually is desirable to indicate in some way the conditions or circumstances under which the activity is performed, such as: "At the end of each month balances the books . . ." "When requested by customer, arranges for . . ." "When observing that generator is discharging . . ."

Further, this section should bring out somehow the way in which any tools, equipment, and materials are involved in the job. There usually is provision for listing these (as in item 13 of Figure 4–1), and therefore their use should be reflected in the description of the tasks.

In writing job description material (as in describing tasks), certain types of information usually should be included (sometimes referred to as the *what, how,* and *why* of job analysis procedures), and there is a somewhat standardized style of writing. The writing of such material will be discussed in a later section of this chapter.

Physical demands and environmental conditions. The job analysis procedures of the USES provide for the completion of a form (Figure 4–4) for recording and explaining the physical demands and environmental conditions, and for entering certain codes relating to these on the job analysis schedule. The responses to some items are to be given in percents, weights, and (in the case of noise) in decibels. For most items, however, the following code symbols are used:

NP Not present (the activity or condition does not exist)
 O Occasionally (activity or condition exists up to 1/3 of the time)
 F Frequently (activity or condition exists from 1/3 to 2/3 of the time)
 C Constantly (activity or condition exists 2/3 or more of the time)

Comments about the activities or conditions, identified by number and letter, are to be entered in the righthand column of the form. (Appendix B includes definitions of the specific physical demands and environmental conditions incorporated in the USES form as presented in Figure 4–4).

In the case of some other job analysis procedures there is also provision for recording information on physical demands and environmental conditions. For example, in the *Summary of National Job Analysis Methods Survey* it was reported that the following items were provided for by the percents of respondents indicated:

Item	Salaried	Hourly
Comfort variables (temperature, humidity, noise, etc.)	35%	61%
Hazards (physical health)	36%	68%

The Use of Questionnaires in Conventional Job Analysis

Some job analysis programs involve the completion by job incumbents of a preliminary questionnaire in which they describe their own jobs. Usually such questionnaires provide for giving the same type of information as that to be included in the final job description (such as provided for in the job analysis schedule shown in Figure 4–1). The purpose of these questionnaires is to provide the analyst with a first draft of a job description. Although this procedure may give some employees a feeling of participation in the program, it usually has some limitations. For example, some employees may not welcome the opportunity to describe their jobs, and some do not have the verbal skills necessary to describe their jobs adequately. Further, there may be a tendency on the part of some employees to "inflate" their jobs by, for example, indicating that they have more responsibility than is actually the case; conversely, some employees may tend to understate their responsibilities.

When a questionnaire is employed, it may be useful to ask the employees to maintain a record of their daily activities (including their time allocation) in advance of the actual completion of the questionnaire, as an aid to them in preparing it. Further, they should be encouraged to express themselves in their own words and to complete the questionnaires entirely independently. Normally, such questionnaires can be completed more adequately by salaried personnel (supervisors, or office personnel) than by hourly paid personnel; this suggests that questionnaires normally should be used with salaried personnel rather than with hourly paid employees.

When such questionnaires are used, the job analyst usually follows up by interviewing and possibly observing the job incumbents in order to clarify doubtful items of information and to fill in additional information about the job.

Writing Job Descriptions and Related Material

The description of work activities can be pitched at various levels, perhaps most typically at the level of job summaries or of descriptions of tasks. Whatever the intended level might be, the descrip-

Figure 4-4. Physical demands and environmental conditions forms used by the USES in its job analysis procedures. (Source: *Handbook for Analyzing Jobs*, pp. 340-341)

ESTAB. JOB TITLE   ESTAB. & SCHED. NO.

DOT TITLE AND CODE

PHYSICAL DEMANDS	COMMENTS
1. STRENGTH	
a. Standing _____ %	
Walking _____ %	
Sitting _____ %	
b. Weight	
Lifting	
Carrying	
Pushing	
Pulling	
2. CLIMBING	
BALANCING	
3. STOOPING	
KNEELING	
CROUCHING	
CRAWLING	
4. REACHING	
HANDLING	
FINGERING	
FEELING	
5. TALKING	
Ordinary	
Other	
HEARING	
Ordinary Conversation	
Other Sounds	
6. SEEING	
Acuity, Near	
Acuity, Far	
Depth Perception	
Accommodation	
Color Vision	
Field of Vision	

RATINGS: P.D.:   S L M H VH 2 3 4 5 6

Analyst _____ Date _____ Estab. Reviewer _____

E.S. Reviewer _____ Date _____ Title _____ Date _____

ENVIRONMENTAL CONDITIONS		COMMENTS
1. ENVIRONMENT Inside _____ % Outside _____ %		
2. EXTREME COLD WITH OR WITHOUT TEMPERATURE CHANGES		
3. EXTREME HEAT WITH OR WITHOUT TEMPERATURE CHANGES		
4. WET AND/OR HUMID		

5. NOISE
     Estimated maximum
     number of decibels		

VIBRATION		
6. HAZARDS		
Mechanical		
Electrical		
Burns		
Explosives		
Radiant Energy		
Other		
7. ATMOSPHERIC CONDITIONS		
Fumes		
Odors		
Dusts		
Mists		
Gases		
Poor Ventilation		
Other		

RATINGS: E. C.:   I O B 2 3 4 5 6 7

PROTECTIVE CLOTHING OR PERSONAL DEVICES

tion of the work activities is intended to convey to the reader information about the jobs in question. How well this information is transmitted to the reader depends very much upon the content of the descriptive material and how it is written (its style).

Content of Job Description Material

In job analysis jargon one frequently hears reference to the *what, how,* and *why* of job analysis processes. In describing human work, the analyst must be sure that the description covers *what* the worker does, *how* he does it, and *why* he does it. Although in some circumstances the *how* and *why* may be implicitly obvious, if there is any question at all about these aspects they should be explicitly brought out in the description.

What the worker does is characterized by statements regarding the physical and mental activities that are performed on the job. As Butler points out, physically the worker may transport materials, cut, grind, set up, regulate, finish, or otherwise change the position, shape, or condition of the work by the expenditure of physical effort; and mentally he may engage in such activities as planning, computing, judging, or directing, including in some instances the governing of the expenditure of his own or others' physical effort. In describing the *what* of the job Butler suggests that the analyst should ask himself the following questions:

- ☐ What tasks have been observed during the performance of the job?
- ☐ Are the tasks included for this job performed by all workers designated by the job title?
- ☐ What is the frequency with which the tasks are performed?
- ☐ What is the relative difficulty of each task as compared with the rest of the tasks on the job?
- ☐ Are there additional tasks which have not been observed?
- ☐ Are there additional tasks customary to all workers on the job?
- ☐ Have the data obtained by observation been verified?

The *how* of the work activities performed deals with the methods or procedures used to carry out the job tasks. In the case of physical activities, this may involve the use of machinery and tools or other equipment, the following of certain procedures or routines, or the execution of certain physical responses such as hand movements. In the case of mental activities, this may involve the use of calculations or formulas, the exercise of judgment, or the selection and transmittal of thought. In considering the *how* of the job, Butler suggests that the analyst should try to cover the following questions:

- ☐ What tools, materials, and equipment have been used to accomplish all of the tasks of the job?
- ☐ Are there other tools, materials, and equipment which have not been observed? If so, how do they work?
- ☐ What methods or processes have been used to accomplish the tasks of the job?
- ☐ Are there other methods or processes by which the same work can be done?

The *why* of the job analysis process goes back to the objective of the job as emphasized by Bouchard and discussed earlier in this chapter (Job Summary). The basic purpose(s) of the job should be one of the first things the analyst should seek to determine and should be brought out in any job summary. Aside from setting forth in the job summary the overall purpose of the job (that is, why the job exists), the description of the specific tasks should also include some indication as to *why* the individual tasks are performed, in case this is not manifest or is not clearly implied in the description of *what* and *how*. The *why* of each individual task generally would characterize the purpose of the task as related to the fulfillment of the overall objectives of the job as incorporated in the job summary.

Butler illustrates the manner in which the *what, how,* and *why* are brought out in the portions of a job description given below, which deal with the job summary and a couple of tasks.

Job: ENGINE LATHE OPERATOR—FIRST CLASS

Job summary: Sets up and operates an engine lathe to turn small airplane fittings from brass or steel bar stock or from unfinished aluminum or magnesium alloy castings *(why)*, finishing fitting down to specified close tolerances *(what, how)*.

Work performed (descriptions of two tasks):

1. Sets up lathe *(what);* carefully examines blueprints *(what)* to determine the dimensions of the part to be machined *(why)*, using shop mechanics *(how)* to calculate any dimensions *(what)* not given directly on the print *(why)* or to calculate machine settings *(why)*.

2. Sets up lathe to turn stock held in chuck *(what);* attaches to lathe the accessories such as chuck and tool holder *(what)* necessary to perform the machining *(why)* threading and locking the chuck and the head stock spindle *(how)* and setting.

In writing job description material there sometimes is a problem in determining the degree of specificity. The *Handbook for Analyzing Jobs* includes the following observations in its discussion of the description of tasks:

> The analyst should keep in mind the necessity for stating a task completely but should not allow the explanation to develop into a motion study. For example, regarding an inspector of small parts, it may be said, "Slides fingertips over machine edges to detect ragged edges and burrs."

> On the other hand, it would be absurd to state, "Raises right hand one foot to table height, superimposes hand over mechanical part and, by depressing the first and second fingers to the machined part and moving the arm slowly sidewise about six inches, feels with his fingertips for snags or pricks that are indicative of surface irregularities."

Writing Style in Job Analysis

The writing style for conventional job descriptions is described in the *Handbook for Analyzing Jobs* as follows:

    a. A terse, direct style should be used.
    b. The present tense should be used throughout.
    c. Each sentence should begin with an active verb.
    d. Each sentence must reflect an objective, either specifically stated or implied in such manner as to be obvious to the reader. A single verb may sometimes reflect both objective and worker action.
    e. All words should impart necessary information; others should be omitted. Every precaution should be taken to use words that have only one possible connotation and that specifically describe the manner in which the work is accomplished.
    f. The description of tasks should reflect the assigned work performed and worker traits ratings.

The last rule relates specifically to the practice of the USES in assigning Work Performed and Worker Traits ratings (as discussed earlier in this chapter) and would also be applicable for other organizations that provide for any type of similar ratings. Even if such ratings are not required, however, the task descriptions should reflect the same substance as such ratings would cover.

As indicated by rule *c*, each sentence usually should begin with an active verb. The worker is the assumed—but unstated—subject. Here are some examples from the *Handbook for Analyzing Jobs:*

Drives tractor to plow . . .
Demonstrates . . . merchandise, such as, . . . to sell . . .
Turns valves to regulate coolant flow . . .
Feeds material into machine that stamps out parts . . .
Devises and installs accounting systems to maintain records of . . .
Compiles reports to show . . .
Talks with supervisors to obtain information . . .
Analyzes medical data to diagnose . . .

There are, however, circumstances in which some qualifying word or phrase should precede the verb, for example, to specify the circumstances under which a particular activity is performed: "At the end of each week compiles reports to show . . ." or "Verbally assigns . . ."

Basic sentence structure. Most job description material has a basic, somewhat standardized sentence structure. This basic sentence structure, as set forth in the *Handbook for Analyzing Jobs,* is given in Figure 4–5 with an example of a "job worker" situation, the opera-

Figure 4-5. Example of the analysis of the sentence structure for describing job activities, namely, the verb, the immediate object, and an infinitive phrase. (Source: *Handbook for Analyzing Jobs*, p. 201)

Job Worker Situation: Operates cord or cordless switchboard to relay incoming, outgoing, and interoffice calls. On cordless switchboard, pushes switch keys to make connections and relay calls. On cord type equipment, plugs cord in jacks mounted on switchboard. Supplies information to callers and records messages.

Analysis

VERB (WORKER FUNCTION)	IMMEDIATE OBJECT	INIFINITIVE PHRASE	
		INFINITIVE (WORK FIELD)	OBJECT OF INFINITIVE (MPSMS)
Compares	switchboard operation with standards	to relay	calls
Converses with	callers	to convey, to receive	information
Operates	cord or cordless switchboard	to relay	incoming, outgoing, and interoffice calls

Classification

HIERARCHY	WORKER FUNCTION	WORK FIELD	CODE	MPSMS	CODE
Data	Comparing (6)	System Communicating	281	Telephone Services	864
People	Speaking-Signaling (6)				
Things	Operating-Controlling (2)				

tion of a telephone switchboard. The job worker situation is defined briefly, and the analysis consists of the following components:

Verb (the worker function)
Immediate object (typically materials, tools, equipment or work aids, data, or people)
Infinitive phrase
    Infinitive (a work field)
    Object of the infinitive (some material, product, subject matter, or service)

Some further examples of such sentence structure are given in Table 4–2.

The lower part of Figure 4–5 shows the USES classification of job activities in terms of the data, people, things hierarchy, worker function, work field, and MPSMS (materials, products, subject matter, and services). In typical job analysis programs within individual organizations, such classification procedures usually would not be relevant.

In describing most work activities, the analyst should keep in mind the writing style and the type of sentence structure discussed

TABLE 4–2. Examples of sentence analysis as used by USES, showing how sentences can be structured in terms of the verb, the immediate object, and an infinitive phrase. (Source: *Handbook for Analyzing Jobs*)

Verb (Worker Function)	Immediate Object	Infinitive Phrase	
		Infinitive (Work Field)	Object of Infinitive (MPSMS)
Analyzes	examination papers	to evaluate	knowledge of law candidates.
Compiles	credit information	to determine	credit rating.
Computes	hours, pay scale, etc.	to calculate and post	wages.
Compares	appearance of hides with specifications	to grade	hides.
Describes	features of interest	to inform	visitors to factory.
Sets up	metal-working machines	to machine	metal patterns, core boxes.
Works	tooth-cleaning instruments	to clean	teeth.
Operates	saw	to cut to size	metal materials.
Tends	sanding machine	to smooth	broomsticks.
Feeds	blending machine	to blend	flour.
Handles	shovel, pick	to fill	holes in road.

above, characteristically using a worker function verb, indicating the immediate object of the verb, followed by an infinitive phrase (infinitive plus object) to reflect the purpose or the why of the activity. The analysis in Figure 4–5 and the other examples in Table 4–2 are admittedly rather stilted. Such a sentence structure, when used in actual job descriptions, usually would be more explanatory and detailed and would be worded in such a fashion as to fit in with other descriptive material. In some instances the substance of the infinitive phrase would be sufficiently implied or covered in other material that it could be omitted. The essential point in focusing attention on this basic structure is that in typical job description material, these components need somehow to be worked in or to be so manifest that they would be unduly redundant if they were overtly stated.

Functional Job Analysis (FJA) as used by the USES has been further developed by Dr. Sidney A. Fine. The system is discussed in more detail in Chapter 6, but one aspect of this system is relevant to our present discussion. The use of the FJA system is predicated in part on the careful description of tasks. In this regard Dr. Fine provides for incorporating into the sentence structure some indication of the nature of the instructions that serve as the basis for the worker's actions, in addition to the components discussed above. Figure 4–6 shows the form used. Certain examples of task statements prepared in the framework of the FJA system are given below. These examples come from jobs involved in the social welfare field (Fine et al.).

1. Calculates/performs statistical analysis of population movements within state's correctional facilities, using a desk calculator, in order to compute data to be used in report requested by the bureau director.

2. Advises/counsels mother on emotional and legal consequences of decision to place her child in adoptive home, listening to mother, asking questions, and reflecting her feelings, and suggesting ways of coping with problems, guilt, and anxieties arising from separation, in order to help mother adjust to permanent separation from child.

3. Visually inspects applicants' files, noting missing information, and indicates omissions on form letters, in order to complete form letters to applicants requesting the missing information by return mail.

4. Verbally assigns tasks/gives directions to the clerical staff worker, explaining and answering questions about prescribed and discretionary elements of procedures and performance requirements, based upon prior assessment of operation flow, workload, and worker's capabilities, in order to ensure that the worker understands his duties and responsibilities.

Model Sentence Worksheet for Task Statement Analyst_____					
Who?	Performs what action?	To whom or what?	Upon what instructions? (Source? How specific?)	Using what tools, equipment, work aids?	To produce/ achieve what? (expected output)
Subject	Action verbs	Object of verb	Phrase	Phrase	In order to . . .
the worker					
Task statement					

Figure 4-6. Worksheet of sentence structure used in connection with Functional Job Analysis (FJA) system. (Source: Fine et al., p. 12)

Although the further elaboration of task descriptions to incorporate provision for the instructions on which actions are to be based is especially relevant in the use of the FJA system, such elaboration can also be very useful in the preparation of conventional job descriptions.

Standardization of Job Analysis Terminology

Since individual words can have different meanings, and since different words can be used to express the same meaning, some type of standardization of terminology can contribute to the clarity of job description material.

There are two ways to achieve some level of standardization of terminology. One way is to carefully select and define relevant categories or specified items that are sometimes used in various job analysis formats. The USES definition of physical activities and working conditions in its Physical Demands and Environmental Conditions Form (Figure 4–4) represent examples of this type of standardization. (The definitions are given in Appendix B.)

The other way to standardize terminology is to suggest uses of specific job-related terms (which sometimes are individually defined) in job descriptions and other job-related materials. One set of such standardized terminology used by the USES and included in the *Handbook for Analyzing Jobs* consists of a list of work fields to be used by job analysts, when appropriate, in describing job activities, along with a listing for each work field of several *method verbs* relevant to the work field. The complete material relating to one work field was given in Figure 4–3. Following are listings of two other work fields with examples of certain of the methods verbs associated with them:

Work Field	*Methods Verbs*
Weaving	Doffing
	Drawing
	Picking
Stock checking	Cataloging
	Counting
	Requisitioning

The USES *Handbook* also contains a list of functional verbs for use in preparing occupational analyses, with definitions for each. A few examples are given below.

Anneals. Subjects to high heat, with subsequent cooling, for the purpose of softening thoroughly and rendering less brittle.

Calibrates. Ascertains the caliber of, determines, rectifies or marks the graduations of; adjusts in accordance with a previously defined standard.

Diagnoses. Recognizes, analyzes and identifies (usually a disease, but also other states or conditions) by examination or observation.

Prescribes. Lays down or sets as a guide, directions or rules of action; e.g., procedures, regulations, etc.

Splices. Joins or unites (wires and ropes) by weaving together the end strands.

Still another example of such standardization comes from Stone and Yoder. As one phase of a broader project they developed definitions of certain verbs which represent specific types of job activities that fall within the categories of certain of the worker functions given in Figure 4–2. For example, for the worker function of copying, Stone and Yoder identified various verbs which characterize specific aspects of copying, and have defined these as follows:

COPYING	Transcribing, entering, or posting data
RECORD	To make a written note or account of
post	To transfer (an entry or item) from one record to another

tabulate	To put into tabular form
list	To enumerate one after another
transpose	To change the relative place or normal order of
DUPLICATE	To make a duplicate, copy, or transcript of
transcribe	To make a copy of (dictated or recorded matter) in longhand or on a typewriter
quote	To write (a passage) from another usually with credit acknowledgment

Discussion

The shortcomings of job descriptions resulting from conventional job analysis procedures are certainly well recognized. At the same time it must be recognized that they do serve certain useful purposes which other methods cannot serve, such as presenting an organized description of individual jobs and reflecting the role of individual jobs within organizations. Thus, although conventional job descriptions are far from perfect, we should not throw up our hands in despair and abandon any effort to prepare and use them. Rather, it behooves the analysts who prepare them to obtain all relevant information about any given job and to prepare as good a description as possible.

References

Bouchard, T. J. *A Manual for Job Analysis.* Minneapolis: Minnesota Civil Service Department, 1972.

Butler, J. L. "Job Analysis: (What + How + Why = Skills Involved)." Unpublished manuscript, Stamford, Conn., 1975.

Fine, S. A.; Holt, A. M.; and Hutchinson, M. F. *Functional Job Analysis: How to Standardize Task Statements.* Kalamazoo, Mich.: W. E. Upjohn Institute for Employment Research, 1974.

Handbook for Analyzing Jobs. U.S. Department of Labor, Manpower Administration, Washington, D.C.: U.S. Government Printing Office (Stock No. 2900–0131), 1972.

Stone, C. H., and Yoder D. *Job Analysis, 1970.* Long Beach: California State College, 1970.

Summary of National Job Analysis Methods Survey. Bureau of Business Research, Long Beach: California State College, 1968.

5

Methods and
Task Analysis

CONVENTIONAL job analysis procedures usually result in job descriptions prepared in essay form or in discursive fashion. For some purposes, however, the work performed in jobs is better characterized in terms of individually identified activity *units*. There are many variations on this theme, one of which is the *level* of description. In most instances such descriptions are pitched at the *task* level or subunits thereof, such as subtasks and elemental motions of the body members. Some variations provide for the organization of the activities into a sequence, whereas others do not. In addition, some variations provide for the recording of certain information related to each activity. The common denominator, however, is that work is dissected into individually identified units.

Although the different approaches have much in common (and thus defy any nice, orderly classification scheme), we will divide our discussion into two general categories, namely, methods analysis and related techniques (dealing essentially with various industrial engineering procedures related to work analysis), and certain other approaches commonly referred to as task analysis.

Methods Analysis and Related Techniques

The techniques of industrial engineering had their origins in the early work of Frank and Lillian Gilbreth. In particular they developed some of the early methods of motion study, or what is now commonly referred to as methods analysis.

Methods Analysis

There are several different forms of methods analysis, most of which provide for the analysis of existing work activities with the view toward their improvement. These methods include operation charts, man and machine charts, and micromotion study.

Operation charts. An operation chart is used to represent the activities of a worker when working at essentially one location, especially for operations involving assembly work and inspection when no machine is involved. In the use of operation charts (and other techniques as well) a set of standardized symbols for certain types of activities usually is used. One set of such symbols (Amrine et al., reprinted with permission) is as follows:

Symbol	Name	Activities Represented
○	Operation	Modification of object at one workplace. Object may be changed in any of its physical or chemical characteristics, assembled or disassembled, or arranged for another operation, transportation, inspection, or storage.
⇨	Transportation	Change in location of object from one place to another.
☐	Inspection	Examination of object to check on quality or quantity characteristics.
D	Delay	Retention of object in a location awaiting next activity. No authorization is required to perform the next activity.
▽	Storage	Retention of object in location in which it is protected against unauthorized removal.

Operation charts usually show the separate actions of the right hand and left hand. An example is shown in Figure 5–1, which represents the assembly of a ballpoint pen.

Man and machine charts. A man and machine chart shows the relationship between the actions of a machine operator and the functions of the machine. As in the case of other methods analysis procedures, the man and machine chart is used to represent the job as it exists, with the view toward possible improvement. In the example of a man and machine chart in Figure 5–2, it can be seen that the vertical scale represents time, with the various segments involved in different operations for the left hand, right hand, and the machine.

Micromotion study. Micromotion study is the analysis of basic body motions from motion picture films taken of a worker performing a job. It is most appropriate for use in the analysis of operations that are short in cycle, that involve rapid movements of body members, and that involve high production over a long period of time, such as sewing, and assembling small parts. The operations are analyzed in terms of any one of several sets of specified body motions. Perhaps the most commonly used such set consists of the therbligs* as set forth by Gilbreth years ago. These are listed in Table 5–1 along with their symbols, their color codes, and definitions.

The typical procedures used in micromotion study include taking motion pictures of the operation in question, analyzing the film in terms of the basic motions, and preparing a *simo* (simultaneous motion cycle) chart, such as the one shown in Figure 5–3. The chart includes a brief description of the motion of each hand, an identification of the basic body motion (e.g., therblig), and an indication of the time involved in the motion, usually expressed in terms of 1/2000 of a minute. (The time can be determined by reading a microchronometer that is set beside the operator and is shown in the film, or more commonly by the use of a camera driven by a constant speed motor that results in each frame representing a specified time interval, such as 1/2000 minute.

Since simo charts depict the simultaneous actions of the two hands, they can provide the basis for improving work methods, especially by eliminating or reducing the motions which are nonproductive (hold, avoidable delay, plan, rest, select, and search), as well as by shortening those which are productive.

Principles of Motion Economy

On the basis of the early work of Gilbreth and the later experience and research of other investigators, various sets of guidelines of

---

*The term *therblig* is Gilbreth spelled backward except for a minor inversion of letters.

Figure 5-1. Operation chart showing the right and left hand actions in assembling a ballpoint pen. (Source: Amrine et al., p. 123. Reprinted with permission)

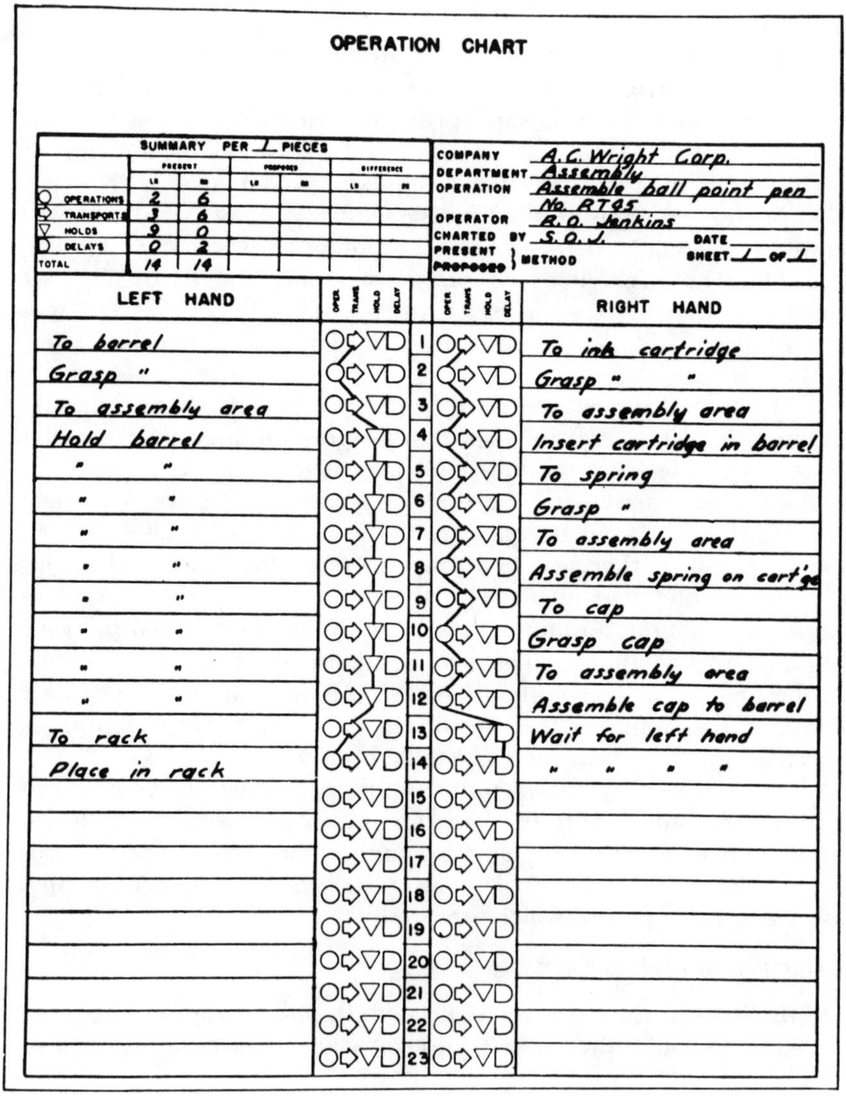

OPERATION CHART

SUMMARY PER _1_ PIECES

	PRESENT		PROPOSED		DIFFERENCE	
	LH	RH	LH	RH	LH	RH
OPERATIONS	2	6				
TRANSPORTS	3	6				
HOLDS	9	0				
DELAYS	0	2				
TOTAL	14	14				

COMPANY _A. C. Wright Corp._
DEPARTMENT _Assembly_
OPERATION _Assemble ball point pen_ _No. RT45_
OPERATOR _R. O. Jenkins_
CHARTED BY _S. O. J._ DATE ____
PRESENT } METHOD SHEET _1_ OF _1_
PROPOSED }

LEFT HAND	OPER. TRANS. HOLD DELAY		OPER. TRANS. HOLD DELAY	RIGHT HAND
To barrel	○⇨▽D	1	O⇨▽D	To ink cartridge
Grasp "	○⇨▽D	2	○⇨▽D	Grasp " "
To assembly area	O⇨▽D	3	O⇨▽D	To assembly area
Hold barrel	O⇨▽D	4	○⇨▽D	Insert cartridge in barrel
" "	O⇨▽D	5	O⇨▽D	To spring
" "	O⇨▽D	6	○⇨▽D	Grasp "
" "	O⇨▽D	7	O⇨▽D	To assembly area
" "	O⇨▽D	8	○⇨▽D	Assemble spring on cart'ge
" "	O⇨▽D	9	O⇨▽D	To cap
" "	O⇨▽D	10	○⇨▽D	Grasp cap
" "	O⇨▽D	11	O⇨▽D	To assembly area
" "	O⇨▽D	12	○⇨▽D	Assemble cap to barrel
To rack	O⇨▽D	13	O⇨▽D	Wait for left hand
Place in rack	O⇨▽D	14	O⇨▽D	" " " "
	O⇨▽D	15	O⇨▽D	
	O⇨▽D	16	O⇨▽D	
	O⇨▽D	17	O⇨▽D	
	O⇨▽D	18	O⇨▽D	
	O⇨▽D	19	O⇨▽D	
	O⇨▽D	20	O⇨▽D	
	O⇨▽D	21	O⇨▽D	
	O⇨▽D	22	O⇨▽D	
	O⇨▽D	23	O⇨▽D	

Figure 5-2. Man and machine chart for drilling wood cleats. (Source: Amrine et al., p. 25. Reprinted with permission)

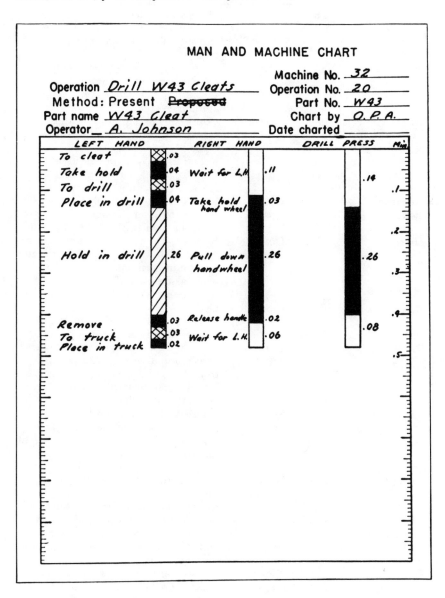

TABLE 5–1. Therbligs (basic body motions) used in micromotion study, along with their symbols, color codes and definitions. (Reprinted with permission)

Name of Symbol	Symbol	Color	Activity Represented
Search	Sh	Black	Occurs when hand or eyes are hunting or groping for something. *Example:* Trying to find or pick a part from a pile.
Select	St	Gray	Occurs when one object is being picked from among several. *Example:* Locating a particular bolt from among several.
Grasp	G	Lake red	Consists of taking hold of an object. *Example:* Closing the fingers around a pencil.
Transport empty	TE	Olive green	Refers to moving the empty hand while reaching for something. *Example:* Reaching for a desk pen.
Transport loaded	TL	Grass green	Refers to moving an object from one place to another. *Example:* Carrying a desk pen from the holder to the paper.
Hold	H	Gold ochre	Refers to the retention of an object in a fixed location. *Example:* Retaining a fountain pen barrel in one hand while assembling the cap to it with the other.
Release load	RL	Carmine red	Occurs when the hand lets go of an object. *Example:* Letting go of a desk pen when it is placed in a holder.
Position	P	Blue	Consists of aligning or orienting an object preparatory to fitting it into some location. *Example:* Aligning a plug preparatory to inserting it into an electrical outlet.
Pre-position	PP	Sky-blue	Consists of locating an object in a predetermined manner and in the correct position for some subsequent motion. *Example:* Lining up a desk pen for insertion into its holder.
Inspect	I	Burnt ochre	Examination of an object to determine some quality such as size, shape, or color. *Example:* Visual examination of finish of a desk.
Assemble	A	Violet, heavy	Consists of combining one object with another. *Example:* Putting a nut on a bolt.
Disassemble	DA	Violet, light	Consists of separating two objects which were combined. *Example:* Removing a nut from a bolt.

Table 5–1 (cont.)

Name of Symbol	Symbol	Color	Activity Represented
Use	U	Purple	Consists of applying or manipulating a tool, control or device for the purpose for which intended. *Example:* Tightening a bolt with a crescent wrench.
Unavoidable delay	UD	Yellow ochre	Refers to a delay by body member which is beyond the control of the operator. *Example:* Right hand pauses during the operation of assembling a mechanical pencil while the left hand asides a completed pencil.
Avoidable delay	AD	Lemon yellow	Refers to a delay by body member which is within the control of the operator. *Example:* An operator pauses or deviates from the normal motion pattern.
Plan	Pn	Brown	Refers to a delay in a motion pattern while the operator decides how to proceed. *Example:* An operator assembling a complex valve pauses to decide which part should be next.
Rest for overcoming fatigue	R	Orange	Occurs when a worker pauses to overcome the fatigue from the previous work. *Example:* An operator pauses to rest after having lifted several heavy metal castings into a metal truck.

motion economy have been developed. Amrine et al. list the following:

1. The movements of the two hands should be balanced and the two hands should begin and end their motions simultaneously.
2. The hands should be doing productive work and should not be idle at the same time except during rest periods.
3. Motions of the hands should be made in opposite and symmetrical directions and at the same time.
4. The work should be arranged to permit it to be performed with an easy and natural rhythm.
5. Momentum and ballistic-type movements should be employed wherever possible in order to reduce muscular effort.
6. There should be a definite location for all tools and materials, and they should be located in front of and close to the worker.

Figure 5-3. Simo chart for assembling dropper bottle tops resulting from a micromotion analysis of a motion picture film. (Source: Mundel, p. 261)

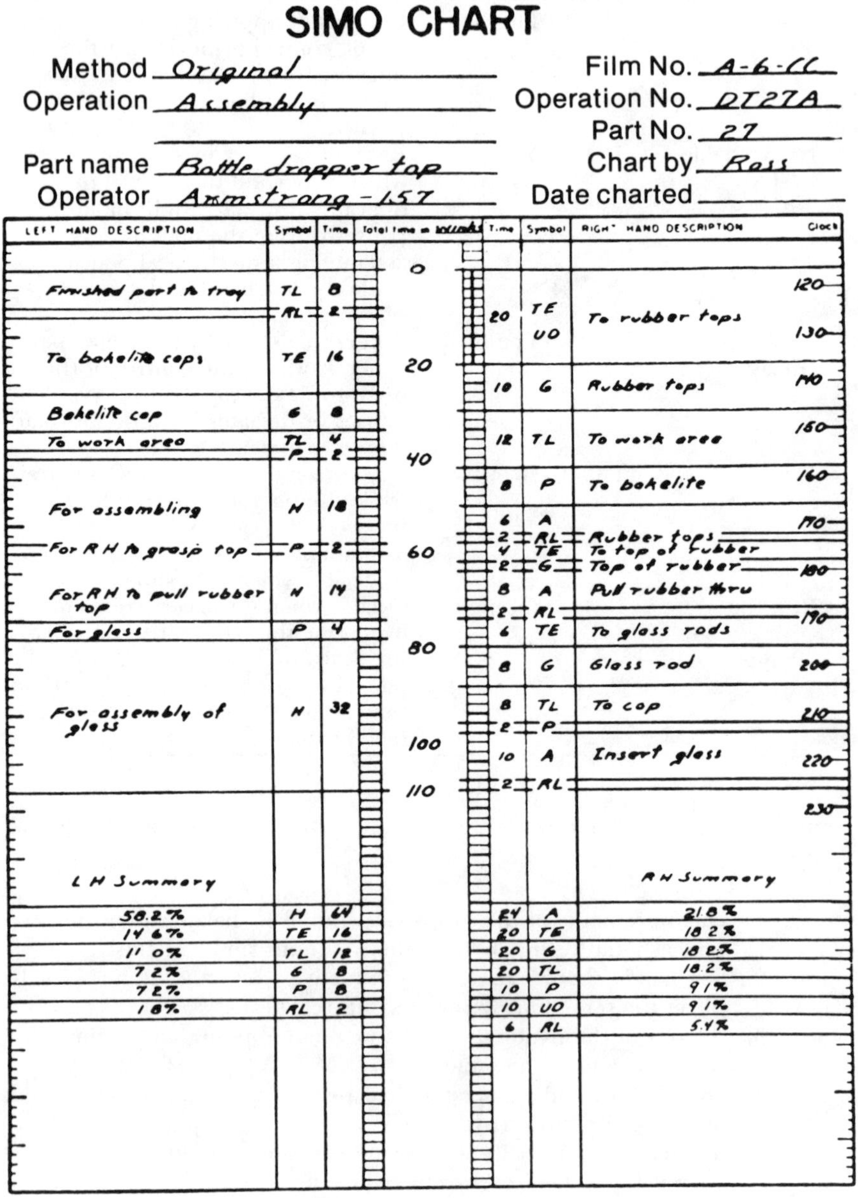

SIMO CHART

Method _Original_

Operation _Assembly_

Part name _Bottle dropper top_

Operator _Armstrong - 157_

Film No. _A-6-CC_

Operation No. _DT27A_

Part No. _27_

Chart by _Ross_

Date charted _____

LEFT HAND DESCRIPTION	Symbol	Time	Total time in 1/100 min	Time	Symbol	RIGHT HAND DESCRIPTION	Clock
Finished part to tray	TL	8	0				120
	RL	2		20	TE	To rubber tops	
					UO		130
To bakelite cops	TE	16	20				
				10	G	Rubber tops	140
Bakelite cap	G	8					
To work area	TL	4		12	TL	To work area	150
	P	2	40				
				8	P	To bakelite	160
For assembling	N	18		6	A		170
				2	RL	Rubber tops	
For RH to grasp top	P	2	60	4	TE	To top of rubber	
				2	G	Top of rubber	180
For RH to pull rubber top	N	14		8	A	Pull rubber thru	
				2	RL		190
For glass	P	4		6	TE	To glass rods	
			80	8	G	Glass rod	200
				8	TL	To cap	210
For assembly of glass	N	32	100	2	P		
				10	A	Insert glass	220
			110	2	RL		
							230
LH Summary						RH Summary	
58.2%	N	64		24	A	21.8%	
14.6%	TE	16		20	TE	18.2%	
11.0%	TL	12		20	G	18.2%	
7.2%	G	8		20	TL	18.2%	
7.2%	P	8		10	P	9.1%	
1.8%	RL	2		10	UO	9.1%	
				6	RL	5.4%	

7. Bins or other devices should be used to deliver the materials close to the point of use.
8. The workplace should be designed to insure adequate illumination, proper workplace height, and provision for alternate standing and sitting by the operator.
9. Wherever possible, jigs, fixtures, or other mechanical devices should be used to relieve the hands of unnecessary work.
10. Tools should be pre-positioned wherever possible in order to facilitate grasping them.

In industrial engineering these principles are applied, when practicable, to modifying jobs for greater motion economy and working efficiency.

Work Measurement

Closely related to methods analysis is the process of work measurement (also called *time study*), which is the basis for the derivation of a *standard* or *allowed* time for each specified unit of work activity. Combining the standard times for all the units of work activity in a given task or job provides a standard time for the task or job. These standard times are used for various purposes, such as:

Providing a basis for wage-incentive plans (incentives generally are given for work performance that takes less than standard time).
Providing a basis for determining costs.
Providing a basis for estimating costs of new products.
Balancing production lines and the work of crews of workers.

Establishing the standard or allowed time for a given unit of work, which represents a problem of some consequence, is based on the amount of time required by a "qualified worker, using a standard method and working at a standard work pace, to perform a specified task." (Amrine et al.) There are essentially four approaches to this process, namely, stop-watch time study, the use of standard times, the use of predetermined time systems, and work sampling.

Stop-watch time study. This method consists of using a stop watch to clock the actual time it takes one or more workers to perform each of the work elements in a task or job (this process typically is preceded by the standardization of the method to be used). Many readings of the element times are recorded, and the mean, median, or mode of these is used as a *representative* time. However, since the worker(s) used in the observation process may be working at a pace that is above or below that of a "qualified worker ... working at a standard work pace," it is the practice to adjust the obtained representative time for an element according to the judged work pace of the worker when he was performing the task or the element. This adjustment is referred to as *leveling* or *pace rating* or simply *rating*. It is based on the analyst's judgment (that is, his rating) of the pace of the worker using a concept of a *standard* or *normal* pace. In some instances certain verbal descriptions of *standard* are used, and in some instances films are used to represent the standard or normal rating expressed as a percent of the normal pace, and the normal time for the element is derived by the following formula:

$$\text{Normal time} = \text{"average" time} \times \frac{\text{percent rating}}{100}$$

The normal time so derived is not used itself as the standard or allowed time. Rather, the standard or allowed time consists of the normal time plus certain additional time allowances such as for interruptions, uncontrolled delays, and personal time. Thus, the standard time for an element is derived with the following formula:

$$\text{Standard time} = \text{normal time} \times \frac{(100 + \text{allowance in percent})}{100}$$

The use of judgments in the rating process obviously could introduce some error into the derivation of normal (and thus of standard) times. In this regard Lifson (1951) carried out a laboratory study to investigate possible sources of error in the rating process. He had four tasks rated by experienced industrial engineers when the tasks were being performed at various paces controlled by the use of a metronome. (The normal paces had been set on the basis of the pace ratings of one sample of industrial engineers.) The subjects then performed the tasks at the normal pace and at metronome-controlled paces of 90, 110, 120, and 130 percent of the normal pace. Generally, Lifson found that some raters tended to rate faster than others, that some workers were rated faster than other workers (even when their paces were controlled with the metronome), that slow (controlled) paces tended to be rated faster than the "true" (normal) paces, and that fast (controlled) paces tended to be rated slower than the "true" paces.

Although there is thus evidence that there are various sources of possible error in the pace rating process, experience with rating in practice presumably has indicated that there is reasonable reliability in the ratings of experienced personnel. The implication is that the magnitude of whatever error arises from these various sources is not of major proportions in actual operational circumstances.

Standard data. Standard (time) data are sometimes developed from time data for common elements consolidated from many different jobs of some general type (such as machining jobs). Usually such data are developed within a given organization and are used on an across-the-board basis for the jobs in the organization to which they apply.

Predetermined time systems. These systems consist of tables of standard time values for various types of basic motions that can be applied in the case of any operation that is to be analyzed to that level of detail. Most of these systems have been developed by management consulting services, and are based on large amounts of data for the basic motions that have been accumulated from many different jobs in various organizations. Among the predetermined time systems are the following: Methods-Time Measurement (MTM), Work Factor (WF), Motion-Time Analysis (MTA), and Basic Motion Time Study (BMT). Such systems consist of tables of time values for most variations of each of the several basic motions represented in the system in question, such as the therbligs listed in Table 5–1.

Figure 5–4 shows a set of simplified predetermined time data for several types of motions; the time study units (TMU) represent 0.00001 hour (0.006 minute or 0.036 second). For some applications of predetermined times more detailed sets of data are available, for example, for variations of the *move* motion: (A) move object to other hand or against stop; (B) move object to approximate or indefinite location; and (C) move object to exact location. Further variations are based on distance moved and the weight of objects moved.

The allowed time for any given operation, then, is based on the sum of the times specified for the several basic motions involved in the operation.

In the use of predetermined time values a basic assumption is that the times specified for the basic motions are in fact additive. However, this assumption has been questioned by some individuals on the grounds that evidence from a few laboratory experiments indicates that in some instances the times required to perform certain individual motions in a sequence of motions are directly de-

Figure 5-4. Examples of predetermined time values of the Methods-Time Measurement System (MTM). (Source: Maynard, pp. 5-17)

METHODS-TIME MEASUREMENT APPLICATION DATA

SIMPLIFIED DATA

(All times on this Simplified Data Table include 15% allowance)

HAND AND ARM MOTIONS	BODY, LEG, AND EYE MOTIONS
REACH or MOVE **TMU** 1″ .... 2 2″ .... 4 3″ to 12″ 4 + length of motion over 12″ 3 + length of motion (For TYPE 2 REACHES AND MOVES use length of motion only)	**TMU** Simple foot motion....... 10 Foot motion with pressure 20 Leg motion 10
	Side step case 1......... 20 Side step case 2......... 40
	Turn body case 1........ 20 Turn body case 2........ 45
POSITION <table><tr><td>Fit</td><td>Symmetrical</td><td>Other</td></tr><tr><td>Loose</td><td>10</td><td>15</td></tr><tr><td>Close</td><td>20</td><td>25</td></tr><tr><td>Exact</td><td>50</td><td>55</td></tr></table>	Eye time............... 10
TURN—APPLY PRESSURE TURN............... 6 APPLY PRESSURE.. 20	Bend, stoop or kneel on one knee............. 35 Arise................... 35
GRASP Simple............... 2 Regrasp or Transfer... 6 Complex............. 10	Kneel on both knees..... 80 Arise................... 90
	Sit..................... 40 Stand.................. 50
DISENGAGE Loose............... 5 Close................ 10 Exact................ 30	Walk per pace.......... 17

	1 TMU = .00001 hour
	      = .0006 minute
	      = .036 second

pendent on each other. This interdependence is primarily associated with the motions that precede and follow any given motion. To the extent to which this might influence the total time values for individual operations (when the allowed times for the motions are added together) the total time values could then be off what they should be. This is a worrisome issue in the use of predetermined time values, at least from the theoretical point of view. However, there are some hints that these disparities tend to even themselves out, thus suggesting that their practical distortion effect may be rather nominal.

Work sampling for determining standard time. Work sampling is still another approach to setting standard times for various work activities. However, since this technique has other uses as well, it is discussed separately in the next section.

Work Sampling

Work sampling is the process of taking instantaneous samples of the work activities of individuals or groups of individuals. The activities of the individuals as recorded from these sample observations are classified according to predetermined categories. A summation of the observations in the individual categories then reflects something about the distribution of time across the categories. Operationally, the observations can be obtained by one of three methods, as follows: (1) an analyst can make a direct observation of the individual(s) at each of many predetermined times; (2) a motion picture camera can be set to take one frame at each predetermined time; and (3) at the sound of a bell everyone can record his activity at that moment. Table 5-2 shows a simple example of work sampling for metal press operators. For any given activity category in the table the percent of observations for that category is taken as the estimated percent of time devoted to it.

Work sampling lends itself to use in the analysis of many types of jobs, in particular those which can reasonably be segmented into relevant activity elements which can be visually observed. Its most straightforward applications are in the cases of jobs that have a fairly well-defined pattern. Such a pattern is by no means a constraint, as long as the relevant activity elements can be differentiated in the analysis process. The method normally cannot be used if the differentiation of the elements cannot be observed—for example, one cannot observe different mental activities, or topics of verbal or written communications. The exceptions to this generality occur when the individual is reporting his own activities, or when

TABLE 5–2. An example of work sampling. (Source: Heiland and Richardson)

Category	Observations
Operating press (all elements)	27.1%
Press and tool adjustment	6.7
Materials handling, into press	20.6
Materials handling, out of press	27.3
Operator absent	5.8
Delay for material supply	3.3
Delay for material removal	5.2
Delay, other	4.0
	100.0

the observer analysts are given special training to be able to recognize distinctions that have been established. A case in point is reported by Hansen, in which observer analysts were trained to recognize differences between the various activities of biological scientists. In this instance some of the categories of activities established were planning conference with supervisor, planning experiments, reading current field literature, reading for background information, preparing media, preparing culture for inoculating, and observing of experiments.

In addition to its use as a method of establishing standard times for various work activities, work sampling can aid in improving the efficiency of operations by determining the time devoted to inefficient worker activities, the so-called down time of a machine, and the like. Further, it can give management a fairly good impression of the allocation of time to various activities for better manpower control.

Work sampling is essentially a statistical procedure, rooted in the laws of probability. In view of this, two conditions need to be fulfilled in order to be able to have confidence in the resulting data. First, the sampling of times for the observations must be random. Such randomization typically is achieved by the use of a table of random numbers. Thorough randomization is especially critical in the case of jobs that have a rather well-defined cycle. In the case of noncyclical jobs, it may be permissible to make the observations at more regular intervals since the activities being performed at various times presumably are randomized. However, there are some statistical risks involved in so doing; in addition, if the subjects being observed learn at what intervals the observations usually take place, they may alter their pattern of activities in order to be busy at the time of the observations.

Second, the size of the sample needs to be large enough to produce the desired level of precision and statistical confidence in the data. The level of precision is expressed as an interval of percent above or below the observed percent, such as ±1 percent, ±2.5 percent, or ±5 percent. The level of statistical confidence is involved in the notion of statistical significance. In very general terms, one can determine, for certain statistical values, the probabilities that a given value could not have occurred by chance. Thus, one can refer to the 99 percent confidence level, meaning that the *true* value would be expected to fall within the specified precision interval 99 times out of 100 if one selected other samples of the same size. Other confidence levels can be similarly interpreted. The 95 percent level is a rather commonly used level.

Statistical basis of the confidence level. The confidence level of a given sample of values is predicated on the estimated standard deviation of the distribution of the means of samples of similar size.

For the moment, let us consider the distribution of values of some variable that forms a reasonably normal distribution. The standard deviation of the values in a sample (sometimes represented by σ or S) is a measure of the variability of the cases in that distribution, as illustrated in Figure 5–5. In general, one standard deviation above or below the mean embraces about 68 percent of the cases, two standard deviations embrace about 95 percent, and three standard deviations embrace about 99.7 percent.

Now, let us consider the proportion of times which might be derived from a work sampling study. For a given category of work activities we derive a proportion, specifically the proportion of the total observations which fall in that category; this is an estimate of the proportion of time devoted to that activity. If we were to repeat the study with another sample of observations the same size we would probably find a somewhat different proportion; and if we were to do this again, and again, several or many times, with samples of the same size, we would usually find still other values. If the size of the samples is small we would expect that the variability in the samples would be much greater than if the size of the samples is large. This is illustrated in Figure 5–6. The estimated standard deviation of such a distribution (that is, the values of proportions expected from numerous samples of any given size) is technically referred to as the *standard error* of a proportion. The standard er-

Figure 5-5. Representation of a normal distribution showing the percentage of cases embraced within 1, 2, and 3 standard deviations (σ) above and below the mean.

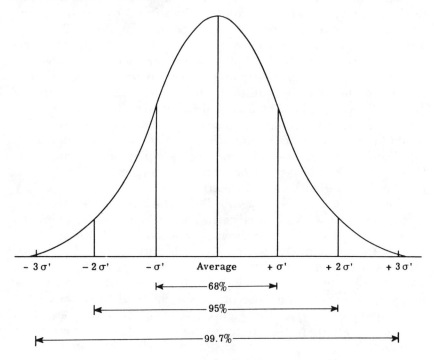

ror is not actually computed from a distribution of the proportions resulting from several or many samples (after all, it usually would be impractical to repeat a study several or many times). Rather, it is estimated from the single sample of the observations which have been made.

The confidence level, as used in work sampling, is based on this estimated standard error, and reflects the odds or probabilities that the "true" value of the proportion (which can never really be known) would fall within the specific precision interval.

Work sampling equation. There are various versions of the basic equation that is used in work sampling (along with various symbols used to represent the specific items in the equation). The following form is from Barnes:

Level of statistical confidence = 68%

$$S_p = \sqrt{\frac{p(1-p)}{N}}$$

where S = desired accuracy (as a percent of p)

p = percentage expressed as a decimal (i.e., a proportion)

N = number of observations (sample size)

This specific equation would apply if the level of statistical confidence were 68 percent, meaning that the true value would fall within the specified range of desired accuracy 68 percent of the time in repeated samples. (This corresponds to $\pm$ 1 σ from the mean.) To establish higher confidence levels, all that is necessary is to multiply the equation by the number of standard deviation units

Figure 5-6. Effects of sample size on the expected distributions of values of proportions. (Source: Hansen, pp. 13, 48. Reprinted with permission)

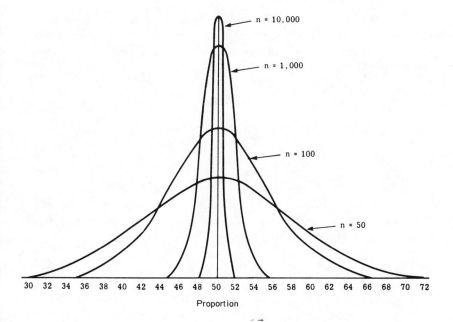

above or below the mean that represent the desired level of statistical confidence, as follows:

Number of σ Units ± the mean	Confidence level
1.00	68%
1.65	90
1.96	95
2.58	99

Thus for the 95 percent and 99 percent confidence levels, the formula would be as follows:

Level of statistical confidence = 95%

$$S_p = 2 \sqrt{\frac{p(1-p)}{N}}$$

Level of statistical confidence = 99%

$$S_p = 3 \sqrt{\frac{p(1-p)}{N}}$$

The 95 percent level of confidence is a rather common one in use. According to Barnes, for this level of confidence, the number of cases (N) would be derived with the following formula, assuming the desired accuracy, $S_{p'} = \pm 5\%$:

$$N = \frac{1600 \, (1-p)}{p}$$

As an example, if p for a given activity element is .80, then

$$N = \frac{1600 \, (1-.80)}{.80} = \frac{320}{.80} = 400$$

Applying this formula for various values of p (again assuming the 95 percent level of confidence and ± 5 percent accuracy) would require the sample sizes (N) indicated here:

p	1	2	5	10	20	30	50
N	158,400	78,400	30,400	14,400	6,400	3,730	1,600

Absolute error. As indicated above, the S_p (the desired accuracy) was represented as the percent of p (the percentage occurrence of any given activity element). Thus, if p were .10, and S_p were ± 5 percent, the desired accuracy would be between .095 and .105. (5% × .10 = .005, so .10 ± .005 = .095 and .105.) Similarly, if p = .40, the corresponding range would be from .380 to .420 (.40 ± .020).

Thus the range of desired accuracy is a function of the value of p, which is a *relative* level of accuracy. However, one could argue for an *absolute* level of accuracy that would be the same regardless of the value of p. Thus, an absolute error of, say, 2.5 percent, would result in acceptable ranges for the two examples used above as follows, showing the ranges for *absolute* versus *relative* accuracy:

<table>
<tr><td></td><td colspan="2" align="center">*Range of Accuracy*</td></tr>
<tr><td>p</td><td align="center">*Absolute*</td><td align="center">*Relative*</td></tr>
<tr><td>.10</td><td>.075 to .125</td><td>.095 to .105</td></tr>
<tr><td>.40</td><td>.375 to .425</td><td>.380 to .420</td></tr>
</table>

The required values for N for a given *absolute* level of desired accuracy are less, especially for small values of p. These are shown graphically in Figure 5–7.

Considerations in establishing sample size. We see that in work sampling a critical consideration is to determine the number of observations (N) that should be made. This determination is contingent upon the following three conditions:

1. The value of p for the activity element in question (the proportion of total time devoted to the activity element).
2. The desired level of accuracy (that is, the S_p value above).
3. The desired level of statistical confidence (as the 95 percent level). This is operationally expressed in terms of standard deviation (σ) units above and below the mean, as follows:

<table>
<tr><td align="center">*No. of σ units*
± *the mean*</td><td align="center">*Confidence*
level</td></tr>
<tr><td align="center">1.00</td><td align="center">68%</td></tr>
<tr><td align="center">1.65</td><td align="center">90</td></tr>
<tr><td align="center">1.96</td><td align="center">95</td></tr>
<tr><td align="center">2.58</td><td align="center">99</td></tr>
</table>

In considering the desired level of accuracy (item 2 above), a determination needs to be made as to whether the percentage of accuracy should be in *relative* terms or in *absolute* terms. If the purposes can be fulfilled with a given *absolute* percentage of accuracy (regardless of the proportion of time devoted to an activity) the

Figure 5-7. Curves for determining the number of observations required in a work sampling program for varying percents of occurrence of the activity elements and for specified percents of desired absolute accuracy. This figure is for the 95% confidence level. (Source: Barnes, pp. 32)

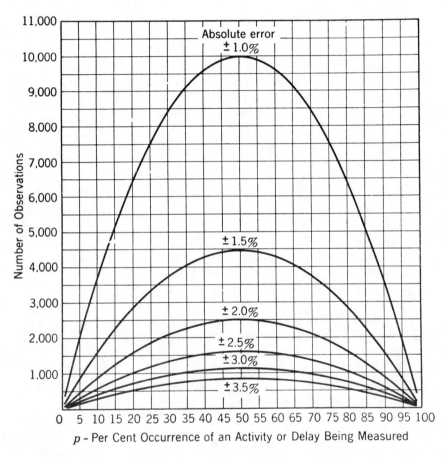

p - Per Cent Occurrence of an Activity or Delay Being Measured

number of observations is considerably less (especially with infrequently occurring activities) than if the desired level of accuracy is expressed as the percentage of the proportion of time for the individual activities. In this latter instance the following simplified formula, as given by Barnes, would apply for the 95 percent confidence level:

$$N = \frac{4(1-p)}{S_p{}^2}$$

where S = desired accuracy

$\quad p$ = percentage occurrence of the activity element expressed as a decimal (e.g., 15% = 0.15)

$\quad N$ = number of random observations required

Procedures for work sampling program. The usual procedures for carrying out a work sampling program include the following:

Establish objectives of study.
Identify the activity elements to be used in the study.
Carry out preliminary study to get estimates of percentages of time of activity elements, or otherwise estimate percentage of time of least frequently occurring element.
Set level of desired accuracy.
Set level of desired statistical significance.
Determine number of observations necessary to fulfill specified conditions.
Determine method of survey and individuals to be surveyed.
Prepare appropriate record forms.
Carry out survey.
Summarize and analyze resulting data.

An example of work sampling results. Work sampling has, of course, been used in the analysis of the activities of people in many kinds of jobs. The results of one such study, dealing with managers in a plant, are summarized in Table 5–3, to illustrate the end result of such studies.

Task Analysis

What is commonly referred to as *task analysis* covers a range of analytic procedures for use in describing human work in terms of *tasks,* a term used rather loosely since the procedures can be applied to the analysis of work at various levels of specificity. (The term *activity analysis* is sometimes used, and is somewhat more applicable because it could apply to various levels of specificity. However, we will use the label of *task analysis* because of its more common usage.)

Task analysis has its roots in the various techniques of methods analysis of the industrial engineers. Although the typical industrial engineering techniques have very important applications, they also have their limitations (as do most methods of work analysis). Thus, some adaptations, elaborations, and extensions of the basic precepts of those methods have been developed. These we discuss under the rubric of task analysis.

The Nature of Task Analysis

The common denominator of task analysis techniques is the description of jobs in terms of identifiable units of activities. Although the level of specificity of analysis and description can vary, many procedures are pitched at the task level. In this regard, a United States Air Force manual (*Handbook for Designers of Instructional Systems*) sets forth the following criteria for identifying tasks,:

A task is a group of related manual activities *directed toward a goal.*

A task usually has a definite beginning and end.

A task involves people's interaction with equipment, other people, and/or media.

TABLE 5–3. Results of a work sampling study of top managers and operating managers in one company. (Source: Hansen. Reprinted with permission)

	Percent of time	
Activity	*Top Managers**	*Operating Managers†*
Talking (oral communication)		
Consultation	10.5	3.6
Deciding on course of action	9.4	6.3
Discussion	6.2	4.0
Interviewing visitors	3.0	3.5
Telephone	8.8	8.2
Dictating	3.7	1.9
Meetings:		
Regularly scheduled	1.4	4.0
Special	8.0	6.0
Luncheon discussions	14.3	11.0
Visiting other offices	14.7	36.1
Writing	9.1	3.8
Reading	13.2	9.2
Miscellaneous	2.7	2.4
Total	100.0	100.0

*General Manager, Plant Manager, Director of Industrial and Public Relations, etc.
†Managers of Operations, Quality Control, Industrial Engineering, etc.

A task, when performed, results in a meaningful product. (Products are not always tangible. For example, a "correct decision" is a meaningful product.)

A task includes a mixture of decisions, perceptions, and/or physical (motor) activities required of one person.

A task may be of any size or degree of complexity. But, it must be directed toward a specific purpose or separate portion of the total duty.

Although task analysis in most instances is restricted to manual activities (as indicated by the above criteria), one can also consider certain mental activities as comprising tasks, although the problem of identifying them may be difficult.

Level of description. At one level, task analysis can consist of a very simple, straightforward listing (or other form of presentation) of tasks performed by an individual. For example, if we were to look at the job of secretary we might identify such tasks as the following:

Takes dictation.
Types letters from stenographic notes.
Types from rough copy.
Types from transcribed tape or disc.
Answers telephone.
Files letters in alphabetical file.
Operates duplicating machine.
Sorts incoming mail.

In the case of many jobs the various tasks may have no prescribed sequence (such as above), whereas in other jobs there may be a specific sequence. And in some jobs the sequence may be conditional upon various circumstances. (This is sometimes referred to as *branching* and is discussed in a later section, Techniques of Task Analysis).

Aside from the listing of tasks as such (whether in sequence or not), some techniques provide for further dissection of tasks into subtasks or more specific actions or activities that are required to complete the task. Usually the actions involved in completing a task do have a specified sequence, such as in the operation of a duplicating machine. In breaking down tasks into more specific activities there is some question as to how specific the activities should be.

The answer to this question depends in large part on the purpose of the analysis. In many instances the purpose is not served by a very detailed breakdown. In certain circumstances, however, the dissection of tasks has been carried out to the point of specifying the nature of relevant input stimuli, the decisions, and responses involved. (Examples of such analyses are given in the Section on Techniques of Task Analysis.) Generally speaking, the more detailed analyses are used for the development of training programs.

At whatever level the work activities are described, the individual activities are described or identified in very abbreviated form, usually consisting of an active verb and its object, but typically not including the infinitive phrase which is characteristic of conventional job descriptions.

Elaborations of task analyses. For some purposes task analysis processes go beyond the simple description of activities. For example, in the development of training programs the analyst may be asked to infer from the description of the activity what knowledges and skills might be required. And for this same purpose, and in some system development programs, provision may be made for the analyst (or others) to rate each task in terms of such constructs as difficulty or criticality, or to judge the amount of time the activity might take.

Uses of Task Analyses

To date, the primary users (and developers) of task analysis techniques have been the military services (especially the United States Air Force) as an integral part of the personnel aspects of existing systems or of those that are being developed. The techniques are used in descriptions of existing jobs, job redesign, personnel selection, the development of training programs, and manpower planning. The techniques have also been used by other types of organizations, and certainly have potential applicability in other contexts.

When it is used as a phase of the development of a new system, task analysis provides data for predicting the nature of the job activities that would be required to operate and maintain the projected system. Such predictions are based on inferences from blueprints, engineering specifications, and related design materials. This approach has two primary purposes. The first is to determine if there are any job activities that would be required on the basis of the tentative design of the system that might be undesirable from a human factors point of view (such as excessively complicated control operations). In such instances the tentative design can be modified to bring it more in line with human performance expectations. The second purpose is to predict the nature of the jobs that would be required when the system becomes operational. The job descriptions based on such predictions are used in turn, to plan personnel selection and training programs, to develop training simulators and job aids, and to estimate required manpower. The intent, in the case of some military systems, is to have trained personnel available upon the production of the systems in question.

In the United States Air Force the procedures directed toward these two objectives were originally called QQPRI (Qualitative and Quantitative Personnel Requirements Information). As it turned out, the full-scale implementation of such programs presumably became excessively cumbersome, so such an approach has not been used as extensively as was originally intended. However, a spinoff from such programs has been the development of task analysis techniques which have practical utility in both the military services and civilian organizations for the personnel aspects of existing systems, if not for systems under development. A major application, for example, is to provide the basis for developing training programs (or what are sometimes called instructional systems).

The Nature of Tasks

Task analysis techniques need to be predicated on the fact that there are certain common characteristics of tasks and that there are different types of tasks.

Common characteristics of tasks. One frame of reference in viewing tasks is the so-called S→O→R model: a *stimulus* (S) acts upon the *organism* (O), to bring about a *response* (R). Such a model is of course most clearly applicable in the case of tasks which involve physical responses, such as operating or maintaining a piece of equipment.

This paradigm had been used by Miller in some of his early work in providing a procedure for use in task-equipment analysis (TEA). His formulation provides for the analysis of tasks in terms of the following aspects:

a. The *discrimination* of stimuli (as from displays).
b. The *decision* required in selecting the most appropriate response.
c. The *action response* (as the operation of control mechanisms).
d. An indication of *response adequacy* (some form of feedback to tell the individual if his action was performed adequately).
e. Indications of *characteristic errors* or *malfunctions*.

Depending upon the nature of the job and the associated tasks, and the purpose of the task analysis, the technique selected might incorporate provision for including only certain of these features, or at least for emphasizing certain ones. (The listing of the tasks of a secretary given above, for example, consists only of the actions taken, and those are described at a rather gross level.)

Types of tasks. Tasks vary, of course, in their involvement of mental activities (including decision making and problem solving), and of physical activities. Most tasks which are dominantly manual may be continuous in nature (as in steering an automobile), or procedural (those involving a number of discrete activities, sometimes in fixed sequence, and sometimes involving alternative courses of action which in turn may involve some sequence of actions). Because of such differences in the nature of tasks, different approaches to task analysis may be in order.

Techniques of Task Analysis

There have been numerous variations in the techniques of task analysis, and in the formats used, which have been developed and used over the years. The *Handbook for Designers of Instructional Systems* has set forth some guidelines for use in the selection of appropriate methods and formats for various types of tasks. These guidelines are given in Figure 5–8. (It should be added that the discussion in that handbook is focused on the use of task analysis as the basis for the development of training programs, or what is referred to as instructional systems.) In this discussion we will touch on a few specific techniques and will illustrate each.

Decision table. Decision tables and flow charts involve complex decision making or problem solving. A decision table sets forth the various possible input conditions (and the combinations thereof), and specifies the action that should be taken in the case of each combination of input conditions. Figure 5–9 illustrates such a table, indicating for each possible combination of three input conditions what action should be taken and in certain instances the sequence of actions.

Decision flow chart. A decision flow chart is something of an elaboration of a decision table, but it is more specifically applicable to a circumstance in which there is a series of alternate action paths, with a "yes" or "no" decision to be made at each of several decision points, depending upon the conditions which exist at each point in time. Such a format represents the *branching* notion referred to in

Figure 5-8. Guideline for selecting appropriate methods and formats for analyzing various types of tasks and activities. (Source: *Handbook for Designers of Instructional Systems*, p. 2-24)

TASKS WHICH INVOLVE	ARE BEST DESCRIBED IN
• Complex decision making • Problem solving	Decision Table/Flow Chart or Outline Format
• Continuous activities (for example, driving a car) • Activities which must be performed in a specific sequence, within a definite time frame	Outline or Time-Line Format
• Step-by-step activities • Identifiable procedures	Column Format*

*The column format will be satisfactory for the vast majority of technical tasks.

Figure 5-9. Hypothetical example of a decision table. (Source: *Handbook for Designers of Instructional Systems*, p. 2-25)

WHAT	INPUT CONDITION	A	Y	Y	N	N	N	Read down columns to find
YOU	INPUT CONDITION	B	N	Y	N	Y	N	what pattern of conditions you have (Y = yes,
HAVE	INPUT CONDITION	C	N	N	N	N	Y	condition exists; N = no, it doesn't exist).
	ACTION	1	X					
WHAT	ACTION	2		X				
YOU	ACTION	3			X	2		Perform the Xed action *or* numbered sequence
DO	ACTION	4				1		of actions.
	ACTION	5					X	

the section on The Nature of Task Analysis. A generalized illustration is given in Figure 5–10. A more specific application of such a flow chart is given in Figure 5–11, which deals with the job of a service station attendant, and which actually depicts certain alternative, or branching, conditions, in addition to those of a distinctly "yes" or "no" nature.

Outline format. In describing some types of tasks, especially those involving some continuous activities, an outline format may be most

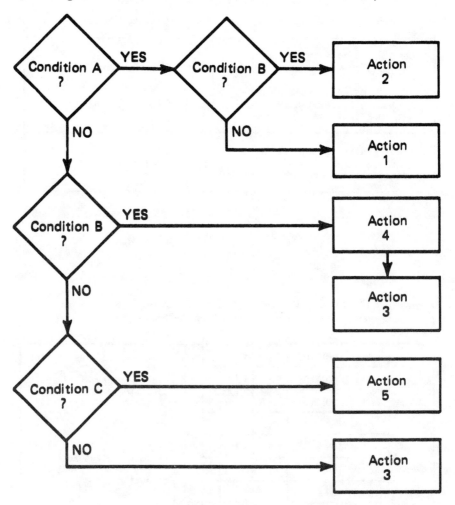

Figure 5-10. Generalized illustration of a decision flowchart. (Source: *Handbook for Designers of Instructional Systems*, p. 2-26)

suitable. Such an outline may well be based on Miller's formulation, which provides for the analysis in terms of discriminations (input from some source), decisions, action responses, indications of response adequacy, and indications of characteristic errors or malfunctions. Such an outline is shown in Figure 5–12, which represents an analysis of the task of passing when driving an automobile. The headings at the left of the figure are those for which entries are to be made.

Time-line format. A time-line format provides for showing, along a time scale, the various activities as they are carried out over time. It is especially suited for the analysis of tasks in which the sequence and time of performance of activities is critical. Depending on the activities in question, the time scale can be expressed in terms of seconds, minutes, hours, or other time units. The activities represented normally would be those depicting input, action, and output functions. A hypothetical example is given in Figure 5–13.

Column format. A column format in task analysis is usually most applicable in the analysis of tasks that are characterized by step-by-step activities and tasks that have identifiable procedures. Some such formats are modeled after Miller's original structure, depicted in Figure 5–14. In this scheme he provides a format for "general" task analysis and a separate one for "continuous" tasks. The format for general tasks is presented in Figure 5–14 with a segment of the analysis of the job of mimeograph operator.

An abbreviated column format is shown in Figure 5–15. This format provides for recording the action (including the item acted upon and any activity support elements such as equipment, materials, and work aids), the inputs(s) and the output(s). This format also provides for other task-relevant information, such as for characterizing the knowledges and skills required (these to be used in the development of training programs).

Other task analysis techniques. There are a number of other task analysis procedures and formats, some of which are variations of those already illustrated. Swain refers to one such variation as *operational sequence diagramming* (OSG). This form of task analysis also is rooted in Miller's basic formulation in that it provides for the identification of input information (stimuli), decision, and action (response) components of work activity. Variations in this theme can provide for indications of feedback (when available), recall, and communication processes.

One format that represents this approach is shown in Figure 5–16 with a simple example of its application to an automobile

Figure 5-11. Part of a decision flow chart for the job of service station attendant, showing branching.

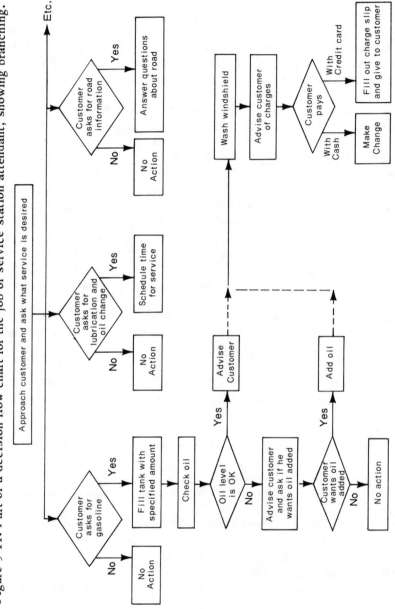

Note: Diamond-shaped figures represent possible conditions; rectangles represent actions.

Figure 5-12. Example of an outline format used in analysis of the task of passing in driving an automobile. (Source: *Handbook for Designers of Instructional Systems*, p. 2-28)

I **INPUTS (Cues)**		Your car (O) is in act of passing car X. Oncoming car Y appears ahead. Car X is to the right and ahead. Assume competing car will not accelerate.
Problem—Critical Cue Variables		1. The absolute rate of car being passed (X). 2. The absolute rate of oncoming car (Y); cars of variable size and speed. 3. The absolute momentary distance between X and Y. 4. The acceleration potential of car O at that speed (knowledge requirement).
Time Values		Critical, since a time of no return will be reached when it is too late to either dive in front of X or to brake. Time is function of 1, 2, 3, and 4 above.
Noise		1. Stress may occur. 2. Worry that X will increase speed while passing.

II **DECISIONS**		Pass now or pass later.

III **ACTIONS**		
Item Acted Upon	Accelerator	Steering Wheel
Specific Action	For rapid access of power, press all the way to floor board past a resistance detent.	
Effect of Action	Downshifts transmission from 3rd to 2nd gear (if below 50-55 mph). More power from faster engine-to-wheel ratio.	

IV **INDICATIONS OF CORRECT ACTION**	
Outputs	Same as inputs, but as X, Y, and O converge, the success or failure of the action becomes more apparent.
Time Delay	Function of acceleration rate of car.
Criterion of Correct Action	Getting back into right lane with "safety margin" (50 ft. plus, depending on speed). (Better criterion would be in terms of time between turning in to right lane and potential collision: 5 sec.)
Critical Value	Collision course perceived imminent.
Corrective Action	Brake and return to right lane or head for ditch on left.

V **CHARACTERISTIC ERRORS**	Misjudges one or more of critical cue variables; hesitates in application of accelerator.

Figure 5-13. Hypothetical illustration of a time-line format for use in task and activity analysis, showing overlapping of various activities. (Source: *Handbook for Designers of Instructional Systems*, p. 2-31)

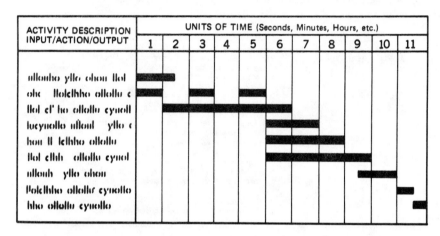

driving task. This particular form provides for representing recall and communication elements (when appropriate) in addition to information, decision, and action elements.

Criteria for reporting and recording task analysis information. Thus, we see that various techniques have been developed for reporting and recording task analysis information. As indicated earlier, certain schemes have particular relevance for use in the analysis of different types of tasks, so there is not any one best way, and one cannot use one particular scheme on an across-the-board basis. Snyder offers some criteria for evaluating different approaches:

> Psychological significance [the information should be presented in a psychologically meaningful manner, referring specifically to the information, decision, action, and feedback aspects]
>
> Reliability in use by different analysts and across jobs.
>
> Comparability [the method should make possible meaningful comparisons of performing the same task with other methods].
>
> Applicability to different tasks.
> Applicability to different stages of system development.
> Ease of revision.
> Prominence of important information.
> Flexibility.
> Provision for unique information.

Figure 5-14. Format of Miller's man-machine task analysis procedure for general tasks. This example illustrates the application of the procedure to one of the gross tasks and a specific subtask for the job of mimeograph operator. (Source: Miller, pp. 33, 37)

Format: Gross Task Analysis

| Task | Display | | Decision | Subtasks | Characteristic errors or malfunction |
	Description	Critical values			
Set up before first run	Position of brake	Not in 9 o'clock position	Release brake — move to 9 o'clock position	1	
	Discrimination required		Decision		

Format: Subtasks

Subtask or task	Display	Control description (or display-control description)	Control action	Indication of response adequacy	Objective criterion of adequacy	Characteristic errors or malfunction
1. Release brake		Brake	Turn clockwise (up)	Brake stop in 9 o'clock position		
	Action response			Indication of response adequacy (feedback)		Characteristic errors or malfunction

Figure 5-15. Part of the format used in a task analysis procedure by the United States Air Force as the basis for the development of instructional systems. (Source: *Handbook for Designers of Instructional Systems*, p. 2-32)

| JPR Code | TASK/ACTIVITY DESCRIPTION | | | |
| | ACTION | | INPUT(S) | OUTPUT(S) |
	Action and Item Acted Upon	Activity Support Elements (Equipment, Materials, Performance Aids)	Action Determinant(s)	Proficiency Requirements
TASK				

Figure 5-16. Operational sequence diagram (OSD) for an automobile driver. (Source: Swain, p. 17)

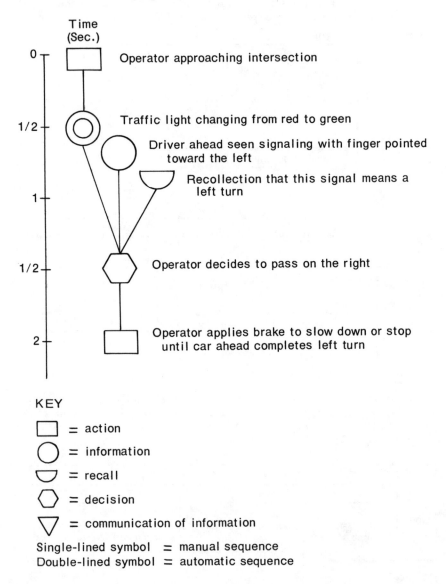

Discussion

Task analysis procedures come in many varieties. Conceptually they all do have a common denominator, namely, the analysis and description of work activities in terms of identifiable units (such as tasks, and subdivisions thereof). In this respect they represent an approach to job description that is reasonably objective and perhaps quantitative. Since no single approach can serve the various possible purposes of task analysis, however, it behooves those who are interested in such methodologies to select, or adapt, or develop that method considered to be most appropriate for the purpose at hand.

References

Amrine, H. T.; Ritchey, J.; and Hulley, O. S. *Manufacturing Organization and Management.* Englewood Cliffs, N.J.: Prentice-Hall, 1975.

Barnes, R. M. *Work Sampling.* 2nd ed. New York: Wiley, 1957.

Handbook for Designers of Instructional Systems, Vol. II. Headquarters, USAF, AFP 50–58. Washington, D.C.: 1973.

Hansen, B. L. *Work Sampling for Modern Management.* Englewood Cliffs, N.J.: Prentice-Hall, 1960.

Heiland, R. F., and Richardson, W. J. *Work Sampling.* New York: McGraw-Hill, 1957.

Lifson, K. A. "A Psychological Approach to Pace Rating." Ph.D. thesis, Purdue University, 1951.

Maynard, H. B. *Industrial Engineering Handbook,* 2nd ed. New York: McGraw-Hill, 1963.

Miller, R. B. *A Method for Man-Machine Task Analysis.* USAF, WADC, TR 53–137. Wright-Patterson AFB, Ohio: 1953.

Mundel, M. E. *Motion and Time Study,* 4th ed. Englewood Cliffs, N.J.: Prentice-Hall, 1970.

Snyder, M. B. "Methods of Recording and Reporting Task Analysis Information." In *Uses of Task Analysis in Deriving Training and Training Equipment Requirements,* pp. 11–31. USAF, WADD, TR 60–593. Wright-Patterson AFB, Ohio, 1960.

Swain, A. D. *System and Task Analysis, a Major Tool for Designing the Personnel Subsystem.* Sandia Corporation, SCR-457. Albuquerque, N. Mex.: 1962.

6

Structured
Job Analysis
Methods

The widespread use of conventional job descriptions is a reflection of their usefulness in personnel management and vocational guidance. They do have limitations, however, which arise primarily from their dependence upon verbal material, largely in essay form, which was characterized by Kershner as a "morass of semantic confusion." Even with the most skillful use of language in essay form there can be some slippage in conveying to the reader the meaning that is intended.

Largely because of such shortcomings, there have been efforts over the years to develop job analysis methods that are more systematic and scientific, methods that tend to be more quantitative then qualitative. These efforts have been aimed at developing procedures to identify and/or measure units of job-related information (such as tasks, or worker attributes). That would make it possible to compare and group jobs according to their similarities and to otherwise manipulate job-related information conceptually and statistically. Such approaches are becoming known as *structured job analysis* procedures.

These efforts have not been carried out with the intent of completely replacing conventional job descriptions with structured job analysis methods. Rather, the intent has been to develop methods that can serve certain purposes better than conventional job descriptions, or that can serve purposes that cannot be served by conventional descriptions. It is expected that conventional job descriptions will continue to be useful for personnel management and other purposes, especially for characterizing the role or objective of jobs and for presenting an integrated impression of the job activities. Some job analysis programs consist (or could consist) of combinations of conventional and structured methods. The procedures used by the USES, for example, although basically of the conventional job analysis approach, use some structured methods.

Bases of Quantification of Job-Related Data

As we envision the quantification of job-related data it is reasonable to be curious about the basic nature of the data that are expressed in quantitative form. In general, such quantification can be based on three different types of underlying data.

The first type includes certain data that by their nature are essentially objective and that typically can be measured in objective, quantitative form. A number of examples come to mind, such as: the time it takes to perform a specific activity; the frequency with which a specific activity is performed; the energy requirements of a given type of work; the accuracy of job performance (for example, in typing or in the making of parts to specified dimensions); the aptitude test scores of successful workers; the average time required by trainees to achieve a given level of performance; and the noise level and temperature of the working conditions.

The second type of job-related data may be essentially objective in nature but for one reason or another the quantification of such data is derived on the basis of someone's judgment, usually because of the practical problems of deriving strictly objective measurements. For example, we could determine experimentally the average time required to learn each of a number of jobs, but the experimental determination of such measures of mean learning time might be so complicated or costly that we would resort to the use of judgments (for example, of supervisors) about the learning time for the individual jobs.

The third type of job-related data that one might quantify is essentially subjective in nature, for example, the perceived difficulty of various tasks, preferences of people for different types of work, the prestige values of jobs, and the judged importance of various job activities. Such data, although essentially subjective in nature, can be expressed in quantitative form by any of a number of methods, such as various types of ratings.

Form of Quantification*

When objective measurements of essentially objective types of job-related data are available (such as the time it takes to perform a task, or the amount of oxygen consumed when performing a task), they should be used if they are relevant to the purpose at hand. Perhaps more typically, however, the job-related data used in the study of human work need to be quantified on the basis of human judgments (the second and third types mentioned above). To obtain such judgments there are four types of *measurements,* or what are commonly called *scales:* nominal, ordinal, interval, and ratio scales. Measurement in this sense has been characterized as the process of assigning numerals to objects according to rules.

Nominal Scale

A nominal scale consists of several mutually exclusive categories or classes of objects, each with some type of identifying label. . . . Thus, we could characterize jobs in terms of various classes, such as professional, managerial, supervisory, office, sales, production, etc. Or we could characterize job activities in terms of a wide range of activities such as handling, computing, reading, negotiating, supervising, etc. Each "class" in a nominal scale is in some respects different from every other class, although there may be some problems in differentiating among cases that fall at the borderline between two somewhat related classes.

The classes so established can be identified by labels or symbols, such as "3," "III," or "C," but these do not have any fixed numerical or systematic relationship to any other labels or symbols. In a sense, the process of assigning objects (such as jobs) to individual classes is essentially a classification or identification process (identi-

---

*Material on the four types of scales discussed in this section was originally prepared by the author for the *ASPA Handbook of Personnel and Industrial Relations.*

fying the class in which any given object falls). Although this classification does not strictly involve the assignment of quantitative values to the objects, we can nonetheless think of this as a form of
measurement.

Ordinal Scale

If two objects (or jobs) differ in terms of some given quality, they
can be ordered with respect to each other according to the
"amount" of that quality. Thus, jobs could be ordered in terms of
judgments of their relative difficulty, decision-making responsibilities, degree of supervision received, or endurance requirements.
However, an ordinal scale simply indicates that one case is greater
than the next case for the quality in question; it implies nothing
about the magnitude of the differences between adjacent cases.
Thus, the difference between the first job and the second on some
ordinal scale might be much less than the difference between the
second and third. Incidentally, the symbols $>$ or $<$ are used to indicate the direction of ordinal differences. $A > B$ means that A is
greater than B, or has more of the quality on which they are compared. In turn, $A < B$ means that A has less of the quality than B.

Interval Scale

In an interval scale, individual cases (for example, jobs) are characterized in terms of some unit of measurement. In a true interval
scale there is no absolute zero, but each unit is equal to every other
unit. The Fahrenheit and Celsius temperature scales are examples
of true interval scales; the difference between any two adjacent degrees is the same as between any two other adjacent degrees, but
the zero used in these scales is not an absolute zero.

Some tests are basically interval scales. An arithmetic test that
consists of many problems could serve as the basis for a scale of
arithmetic computation ability, with students falling at various positions along the scale depending on their test scores. Although one
could receive a zero on the test, such a score would not necessarily
indicate a complete lack of mathematical ability. For job-related
data we could assign jobs values along a quantitative scale of the
difficulty of a task that would reflect the judgments of analysts in
terms of equal intervals of "difficulty."

The condition of maintaining equal units along the scale is not
rigorously fulfilled in the case of many scales, such as those based
on test scores or on judgments of people about objects of some
class.

Ratio Scale

Like an interval scale, a ratio scale is characterized by units of measurement, but a ratio scale does have an absolute zero. In a job-related context, the factors that could be measured on a ratio scale might include completion time for an activity or the number of parts produced. In such instances the numerical properties of the scales developed would allow you to express differences in speed or parts produced as ratios by saying, "John is twice as fast in doing a job as Henry," or "Jane produced half again as many products as Lucille."

Discussion

Some of the methods of measurement described above have been used to classify jobs into categories (using a nominal scale) or to evaluate jobs on the basis of some quality or factor (using an interval scale). However, such quantification has not been employed as commonly in the study of human work as it ought to be.

The development of structured job analysis procedures is based on the notion of measurement of various aspects or characteristics, usually by one or another of the four scales, perhaps most commonly by nominal scales and interval scales (although the specification of equal difference between intervals of interval scales probably is not rigorously fulfilled in many cases). The rest of this chapter is devoted to descriptions of the more important examples of structured job analysis procedures.

Functional Job Analysis (FJA)

In the discussion in Chapter 4 of the job analysis procedures of the USES, reference was made to the worker functions as provided for in writing job summaries and in completing the work performance ratings. The USES worker function hierarchies of data, people, and things were given in Figure 4–2.

The basic concept of these worker functions and the three hierarchies was developed during the early 1950s when the USES was involved in an intensive research program directed toward producing the 1965 edition of the *Dictionary of Occupational Titles (DOT)* and a new job classification system for it.* The 1965 formulation was modified slightly for the 1977 edition of the DOT and is incor-

---

*Dr. Sidney A. Fine, who was then with the USES, was primarily involved in the formulation and development of the concept.

porated in the coding structure of the DOT as used by the public employment offices throughout the United States. Further modifications by Fine (Fine and Wiley) produced a formulation that serves as the basis for an operational system that is used by a number of private and government organizations as a job analysis procedure. The data, people, and things hierarchies of the modified structure are shown in Figure 6–1, and the individual functions are defined in Table 6–1.

Fine proposed the use of functional job analysis (FJA) as an approach to a technology for manpower planning (Fine, 1974). In our present context, however, we will focus our attention on the primary features of the job analysis aspects of the system.

FJA has been characterized by Fine and Wiley as "both a conceptual system for defining the dimensions of worker activity and a method of measuring levels of worker activity." The primary premises of the FJA conceptual system, as they characterized it, include the following:

1. A fundamental distinction must be made between *what gets done* and *what workers do* to get things done. The bus driver does not carry passengers; what he does is perform a number of sequenced tasks to drive a vehicle and collect fares.

2. What workers do, insofar as their job context is concerned, they do in relation to three primitives: Data, People, and Things.

3. In relation to each primitive, workers function in unique ways. Thus, in relation to things, workers draw upon physical resources; in relation to data, on mental resources; and in relation to people, on interpersonal resources.

4. All jobs require the worker to relate to each of these primitives in some degree.

5. Although the behavior of workers or the tasks performed by them apparently can be described in an infinite number of ways, there are only a few definitive functions involved. Thus, in interacting with machines, workers function to feed, tend, operate, or set up; and in the case of vehicles or related machines, to drive-control them. Although each of these functions occurs over a range of difficulty and content, essentially each draws on a relatively narrow and specific range of similar kinds and degrees of worker characteristics and qualifications for effective performance.

6. The functions appropriate to each primitive are hierarchial and ordinal, proceeding from the simple to the complex. Thus, to indicate a particular function, say compiling (data), as reflecting the requirements of a job is to say that it includes the requirements of lower functions such as comparing and excludes the requirements of higher functions such as analyzing.

Figure 6-1. Summary chart of worker function scales. (Source: Fine, 1974, p. 817)

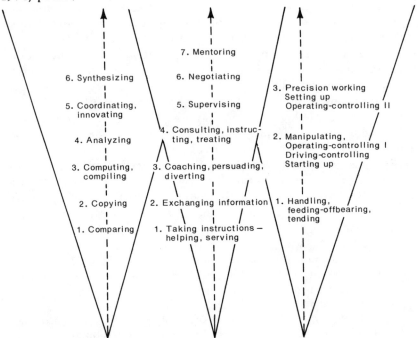

The three hierarchies mentioned above (data, people, and things) form the worker-function scales of the functional job analysis approach. Each of these consists of several specific functions that represent the various ordinal positions along the hierarchy. It should be noted that the hierarchies used in the job-analysis procedures of the USES (that are incorporated in the DOT and given in Figure 4–2) and those presented by Fine and Wiley, are basically the same, but they differ in some of the specific functions and in their numbering systems. The formulation by Fine and Wiley as given in Figure 6–1 is the one that is being used operationally by Fine.

Worker Function Scales of Functional Job Analysis

The functional job analysis approach of Fine and Wiley provides for the analysis of jobs in terms of two worker function scales, namely, the *level* and the *orientation* of involvement with the three hierarchies. The level of involvement is indicated by the specific function of each hierarchy that is considered to be applicable to the job in question. The level of involvement is also reflected in the same manner in the procedures used by the USES, as shown in the example of a job analysis schedule in Figure 4–1. In the use of the functional job analysis approach of Fine and Wiley, the orientation reflects the relative involvement of the worker, and is expressed by the analyst by assigning a percentage of units of 5 to each of the three functions, adding up to 100 percent. An example as applied to a particular task (in the social welfare field) is given below (Fine and Wiley).

> TASK: Asks client questions, listens to responses, and writes answers on standard intake form, exercising leeway as to sequence of questions, in order to record basic identifying information.

ANALYSIS OF TASK:

Area	Functional Level	Orientation
Data	Copying	50%
People	Exchanging Information	40
Things	Handling	10

It should be pointed out that the practice of USES in the use of functional job analysis consists of assigning levels to jobs, reflected in the code number assigned to a job in the DOT, on the basis of the analysis of the total job. On the other hand, Fine and Wiley propose the application of the formulation to individual tasks, and, by integration across tasks, to the entire job; and in addition they provide for the assignment of the orientation percentages.

Other Scales Used with FJA System

In addition to the data, people, and things scales, the FJA system provides for characterizing each job in terms of the following four scales (Fine, 1973): worker instructions; reasoning development; mathematical development; and language development (the last three scales are modifications of the General Educational Development Scales—GED of the USES).

Structure of Task Statements

An additional important facet of the system developed by Fine is the systematic practice of writing task statements, the fundamental units of observation. Fine (1974) makes the point that, to make a task statement meaningful, the action verb is modified by the means (tools, methods, equipment) required by the immediate objective of the action (if different from the result expected of the action), and by some indication of prescription/discretion in the worker instructions.

TABLE 6-1. Worker function scales of functional job analysis. (Source: Fine, 1973)

	DATA FUNCTION SCALE
1. *Comparing*	Selects, sorts, or arranges data, people, or things, judging whether their readily observable functional, structural, or compositional characteristics are similar to or different from prescribed standards.
2. *Copying*	Transcribes, enters, and/or posts data, following a schema or plan to assemble or make things and using a variety of work aids.
3A. *Computing*	Performs arithmetic operations and makes reports and/or carries out a prescribed action in relation to them.
3B. *Compiling*	Gathers, collates, or classifies information about data, people, or things, following a schema or system but using discretion in application.
4. *Analyzing*	Examines and evaluates data (about things, data, or people) with reference to the criteria, standards, and/or requirements of a particular discipline, art, technique, or craft to determine interaction effects (consequences) and to consider alternatives.
5A. *Innovating*	Modifies, alters, and/or adapts existing designs, procedures, or methods to meet unique specifications, unusual conditions, or specific standards of effectiveness within the overall framework of operating theories, principles, and/or organizational contexts.
5B. *Coordinating*	Decides time, place, and sequence of operations of a process, system, or organization, and/or the need for revision of goals, policies (boundary conditions), or procedures on the basis of analysis of data and of performance review of pertinent objectives and requirements. Includes overseeing and/or executing decisions and/or reporting on events.
6. *Synthesizing*	Takes off in new directions on the basis of personal intuitions, feelings, and ideas (with or without regard for tradition, experience, and existing parameters) to conceive new approaches to or statements of problems and the development of system, operational, or aesthetic "solutions" or "resolutions" of them, typically outside of existing theoretical stylistic, or organizational context.
	PEOPLE FUNCTION SCALE
1A. *Taking instructions-helping*	Attends to the work assignment, instructions, or orders of supervisor. No immediate response or verbal exchange is required unless clarification of instruction is needed.
1B. *Serving*	Attends to the needs or requests of people or animals, or to the expressed or implicit wishes of people. Immediate response is involved.

Table 6-1 (cont.)

2.	*Exchanging information*	Talks to, converses with, and/or signals people to obtain information, or to clarify and work out details of an assignment within the framework of well-established procedures.
3A.	*Coaching*	Befriends and encourages individuals on a personal, caring basis by approximating a peer or family-type relationship either in a one-to-one or small group situation; gives instruction, advice, and personal assistance concerning activities of daily living, the use of various institutional services, and participation in groups.
3B.	*Persuading*	Influences others in favor of a product, service, or point of view by talks or demonstrations.
3C.	*Diverting*	Amuses to entertain or distract individuals and/or audiences or to lighten a situation.
4A.	*Consulting*	Serves as a source of technical information and gives such information or provides ideas to define, clarify, enlarge upon, or sharpen procedures, capabilities, or product specifications (e.g., informs individuals/families about details of working out objectives such as adoption, school selection, and vocational rehabilitation; assists them in working out plans and guides implementation of plans).
4B.	*Instructing*	Teaches subject matter to others or trains others, including animals, through explanation, demonstration, and test.
4C.	*Treating*	Acts on or interacts with individuals or small groups of people or animals who need help (as in sickness) to carry out specialized therapeutic or adjustment procedures. Systematically observes results of treatment within the framework of total personal behavior because unique individual reactions to prescriptions (chemical, physical, or behavioral) may not fall within the range of prediction. Motivates, supports, and instructs individuals to accept or cooperate with therapeutic adjustment procedures when necessary.
5.	*Supervising*	Determines and/or interprets work procedure for a group of workers; assigns specific duties to them (delineating prescribed and discretionary content); maintains harmonious relations among them; evaluates performance (both prescribed and discretionary) and promotes efficiency and other organizational values; makes decisions on procedural and technical levels.
6.	*Negotiating*	Bargains and discusses on a formal basis as a representative of one side of a transaction for advantages in resources, rights, privileges, and/or contractual obligations, "giving and taking" within the limits provided by authority or within the framework of the perceived requirements and integrity of a program.

Table 6-1 (cont.)

7. *Mentoring*	Works with individuals having problems affecting their life adjustment in order to advise, counsel, and/or guide them according to legal, scientific, clinical, spiritual, and/or other professional principles. Advises clients on implications of analyses or diagnoses made of problems, courses of action open to deal with them, and merits of one strategy over another.

THINGS FUNCTION SCALE

1A. *Handling*	Works (cuts, shapes, assembles, etc.), digs, moves, or carries objects or materials where objects, materials, tools, etc., are one or a few in number and are the primary involvement of the worker. Precision requirements are relatively gross. Includes the use of dollies, handtrucks, and the like. (Use this rating for situations involving casual use of tangibles.)
1B *Feeding-offbearing*	Inserts, throws, dumps, or places materials into, or removes them from, machines or equipment which are automatic or tended/operated by other workers. Precision requirements are built in, largely out of control of worker.
1C. *Tending*	Starts, stops, and monitors the functioning of machines and equipment set up by other workers where the precision of output depends on keeping one to several controls in adjustment, in response to automatic signals according to specifications. Includes all machine situations where there is no significant setup or change of setup, where cycles are very short, alternatives to nonstandard performance are few, and adjustments are highly prescribed. (Includes electrostatic and wet-copying machines and PBX switchboards.)
2A. *Manipulating*	Works (cuts, shapes, assembles, etc.), digs, moves, guides, or places objects or materials where objects, tools, controls, etc., are several in number. Precision requirements range from gross to fine. Includes waiting on tables and the use of ordinary portable power tools with interchangeable parts and ordinary tools around the home, such as kitchen and garden tools.
2B. *Operating-controlling*	Starts, stops, controls, and adjusts a machine or equipment designed to fabricate and/or process data, people, or things. The worker may be involved in activating the machine, as in typing or turning wood, or the involvement may occur primarily at startup and stop as with a semiautomatic machine. Operating a machine involves readying and adjusting the machine and/or material as work progresses. Controlling equipment involves monitoring gauges, dials, etc., and turning valves and other devices to control such items as temperature, pressure, flow of liquids, speed of

Table 6–1 (cont.)

	pumps, and reactions of materials. Includes the operation of typewriters, mimeograph machines, and other office equipment where readying or adjusting the machine requires more than cursory demonstration and checkout. (This rating is to be used only for operations of one machine or one unit of equipment.)
2C. *Driving-controlling*	Starts, stops, and controls the actions of machines for which a course must be steered or guided in order to fabricate, process, and/or move things or people. Actions regulating controls require continuous attention and readiness of response. (Use this rating if use of vehicle is required in job, even if job is concerned with people or data primarily.)
3A. *Precision working*	Works, moves, guides, or places objects or materials according to standard practical procedures where the number of objects, materials, tools, etc., embraces an entire craft and accuracy expected is within final finished tolerances established for the craft. (Use this rating where work primarily involves manual or power hand-tools.)
3B. *Setting up*	Installs machines or equipment; inserts tools; alters jigs, fixtures, and attachments; and/or repairs machines or equipment to ready and/or restore them to their proper functioning according to job order or blueprint specifications. Involves primary responsibility for accuracy. May involve one or a number of machines for other workers or for worker's own operation.

As a further elaboration of the system, Fine (1974) provides for the development of an "application" paradigm that relates task content to performance standards and training content. Figure 6–2 is an example of a task statement presented in this three-way frame of reference. The first part (To do *this* task) includes the worker function (W F) scales (both level and orientation) and the values given for the four scales (instructions, reasoning, mathematics, and language). Fine states that when a task statement is "controlled" (by its structure and related scales) it is then possible to develop the performance standards and training content on the basis of such a statement, as shown in the other two parts of Figure 6–2.

Task Inventories

Task inventories comprise a form of structured job analysis questionnaire that consists of a listing of the tasks within some occupational field. Although the term *task inventory* is generally applied to

Figure 6-2. Example of a task statement and its related ratings as provided for in functional job analysis (FJA). (Source: Fine, 1974, p. 817. Reprinted with permission)

To do this task:

Types/transcribes standard form letter, including specified information from records provided, following S.O.P. for form letter, but adjusting standard form as required for clarity and smoothness, etc., in order to prepare letter for mailing.

Data	People	Things	Data	People	Things		Reas.	Math.	Lang.	
W.F. – LEVEL			W.F. – ORIENTATION			INSTR.	G. E. D.			TASK NO.
3B	1A	2B	70%	5%	25%	2	3	1	4	
GOAL: (To be completed by individual user.)							OBJECTIVE: (To be completed by individual user.)			

To these standards:

Descriptive:

  Types with reasonable speed and accuracy.
  Format of letter is correct.
  Any changes/adjustments are made correctly.

Numerical:

  Completes letter in X period of time.
  No uncorrected typing, mechanical, or adjustment errors per letter.
  Fewer than X omissions of information per X number of letters typed.

The worker needs this training:

Functional:

  How to type letters.
  How to transcribe material, correcting mechanical errors.
  How to combine two written sets of data into one.

Specific:

  How to obtain records and find information in them.
  Knowledge of S.O.P. for standard letter format: how and where to include information.
  Knowledge of information required in letter.
  How to use particular typewriter provided.

such questionnaires, various other terms have also been associated with the questionnaires, such as *functions, skills, activities, operations, duties, worker actions,* and *job elements.*

Such questionnaires, by whatever name, typically provide for job incumbents (or supervisors or analysts) to report some job-related information about the incumbent's involvement with each task. However, they lend themselves to other uses as well, as discussed later in this chapter in the section on secondary rating factors.

Task inventories of one type or another have been developed and used over a period of many years, but their primary development and use has been by the United States Air Force during and since the 1960s, under the direction of Dr. Raymond E. Christal, Air Force Human Resources Laboratory (AFHRL), Brooks

Air Force Base, Texas (Christal, 1972; Morsh; Morsh and Christal; Morsh and Archer). The methodology has also been adopted by certain other military services in the United States and other countries, by certain other government agencies, by some private companies, by universities, and by certain trade and professional organizations.

The Nature of Task Inventories

A task inventory is characterized by two features, namely, a list of tasks for the occupational field in question, and provision for some type of response scale for each task. The list of tasks usually consists of all or most of the tasks that can be performed by incumbents within the occupational field. Typically, the individual task descriptions consist only of a statement of *what* is done, in job-oriented terms. They do not include indications of *how* and *why* or cues or feedback features as provided for in certain task description and analysis procedures used in system development as discussed in Chapter 5. The tasks usually (but not always) are grouped into broader duties (such as, "Maintaining and repairing braking systems"). An example of part of a task inventory is given in Figure 6-3. In its final form a task inventory might include anywhere from a few dozen to a few hundred tasks.

Figure 6-3. Example of a few tasks from a task inventory for automobile mechanics. (Source: Melching and Borcher, p. 35)

AUTOMOTIVE MECHANICS TASK INVENTORY		Page __19__ of __23__ Pages	
		CHECK	**TIME SPENT**
LISTED BELOW ARE A DUTY AND THE TASKS WHICH IT INCLUDES. CHECK ALL TASKS WHICH YOU PERFORM. ADD ANY TASKS YOU DO WHICH ARE NOT LISTED, THEN RATE THE TASKS YOU HAVE CHECKED.			1. Very Much Below Average
			2. Below Average
		✓	3. Slightly Below Average
			4. About Average
M. MAINTAINING AND REPAIRING BRAKING SYSTEMS		If Done	5. Slightly Above Average
			6. Above Average
			7. Very Much Above Average
1. Repair master cylinder			
2. Repair wheel cylinder		✓	4
3. Replace brake hoses and lines		✓	1
4. Replace brake shoes		✓	6
5. Resurface brake drums			
6. *Adjust brakes*		✓	7

Response Scales Used with Task Inventories

There are essentially two types of response scales that can be provided for with task inventories. The first type provides for some indication of the involvement (if any) of a job incumbent with each task. The second type provides for some response about the task as such (such as a judgment about it, or an attitude toward it).

Primary rating factors. Response scales of the first type (the involvement of job incumbents with specific tasks) are sometimes referred to as *primary* rating factors (Morsh and Archer). Various types of scales can be used, such as the following, which is taken from Morsh and Archer.

□ Importance [of the task to the job]
□ Part-of-job scale [developed by Hemphill for use in obtaining dimensions of executive positions]. This scale is given below:

  0 Definitely not a part of the position
  1 Under unusual circumstances may be a minor part of the position
  2
  3
  4 A substantial part of the position
  5
  6
  7 A most significant part of the position

□ Performance [whether the incumbent does or does not perform the task]
□ Frequency of performance [how often the task is performed per unit of time such as per day, per week, or per month]
□ Time spent [time spent on the task when it is performed, as in minutes]
□ Relative time spent [estimated time spent on each task relative to time spent on other tasks].
  The United States Air Force uses the following scale:

  1. Very much below average
  2. Below average
  3. Slightly below average
  4. About average
  5. Slightly above average
  6. Above average
  7. Very much above average

Another variation of the relative time-spent scale (using nine instead of seven categories) is given below:

1. Very small amount
2. Much below average
3. Below average
4. Slightly below average
5. About average
6. Slightly above average
7. Above average
8. Much above average
9. Very much above average

Variations of these themes can of course be developed, such as the total time spent on a task during the individual's total work career (as contrasted with the time spent on it in the present job).

In reporting time spent on various tasks, it has been the experience of the Air Force that a *relative* time-spent scale (such as shown above) usually is better than an *absolute* (or percentage) time-spent scale. When a relative time-spent scale is used, the responses can be converted into an estimate of percentage of work time. The procedure for estimating these percentages is given by Archer as follows:

> To permit comparisons across incumbents on specific tasks, the relative time-spent ratings are converted to percentage values. These values are regarded as estimates of the percentage of work time spent by each encumbent on each task. It is assumed that the total of an incumbent's raw ratings represents 100% of his work time; and each raw rating is expressed as a percentage of that total. Where r is the rating provided by the incumbent on task i, and
>
> $$\sum_{i=1}^{n} r_i$$
>
> is the sum of his ratings on the n tasks in the inventory, the "percent time spent" by the incumbent on task i is
>
> $$\frac{r_2}{\sum_{i=1}^{n} r_i} \times 100$$

Most typically task inventories are completed by job incumbents in indicating their own involvement with the individual tasks. However, under some circumstances supervisors or analysts complete the inventory as it applies to the jobs of individual incumbents.

Secondary rating factors. The second type of response scale (sometimes referred to as *secondary* task-rating factors) provides for giving essentially judgmental or subjective responses about the tasks themselves, as contrasted with reports about the involvement of incumbents with the tasks. Some of the secondary rating factors that have been used are:

Complexity of the task
Criticality of the task
Difficulty of learning the task
Where the incumbent learned the task (training course, on the job, etc.)
Where the respondent believes the task should be learned
Special training required (amount) to do the task
Time considered necessary to learn the task (ranging from "can do now" to "can learn in a few hours," etc. to "would take more than a year to learn")
Difficulty of performing the task
Technical assistance required in task performance
Supervision required in task performance
Satisfaction in performing task

Such secondary rating factors most typically are incorporated in task inventories to be completed by job incumbents. Thus, an incumbent might be asked to use one primary rating factor (such as a relative time spent on individual tasks) and also to use one or more secondary rating factors (such as difficulty of learning the task or satisfaction in performing the task). However, such secondary rating scales can be completed by supervisors, experts, or others to elicit their judgments about, or subjective reactions to, the individual tasks in the abstract. In either case the responses to the secondary rating scales can be used to derive an index of the factor as related to the task. An example of such an index comes from an occupational survey of the Security Police Career Field of the Air Force (Burton and Driskill). As one phase of this survey, experienced supervisory personnel were asked to rate the tasks in the inventory on a task difficulty, using a 7-point scale. An average difficulty rating for each task was derived from the several ratings. The original ratings were converted to a new range of values with an arbitrary mean of five and a standard deviation of one. These indices are shown below for a few of the most difficult tasks:

Task	*Difficulty index*
Draft base emergency or defense plans	9.09
Draft budget and financial requirements	8.64
Plan correctional or retaining programs	7.24

Task	Difficulty index
Investigate major accidents or incidents	6.95
Develop rehabilitation programs for personnel in correctional custody	6.57
Direct law enforcement flight activities	6.43

Development of Task Inventories

For a more extensive discussion of the development and use of task inventories, the reader is referred to *Procedures for Constructing and Using Task Inventories* by Melching and Borcher. This manual is based in large part on the procedural guide previously developed by Morsh and Archer.

A task inventory is usually developed for an occupational area. Since this is a time-consuming chore, it should be undertaken only when the scope and importance of its use would justify the effort. Archer and Fruchter report that "typical" preliminary inventories should be completed in three to four weeks, but that those for more complex technical jobs might take about twice that long. A final inventory is usually produced by a job analyst and technical advisors.

In discussing the construction and use of task inventories, Melching and Borcher set forth a number of steps. Although their major focus is on the ultimate use of task inventories in training curriculum development, the steps they set forth would generally be applicable for task inventories to be used for other purposes as well. The following discussion of the development of task inventories is based in part on the steps they have crystallized, but it has been substantially abbreviated, and in certain instances other relevant material has been brought in.

1. *Define scope of performance situation.* This step basically consists of deciding on the breadth of the occupational area to be covered by the inventory.

2. *Locate written sources of activity statements.* As a starter, the job analyst responsible for the development of an inventory usually locates source materials that may be descriptive of the occupational area. Such source materials might consist of training materials of various types, instructional materials relating to the occupational field, instruction manuals relating to equipment used, relevant texts, and previously constructed task inventories and job analyses relating to the occupational area.

3. *Develop preliminary inventory.* There are essentially two general approaches to the development of a preliminary task inventory. In the first general approach the analyst develops the preliminary inventory on the basis of whatever source materials he has pulled together. There are two variations on this theme, as discussed by Archer and Fruchter. One is to develop a large pool of task statements from the source materials and then organize them into duty groupings. The other is to start off with a duty outline, and then to develop task statements within the framework of each duty or subduty. For various reasons they propose the second strategy.

In the second general approach, the analyst develops the preliminary inventory by asking a sample of job incumbents to list activities they perform, or by asking technical experts to list the activities they know to be performed in the occupational area in question. In either case, the analyst then consolidates the statements, eliminating duplications to end up with a single list of tasks. In addition, he edits the statements, working them into a reasonably consistent form.

Regardless of which approach is used, there are two major considerations in developing a preliminary inventory, the first dealing with the specificity of the tasks to be included, and the second dealing with the wording of the task statements. Generally, one would tend to characterize as tasks those job activities that are reasonably identifiable as discrete units of work, that have discernible beginnings and endings, and that in the normal course of events are executed completely by an individual. However, one should avoid the Scylla of excessive minutiae (such as, "Remove bolts that hold generator") and the Charybdis of excessive generality (such as, "Repair motor vehicles"), and rather seek an intermediate level on the specificity-to-generality scale (such as, "Repair generators"). Fruchter et al. state that it would be theoretically laudable to have all task statements equal in specificity, but they conclude that this is an almost impossible goal to achieve. They therefore offer the rather pragmatic suggestion that the level of specificity one needs in a given situation (to fulfill the objectives in mind) should serve as the basis for the criterion of adequacy, expressing the opinion that there is probably no one ideal level of specificity.

Closely related to the question of specificity is the matter of the total number of tasks which can reasonably be incorporated into a task inventory. Melching and Borcher suggest that inventories should include at least 200 but no more than 600 tasks. They suggest 600 as a maximum that job incumbents can be expected to respond to on a voluntary basis (although there are some inventories that are longer, and that presumably have been used successfully). For most occupational fields, the minimum of 200 is suggested because resulting task statements from fewer than 200 tasks might be so general that they would yield little information about specific jobs. However, since the minimum number should be very much a function of the range and variety of tasks within the occupational area in question, such a lower limit should not be considered absolute. There are a number of inventories that do have fewer than 200 tasks.

Task statements used in inventories have a fairly characteristic nature. They typically have a straightforward verb-object construction (as "Repair fuel pumps"), usually eliminating modifying phrases (as "Check fuel system *for cleanliness*"), unless there is some particular reason for including such modifiers. Further, multiple verbs are usually avoided (such as "remove and replace," "type and proofread"). Melching and Borcher set forth a number of guidelines to follow in preparing task statements. These are given below:

The task statement must be clear so that it is easily understood by the worker.

The task statement must be stated using terminology that is consistent with current usage in the occupational area.

The task statement should be brief to save reading time of the worker.

The task statement must be written clearly so that it has the same meaning for all workers in the occupational area.

Abbreviations must be used cautiously since they may not be understood throughout the occupational area. It is good practice to spell out the term and follow it by the abbreviation in parentheses where it first appears in the inventory. In later usage the abbreviation may stand alone. However, it is best to avoid abbreviations whenever possible.

The task statement must be worded so that the task rating scales make good sense when applied to it.

The task statement must be ratable in terms of time spent and other rating factors. This eliminates skill, knowledge, and responsibility items that begin with such words as "Have responsibility for," "Know how to," "Understand," "Have knowledge of." Such statements found in source materials should be written as specific activity task statements (e.g., "Maintain files" or "Supervise maintenance of files," NOT "Have responsibility for maintaining files.").

Vague or ambiguous words, such as "check," "assist," "coordinate," "recommend," "determine," "assure," should be avoided.

Short words should be used in preference to long words or expressions (e.g., "Fill out work orders," NOT "Prepare forms for vehicle repairs to be accomplished by mechanics.").

The qualifications a worker has, such as intelligence, aptitude, knowledge, education, skill, training, and experience are not tasks and are not included in the duty-task section of the job inventory. Information with regard to certain qualifications, such as training, education, and work experience, however, may be obtained by including appropriate items in the background information section of the inventory.

Receiving instruction is not included as a duty or task unless actual useful work is performed during the training. Thus, classroom instruction, laboratory or shop instruction, and the coaching a person receives are not tasks. On-the-job training, however, may include the performance of tasks under a supervisor. These tasks are listed in the inventory the same as any other tasks. Giving instruction, which is a supervisory duty, is included under "Training."

The task statement should begin with a present tense action word with the subject "I" understood (e.g., "Operate," "Write," "Clean," NOT "Operates, "Writes," "Cleans.").

Task statements are arranged alphabetically under each duty. This order shortens the incumbent's reading time and assists him in recalling tasks that are not listed. For example, the incumbent can easily scan through a list of tasks beginning with the word "Inspect" to make sure that all the inspections he performs are in the inventory. The alphabetical arrangement also helps the inventory constructor eliminate duplicate tasks.

Murphy carried out a study comparing the reliability of responses to task statements as originally written to that of the same statements after they had been rewritten in line with certain readability guidelines. (Reliability was determined by comparison of two sets of responses of the same job incumbents using the same inventory about a month apart.) The results tended to indicate that the rewritten statements were used with somewhat greater reliability than the original statements. On the basis of his study, Murphy proposed the following rules for preparing statements to enhance their reliability. Certain of these tend to overlap some of the guidelines given above.

   a. Reduce total word value per task statement. [The "word values" come from Thorndike and Lorge, who derived values for 30,000 words on the basis of their frequency of use.]

b. Reduce average word value per statement.
c. Reduce the number of syllables per word.
d. Reduce the number of syllables per task statement.
e. Use double conjunction "and/or" to replace instances in which a task is composed of parts which may be performed independently.
f. Do not use technical terminology where the range of incumbents' experience may vary greatly.
g. Wording of task statements should not be so specific as to include the recipient of the work performed.
h. Task statements which appear to be very general should be rewritten in a manner which confines the task for the total job.

In most task inventories the tasks are organized into duties that cover a relatively large segment of work. Melching and Borcher point out that there are generally two types of duties in task inventories: (1) supervisory activities (such as supervising, organizing, planning, directing, implementing, training, inspecting, and evaluating), and (2) work performance activities (such as performing, maintaining, troubleshooting, repairing, removing and replacing, adjusting, and installing). A few examples of duty statements are given below from Melching and Borcher:

Automotive Mechanics task inventory
Performing engine overhaul activities
Maintaining and repairing cooling system
Business Data Processing task inventory
Supervising programming
Operating automatic data processing equipment
Performing systems programming
Secretarial Science task inventory
Performing bookkeeping and accounting activities
Preparing forms and publications
Maintaining files and library

4. *Review of preliminary inventories.* When the preliminary inventory is completed, it should then be reviewed by several or many technical advisors (experts in the occupational area) to add (write in) tasks that have been omitted; to indicate if any listed tasks should be consolidated, broken down further, or eliminated; and to judge whether the task statements as given are clear in their meaning, or whether they should be reworded to make them more understandable to an incumbent. Such a review may take place by mail, or it might be carried out during an interview with the technical advisors either individually or as a group.

Melching and Borcher suggest the following questions to keep in mind when reviewing the preliminary inventory:

☐ Is the task statement clear: Will everyone understand what it means?
☐ Is this task statement covered by a previous task statement?
☐ Does this task fit better under another duty?
☐ Are there any other tasks that should be under this duty?
☐ Is this task performed in your organization?
☐ Is this task performed by any workers in the occupational area?

5. *Prepare revised draft of inventory.* Once the information from the expert reviewers is in hand, the analyst reviews all the suggested modifications, taking advantage of them to work up a draft of what will generally be the final form of the inventory. In case of questions or significant differences between and among advisors, the review process might be repeated with an intermediate form of the inventory before preparation of a final form.

In the final form there usually is provision for job incumbents to write in tasks that are not in the inventory. This not only makes it possible for the analyst to spot tasks that may have been missed somewhere along the line, but it also helps him identify new tasks and furnishes data for updating inventories with dynamic changes in an occupational area.

In the preparation of the final form of an inventory there is usually provision for the incumbent to record certain types of biographical data, in particular those which might be relevant in statistical summaries and analyses to be carried out later.

6. *Select scales to be used.* The nature of an inventory usually is related to the purpose for which the inventory is to be used. Under normal circumstances there would be provision for incumbents to use one or more primary rating scales which reflect their involvement with each task. Several such scales were mentioned earlier in this chapter, in the section headed Task Inventories. Figure 6–3 illustrates two such scales used in combination, one providing for the incumbent simply to check each task he performs, and the other providing for reporting relative time spent on those which he does do. In some instances a secondary scale is also used, such as one of those listed earlier in the chapter.

7. *Administer a pilot test of inventory.* Before putting the inventory into a formal printed form it is usually a good idea to try it out with a few other incumbents in order to obtain any firsthand feedback from them that may be useful in a final revision. If the pilot test indicates that the inventory is satisfactory in its present form, it

is then reproduced for use. Otherwise, additional modifications are made before reproduction.

8. *Print inventory.*

9. *Administer inventory.* Some task inventories are mailed to subjects (usually job incumbents), whereas the administration of others is arranged for within the organization. When they are to be completed by job incumbents, they can be administered to the incumbents as a group or they can be given to incumbents to complete on their own. In the case of personnel in supervisory, management, professional, and related positions self-administration is usually satisfactory, but with hourly paid, blue collar workers group administration usually is desirable in order to give greater assurance that the instructions are being followed.

In most instances in which task inventories are used the respondents are asked to record their responses on forms that can facilitate any subsequent analysis. Thus, mark-sensing forms or optical scanning forms are used frequently, in order to facilitate the later computer processing of the resulting data.

In planning the administration of task inventories there may be a problem of selection of a sample in case all the incumbents within the occupational area are not to be surveyed. In the military services and other large organizations, for example, a sampling usually would be planned.

Sampling can be a fairly critical matter, especially if the sample represents only a small portion of the total population of people in the occupational area to be sampled. Farrell et al. make the point that there are three basic considerations which should be assured in any sample design, as follows: (1) the sample should be *representative* of the population from which it is drawn; (2) it should be obtained by some systematic *probability process;* and (3) it should be *as small* as considerations of precision and dependability permit.

In some circumstances a strictly random sample can be drawn from the basic population. (The basic population is the total personnel in the occupational area of interest, such as those in the specified occupational area within a specific organization or within a specific geographical area.) More typically, however, a stratified sample would be in order. In drawing a stratified sample the total population is subdivided into one or more strata (categories) that are considered potentially relevant. In an evaluation of the Marine Corps task analysis program, Farrell et al. propose strata based on three factors, namely, the echelon of the facility, rank (that is, pay scale) of the incumbents, and location (East coast, West coast, and overseas). In nonmilitary circumstances, corresponding strata may be thought of in terms of type and/or level of the organizational unit in which people work, pay grade or other indication of level of individuals within an organization, and geographical locations (if relevant). In some circumstances other bases may be appropriate.

Given information about the number of individuals within each stratum or combination of strata (if there are two or more strata used), the sampling may consist of some predetermined proportion, or number, within the different categories. In most sampling schemes the same proportion of cases is selected from each of the combinations of strata. Following this strategy, if the total sample is to consist of 20 percent of the individuals within each of the strata, categories would be selected by the use of random numbers.

In the case of the Marine Corps study, however, the recommendation was made to select the same number (specifically 50), from each of eight pay grades, rather than choosing a sample that would be proportionately representative of the number within each pay grade in the total population. There are statistical arguments on both sides of this fence, but the equal-number strategy in this situation tends to equalize the sample in terms of *different types of jobs* (as reflected by pay grade) rather than *numbers of people* within jobs.

In connection with the size of the sample to be drawn, Farrell et al. carried out a rather extensive analysis of the stability of the results obtained from various sample sizes (20, 30, 40, 50, 60, 70, 80, 90, 100, 150, 200, 250, 300, 320, 400, 500, and 700). In particular, they drew two random samples of each size and compared the distributions of responses of Marine Corps personnel to each of 20 tasks in a task inventory. For each pair of samples they compared the mean responses and the standard deviations, and found that these two values tended to become stabilized with samples of about 400. Larger sample sizes did not increase the stability appreciably. Incidentally, they present mathematical evidence that generally corresponds with their empirical evidence that sample sizes of 400 are usually the optimum.

Discussion. Once a task inventory has been administered and the results obtained, the data are subjected to any of a number of statistical analyses, some of which are illustrated in Chapter 8. Such statistical processing usually is carried out with computers, unless the project is a very small one.

Reliability of Task Inventory Information

In considering the use of task inventory information one may wonder how reliable such data are. The reliability of measurement refers in a general way to the consistency or dependability of measurements of some variable. There are several types of reliability and, as applied to task inventory information, several bases for deriving estimates of reliability. For our purposes here, let us consider the reliability (that is, the consistency) of the responses given by persons who complete task inventories. The preferable basis for determining such reliability is by a comparison of the responses of a sample of people when the inventory is administered twice, say a week or two apart. (In the case of responses from job incumbents, the time interval should not be very long if there is any possibility of changes in job content during the interval.) Reliability in such instances usually is expressed as a coefficient of correlations.*

The reliability of responses to two administrations of an inventory across a sample of subjects can be computed in either of two ways, as follows:

1. Using individual tasks across incumbents as the basis of reliability, the response (for a single task) is:

	Administration	
Incumbent	*1st*	*2nd*
1	3	4
2	7	7
3	1	2
⋮	⋮	⋮
n	5	3

2. Using individual subjects across tasks as the basis of reliability the response (for a single subject) is:

	Administration	
Task	*1st*	*2nd*
1	6	5
2	2	2
3	4	5
⋮	⋮	⋮
n	3	3

Given the reliability coefficients for the individual tasks (or individual subjects) it is possible to derive an average coefficient for all

---

*A coefficient of correlations is an index of the degree of relationship between two variables over a sample of cases. It can range from +1.00 (a perfect positive relationship) through lower positive values to zero (the absence of any relationship) through increasing negative values (which reflect a negative relationship) to −1.00 a perfect negative relationship).

tasks (or for all subjects). Some examples of average coefficients for all tasks in certain inventories are given below, in particular those of (a) McCormick and Ammerman, (b) Birt, and (c) Cragun and McCormick.

Response scale	(a)	(b)	(c)
Task occurrence	.70 & .73	.87	.63, .64 & .65
Time spent on task	.61	.83	.62
Part-of-position (of task)		.83	.63
Importance (of task)			.56
Difficulty (of task)	.47		.35

The time span between the two administrations in the case of the coefficients from Cragun and McCormick (c) was several weeks, which may account for the somewhat lower coefficients.

In one sense, the reliability of task inventory responses can be viewed in much the same way as responses to a test. The reliability of individual test items typically is relatively moderate, but the collective reliability of the pool of items that comprises a test usually is substantially higher; and the more items, the higher the reliability. Thus, in the study by Cragun and McCormick, estimates of the reliabilities of the pool of tasks in the inventories were derived by the use of the Spearman-Brown prophecy formula (Guilford). Certain of these estimates are given below, as taken from the tasks included within certain duty categories of the aircraft maintenance career field. These are expressed as phi coefficients which can be interpreted in the same manner as correlations.

Duty Category	No. of Tasks	Average for Tasks in Category	Adjusted with Spearman-Brown Formula
Planning	28	.50	.97
Supervising	37	.51	.98
Inspecting	10	.53	.92

As another (perhaps indirect) indication of the reliability of task inventory information, Birt examined the possible effect of differences in inventory responses of 20 airmen as given to two inventories a week apart as such differences might affect their hypothetical assignments to 49 actual vacancies which had been described in terms of the same basic inventory. He used an *affinity* index, which reflected the degree of relationship of a *person* profile to each *job* profile. (Affinity indexes were derived in 13 different ways that need not be described here.) For a given method it was possible to correlate an individual's affinity indexes for the 49 vacancies as these indexes resulted from the two administrations of the inventory. These correlations, averaged across the 20 airmen, ranged from .92 to .99 for the 13 methods, with a median of .96. These results indicate that the possible assignments of airmen, as they might be made by a computer matching of men and positions, would not be markedly affected by whatever differences there are in inventory responses on two different occasions.

Stability of Task Inventory Information

Closely related to the concept of reliability of measurement (as related to task inventory information) is the matter of the stability (or consistency) of the data that are summarized from a sample of subjects in a given occupational field. The question here is whether one would get the same results if one could obtain data from a second sample of similar subjects. This question deals with what Christal (1971) refers to as the stability of consolidated job descriptions based on task inventory survey information. In the analysis in question, task inventory data from ten Air Force career fields were used. The number of respondents in each career field was divided randomly into halves. Consolidated job descriptions were prepared for each half, the descriptions for the incumbents in each half consisting of the "percent performing" the individual tasks and the "percent of time spent by the total group" for the individual tasks. A coefficient of correlation was derived for each of these measures across all the tasks for airmen in 35 specialties in ten career fields (with a total $n = 9,822$). The median and range of these 35 correlations were as follows:

Measure Used	Median	Range
Percent performing	.978	.888 to .997
Percent of time spent	.967	.813 to .996

Validity of Task Inventory Information

The concept of validity as applied to task inventory information refers to the underlying truth or correctness of the data. As applied to the responses of job incumbents, this would deal with the extent to which the data given by incumbents about their involvement with different tasks actually reflects their real involvement. Such data — in hard, cold form — are difficult to come by, and there are very limited instances in which data have actually been obtained. (It would require some means of verifying the responses given by individuals.) In most circumstances one must assume that if task inventory responses are reasonably reliable they are also reasonably valid. Christal (1969) reports briefly the efforts of a group of trainers in the Air Force who refused to accept the validity of occupation survey results in their area, and set about to gather evidence that the data were in error; yet at the end of their investigation they had to accept the inventory results as being basically valid.

Discussion of Task Inventories

Some of the uses of task inventories will be discussed in later chapters. For the moment, however, let us consider certain aspects of the use of task inventories as means of eliciting job-related information, especially from job incumbents.

To begin with, the development of a task inventory is a time-consuming chore and probably can be justified only if it is to be used with a large enough number of individuals to warrant the time and effort required in the development stage. It is more efficient to locate, whenever possible, a task inventory that has already been developed for the occupational field in question and can be used in its present or slightly modified form. An appropriate task inventory may provide for the collection of potentially massive amounts of job-related data with minimum administrative effort. The time costs are largely the time it takes for the incumbents to complete the inventories.*

Once the inventories are completed, the question then arises as to adequacy of the data in terms of such aspects as reliability, stability, and validity. As indicated above, it is usually necessary to assume the validity of such data if they are reasonably reliable. In this regard, although the reliability of responses of individuals to individual tasks tends to be rather moderate, when the many bits and pieces of inventory data are pooled, either for an individual, or especially across individuals, the reliability of the data can generally be regarded as very respectable and fully adequate for use in most of the statistical analyses that are carried out with such data. Further, the data on the stability of consolidated job descriptions indicate that substantial confidence can be placed in the typical statistical summarizations of such data.

*Directories of task inventories have been developed by the Center for Vocational Education, Ohio State University, 1960 Kenny Road, Columbus, Ohio 43210. *Task Analysis Inventories,* published by the Manpower Administration (now the Training and Employment Administration) of the United States Department of Labor, also includes a compilation of task inventories for various occupational areas.

It should be added that, as in the case of most structured job analysis procedures, the end results of task inventories typically are expressed in quantitative terms as related to specific tasks and do not depict the integrated role of individual positions or jobs.

Data from task inventories are particularly useful for certain purposes, such as the identification of job types, or the planning of training curricula. However, task inventories do not lend themselves as effectively for other purposes, so we cannot agree with Moore when he states that this procedure "seems to offer a significant step forward over other forms of occupational analysis." The basic point we are making here is that each of the various individual methods has its own potential uses, and it does not seem reasonable to believe that there is one best method that can serve all purposes.

Job Information Matrix System (JIMS)*

Certain job-analysis procedures, such as the use of task inventories and the functional job-analysis approach, are intended to provide standardized bases for analyzing jobs. Another development for providing standardized job information is what is referred to as the Job Information Matrix System (JIMS), developed by Stone and Yoder and their associates (1970).

The JIMS Concept

The JIMS has undergone a series of evolutionary developments. In its most current form it provides a standardized basis for gathering and recording job information of the following categories:

1. What the worker *does* on his job
2. What the worker *uses*
3. What *knowledge* the worker must have
4. The *responsibilities* of the worker
5. The *working conditions* of the job

For each of these categories of information the JIMS concept provides "modules" or "units" of information, or standardized terms, to be used in the analysis of jobs in presenting job information in these different categories. The JIMS procedure is tailor-made for specific occupational areas. The one that has been

*This section was originally prepared by the author for the *ASPA Handbook of Personnel and Industrial Relations,* and appeared in the chapter "Job Information: Its Development and Application."

developed for experimental and demonstration purposes is an occupational division of the DOT, division 60, metal machining occupations.

What the worker does on his job. The analysis of what the worker does is carried out with a standardized listing of job activities of essentially a job-oriented nature. In essence, these are tasks such as those incorporated in task inventories. Such task listings would be developed for the particular occupational areas in question. A few illustrative tasks for the metal machining occupational area are given below:

1. Interpret engineering drawings
26. Drill center holes
36. Adjust cutting tools and machine attachments
46. Grind tools and drills to specifications
84. Calibrate mechanical or electronic devices

In practice, such tasks would be rated by the job analysts in terms of the relative frequency with which they are performed by a worker.

Aside from the use of the list of tasks in characterizing the job activities, there is provision for describing the major job tasks, those that occupy the most amount of the time on the job. This section is not "structured" in the same sense as the list of tasks mentioned above. Rather, the analyst is asked to describe in an open-ended fashion the "major" tasks of the job, those that occupy a major portion of the worker's time. In doing so, however, the analyst is to use when possible verbs that are related to modified versions of the worker functions of the three hierarchies of the functional job-analysis approach (data, people, and things).

For each of the "data" and "people" hierarchies there is provided a specific list of activity verbs that are elaborations of the hierarchy in question. For any given (modified) worker function there are several more "specific" verbs, thus making it possible for the analyst to describe each such function in terms that are more uniquely appropriate to the activity in question. An example of the activity verbs within one of the worker functions—analyzing—is given here:

Investigate	*Scrutinize*	*Evaluate*	*Report*
research	examine	verify	identify
experiment	audit	appraise	recommend
study	scan	test	summarize
			suggest

Each of these verbs is defined in order that its use may be reasonably standardized. In the case of the "data" and "people" hierarchies the use of such verbs presumably would make it possible to "peg" major tasks at appropriate levels of the hierarchies.

This seems not to be as feasible, however, in the "things" hierarchy since the level of activities described by individual activity verbs depends very much on the object. For example, cutting lumber does not rate the same position in the hierarchy as cutting diamonds. It thus appears that in this area task statements could be ranked in terms of their verbs only when the verbs are considered in the context of the entire task statement. This presumably would have to be done within any given occupational area.

What the worker uses and what he has to know. The items which the individual uses and what he must know are intended to describe how a worker accomplishes his job tasks. In this phase of the analysis the analyst would have available for the occupational area in question a previously prepared listing of machines, tools, equipment, work aids, and so forth that might be used. For example, in the case of metal-machining jobs there would be listings of various types of grinding machines, milling machines, drill presses, and so forth. The entries to be made are related to the individual tasks, as in the following example:

Task: "scribe reference lines and points on work piece"
　Uses: gauges, blueprints, dividers, scribers, templets, straight edge
　Must know: trigonometry, set-up procedures, blueprint reading

Job responsibility. In the analysis of any given job the job responsibilities indicated would be those which are specifically relevant to the occupational area in question. In the case of the machine occupations, for example, there is provision for indicating both the dollar value of the usual product work piece dealt with and the responsibility for equipment such as preventive maintenance, minor repairing, and so forth.

Working conditions. The working-conditions phase of the JIMS essentially parallels the procedures used by the USES in characterizing working conditions, hazards, and so forth, as shown in Figure 4–4.

Discussion

The JIMS system has been applied to the machining occupational area with reasonably promising results. At the present time it is not a "complete" system since certain features of it need to be specifically developed with respect to each occupational area. The extension to a broad range of occupational areas would of course be a major undertaking. At the present stage it probably should be viewed as something of a "demonstration" approach to the analysis of jobs. In this regard, it does provide for considerable standardization in job information in, for example, the use of what are in effect task inventories and in the use of terminology (specifically the use of specified activity verbs) in describing major tasks. The JIMS is relatively easy to use and normally can be used in the analysis of individual jobs by supervisors or others who are thoroughly familiar with the job in question, including the workers themselves in many instances. Although a job analyst would be needed in any program involving the use of the JIMS, his role would be one of monitoring the actual analyses by others. Further, the JIMS as it is envisioned in operation would lend itself to computer storage and retrieval of job data, with the possibility of print-outs of task and other data for individual jobs. The time and cost savings could be substantial over the long run after a JIMS has been developed for any given job family. Although this system has been used experimentally only in the area of machining occupations, its use there can serve as a model for application to other occupational areas.

The Critical Incident Technique

The critical incident technique, developed by Flanagan some years ago, provides for the recording of the job-related behaviors of job incumbents that are critical to job performance, in reflecting either particularly effective (or successful) types of behavior or particularly ineffective (or unsuccessful) types of behavior. Such recordings can be made by supervisors of the job incumbents in question, by observers, by job incumbents themselves; or by interviewers who interview such persons; and they can be made as the behaviors occur, or by recall at some subsequent time (for example, asking individuals to recall such events as they have previously observed them or, in the case of job incumbents, actually engaged in the behaviors). According to Dunnette, in their most complete form such records include some indication of:

1. What led up to the incident.
2. Exactly what the employee did that was so effective (or ineffective).
3. Perceived consequence of the behavior.
4. Whether consequences were within the control of the employee.

Perhaps the primary use of the critical incident technique is as a performance appraisal procedure. However, accumulated data on critical incidents of several or many job incumbents on a given job can serve as a job analysis technique for at least certain purposes. In particular, the critical incident technique can be used as the basis for inferring the human qualities or attributes that are relevant to successful performance.

Dimensions of Critical Incidents

For this and other job analysis purposes, it is usually desirable to obtain hundreds or even thousands of critical incidents (both effective and ineffective) and to categorize them into classes of what are considered to be reasonably homogeneous groups. This is sometimes done by first taking a sample of incidents as recorded on cards, then sorting and resorting them until they form reasonably homogeneous categories (or dimensions) in terms of the types of behavior that are implied. Bouchard sets forth the following procedures which are followed in carrying out what he calls the "dimensionalization" process:

1. Type all behavioral incidents on index cards.
2. The job analyst or someone equally qualified should sort all the cards into homogeneous categories. During this procedure the cards should be laid out in such a way that they can all be read at once (this may require a very large surface). The categorization process is often facilitated if the sorter defines the categories as they develop. They can be defined and redefined as the rating proceeds. Under ideal circumstances a number of judges should carry out the procedure. Categories common to all judges should be set aside and the other categories discussed until there is agreement on how to sort them. It may be that new categories are needed, or that they should be placed into existing categories, or existing categories may have to be subdivided.
3. The categories should now be named and carefully defined with a brief paragraph.

Figure 6-4 illustrates one of the dimensions of critical incidents for the job of clerk typist. This is expressed as the "ability to work accurately and neatly."

If the categories or dimensions are based on the sorting of a sample of incidents, the remaining incidents can then be allocated to these predetermined categories. With respect to the categorizing of the total pool of incidents, Bouchard recommends that, after a

Figure 6-4. Examples of critical incidents for the job of clerk typist in the category of ability to work accurately and neatly. (Source: Mussio and Smith, p. 82)

JOB: Clerk Typist I

DIMENSION: Ability to Work Accurately and Neatly

CRITICAL INCIDENTS:

1. Notices an item in a letter or report that didn't appear to be right, checks it, and corrects it.

2. Produces a manuscript with square margins on each side, making it look like a printed book.

3. Notices and corrects an incorrect address on a mailing roster to clients.

4. Uses a Secretary's Manual whenever in doubt about proper usage.

5. Misfiles charts, letters, etc. on a regular basis.

6. Types key information showing size, location, and other data in reversed order because of carelessness.

7. Continually fails to use the dictionary "when in doubt" of a word's spelling because is never in doubt.

8. Makes typing errors and crooked margins so flagrant as to necessitate the retyping of 600-800 pages.

---

job analyst has initially developed and defined the categories of incidents, a group of independent judges (preferably supervisors of people whose jobs are involved) should sort the incidents into the categories. If this is done, only those incidents which a majority of the judges sort into the same category should be retained. (If in this process a large number of incidents are not agreed upon, the job analyst should reconsider his categories.)

The development of such categories for a particular job can have various uses, one of the most important being to serve as a basis for the selection of personnel tests. (This will be discussed in Chapter 10.) As a prelude to the use of critical incident dimensions for this and other purposes Bouchard proposes that the various dimensions so developed be rated for criticalness or importance as related to the job, using such a scale as the following:

We know that some of these dimensions of job behavior are more important than others, but we want to know how important each is. So please rate on the following scale how important is good performance on each dimension of job behavior for effectively carrying out the entire job.

1 = extremely important
2 = very important
3 = important
4 = only slightly important
5 = hardly important at all

The mean rating of a number of judges can be used to rank the importance of the dimensions.

Other possible uses of the dimensions based on critical incidents include developing performance rating scales, identifying training needs, constructing work sample tests, and vocational counseling.

The Job Element Method of the Civil Service Commission

Over the years Dr. Ernest S. Primoff of the United States Civil Service Commission has developed a procedure for analyzing jobs in terms of job elements for use as the basis for establishing standards for the selection of candidates for jobs in the federal government. Modifications and developments of this procedure have been aimed toward two related objectives. One of these objectives (and in point of time the first) was to develop a structured job analysis method that might provide a basis for identifying, for any given job, the test or tests of a standard battery that should be used for selection of job candidates. The second (and later) objective was to adapt the basic method to serve as the basis for developing tailor-made tests for specific jobs which would tie test content rather directly to specific job characteristics.

The application of what Primoff calls the *job element method* toward these two objectives is discussed in Chapter 10, but in this chapter we discuss the basic job analysis method.

Job Elements for Selection of Tests

Primoff considers as job elements various knowledges, abilities and skills, and personal characteristics which may affect success in jobs. His original formulation made in 1955 incorporated a standard set of 62 job elements (specifically for use with trades and industrial jobs), each of which was defined. Some examples are as follows: Work rapidly, Estimate size of objects, Arithmetic computation, Oral expression, and Reasoning. The analysis of jobs in terms of these elements typically is done by several supervisors of the jobs in question and expert employees, using a simple 3-point scale, as follows:

0 (0) The element is not present in the job.
✔ (1) The element is present in the job but not of extreme importance.
+ (2) The element is present and of extreme importance to the job.

The value of a given element is the sum of the ratings of the several raters (the rating categories having values of 0, 1, or 2, respectively). These values are then used as the basis for deriving an estimate of the validity (called a J-Coefficient) of one or more standardized tests for use in personnel selection.

Primoff later modified the job element method to provide for developing, for any given job, a set of (tentative) job elements that presumably would be relevant to the job in question. Some of these may be developed specifically for the job, and some may be drawn from prepared lists of job elements for two categories of jobs— trades and labor occupations and clerical positions. A few examples of job elements from these lists are given here:

Job elements for trades and labor occupations
   Operation of motor vehicles
   Knowledge of riveting
   Knowledge of welding
   Theory of electronics
   Ability to use electrical drawings
   Trouble-shooting (mechanical)
Job elements for office positions
   Ability to proofread by self
   Ability to help people find things in files
   Ability to meet short deadlines
   Ability to do editorial checking for spelling
   Accurate and rapid typing
   Memory for names and faces of people
   Knowledge of secretarial practices

Job Elements for Development of Tests

The second application of the job element method is to serve as the basis for developing job-relevant tests. For this purpose essentially the same job elements are used (as discussed above), except that the raters are to use four 3-point ratings (instead of one). The rating factors and the rating scale categories are:

Barely acceptable workers now on the job:
+ (2) All have
✔ (1) Some have
0 (0) Almost none have
To pick out acceptable workers the element is:
+ (2) Very important
✔ (1) Valuable
0 (0) Does not differentiate
Trouble likely if the element is not considered:
+ (2) Much trouble
✔ (1) Some trouble
0 (0) Safe to ignore
Practicality. Demanding this element we can fill:
+ (2) All openings
✔ (1) Some openings
0 (0) Almost no openings

These rating factors are incorporated in a job analysis blank shown in Figure 6–5. Using the numerical values assigned to the three rating categories (2, 1, and 0), an Item Index is derived with the formula shown in the last column of the figure. These indices, in turn, are used as the basis for developing the job content of tailor-made tests to be used for the job.

Figure 6-5. Portions of the job element blank used by the United States Civil Service Commission in the selection of job elements to be used as the basis for establishing standards for selection of candidates for specific jobs. (Source: Primoff, 1975, p. 12)

Element No.	Barely acceptable workers (B) + all have √ some have 0 almost none have	To pick out superior workers (S) + very important √ valuable 0 does not differentiate	Trouble likely if not considered (T) + much trouble √ some trouble 0 safe to ignore	Practical. Demanding this element, we can fill (P) + all openings √ some openings 0 almost no openings	S X P	T	Item Index (IT) SP + T

Position Analysis Questionnaire (PAQ)

The Position Analysis Questionnaire (PAQ)* is a structured job analysis questionnaire that provides for analyzing jobs in terms of 187 job elements. The elements are of a worker-oriented nature that tend to characterize, or to imply, the human behaviors that are involved in jobs (McCormick et al.). As such, the PAQ lends itself to use in the analysis of a wide variety of jobs.

Organization of the PAQ

The job elements in the PAQ are organized in six divisions as follows (examples of two job elements from each division are included):

1. *Information input.* (Where and how does the worker get the information he uses in performing his job?)
   Examples: Use of written materials
                 Near-visual differentiation
2. *Mental processes.* (What reasoning, decision-making, planning, and information-processing activities are involved in performing the job?)
   Examples: Level of reasoning in problem solving
                 Coding/decoding
3. *Work output.* (What physical activities does the worker perform and what tools or devices does he use?)
   Examples: Use of keyboard devices
                 Assembling/disassembling
4. *Relationships with other persons.* (What relationships with other people are required in performing the job?)
   Examples: Instructing
                 Contacts with public, customers
5. *Job context.* (In what physical or social contexts is the work performed?)
   Examples: High temperature
                 Interpersonal conflict situations
6. *Other job characteristics.* (What activities, conditions, or characteristics other than those described above are relevant to the job?)

*The Position Analysis Questionnaire (PAQ) is copyrighted by the Purdue Research Foundation. The PAQ and related materials are available through the University Book Store, 360 West State Street, West Lafayette, Indiana 47906. Further information regarding the PAQ is available through PAQ Services, Inc., P.O. Box 3337, Logan, Utah, 84321. Computer processing of PAQ data is available through the PAQ Data Processing Division at that address.

      Examples: Specified work pace
                  Amount of job structure

Rating Scales Used with the PAQ

There is provision for rating each job on each job element. Six types of rating scales are used, as follows:

Letter Identification	Type of Rating Scale
U	Extent of Use
I	Importance to the job
T	Amount of Time
P	Possibility of Occurrence
A	Applicability
S	Special Code (used in the case of a few specific job elements)

A specific rating scale is designated to be used with each job element, in particular the scale considered most appropriate to the content of the element. All but the "A" (Applicability) scale are 6-point scales, with "O" (which is coded as "N") being used for "Does not apply," as illustrated below:

Rating	Importance to the Job
N	Does not apply
1	Very minor (importance)
2	Low
3	Average
4	High
5	Extreme

The "A" scale (Applicability) is a dichotomous scale providing for responses of "Applies" or "Does not apply," and is used only in the case of some of the job context job elements, such as "Regular work hours."

Analysis of Jobs with the PAQ

The analysis of jobs with the PAQ is typically carried out by job analysts, methods analysts, personnel officers, or supervisors, but in some instances job incumbents are asked to analyze their own jobs (especially in the case of managerial, professional, and other white collar workers).

Attribute Profiles of PAQ Job Elements

As one phase of the research with the PAQ (discussed further in Chapter 10), attribute profiles of the PAQ job elements were developed. These profiles were based on the ratings by industrial psychologists of the relevance of each of 76 human attributes to each of the job elements (Marquardt and McCormick; Mecham and McCormick). Some of the attributes for which ratings were obtained were of an aptitude nature (such as verbal comprehension, intelligence, and manual dexterity.) Others were of an "interest" or "temperament" nature, characterized by the types of on-the-job situations to which people must adjust; these are referred to as *situational* attributes. Examples are adjustment to repetitive/shortcycle operations, dealing with people, pressure of time, and working alone. The ratings were on a 6-point scale ranging from 0 to 5.

The median ratings of the attributes as related to each job element form the attribute profiles, as illustrated below:

	Attribute					
Job Element No.	*1*	*2*	*3*	—	—	*74*
1	4.5	1.0	0.0	—	—	2.5
2	3.0	0.0	2.5	—	—	4.0
—	—	—	—	—	—	—
—	—	—	—	—	—	—
187	0.5	3.0	1.0	—	—	0.0

The inter-rater reliability of the ratings used in the development of these profiles was determined. The intraclass coefficients of reliability (adjusted for the number of raters for the attributes in question) were generally quite high, most of them being in the upper .80's and in the .90's, with only nine being below .80 (Marquardt and McCormick).

Reliability of PAQ Job Analyses

The reliability of the analyses of jobs with the PAQ could be derived on the basis of two reported analyses of the same jobs by the same analysts, or on the bases of analyses of the same jobs by independent analysts. One comparison of the reliability of PAQ analyses was based on analyses of 62 jobs, each having been analyzed by two independent analysts (Jeanneret and McCormick). The coefficient of reliability was .79, which reflects a respectable level of consistency on the part of different analysts.

Discussion of the PAQ

Some subsequent studies with the PAQ are discussed in later chapters, but it might be said here that in one of the studies PAQ-based data were used in the derivation of what are called *job dimensions,* each such dimension being characterized primarily by a combination of job elements that tend to occur in common jobs. In certain of the applications of PAQ-based data (such as for establishing aptitude requirements and compensation rates for jobs) scores on these dimensions are computed for individual jobs, and these job dimension scores are then used for the purpose in mind.

Occupation Analysis Inventory (OAI)

The Occupation Analysis Inventory (OAI) was developed by Dr. William J. Cunningham and his associates in the Center for Occupational Education of North Carolina State University as a step toward a scheme for describing and classifying occupations for educational purposes. As Neeb et al. indicate, the increasing variety of jobs renders impracticable the traditional practice of developing separate education programs for each specific occupation. This situation points to the need for a comprehensive taxonomy of human work which could be used to impose some structure and parsimony upon occupational education, thus suggesting the possibility of *occupational clustering*—that is, the clustering of occupations with reasonably similar educational requirements. The OAI was developed as a structured job analysis questionnaire that might be useful in subsequent research aimed toward the later development of such occupational clusters (Cunningham et al.).

Nature of the OAI

The OAI represents a basic job analysis approach similar to that of the Position Analysis Questionnaire (PAQ) with two important differences, which will be discussed later in this section. It consists of 622 work elements grouped into five categories. These are listed here along with a couple of illustrative work elements from each.

Category	No.	Examples of Work Elements
Information received	125	Tables and graphs
		Mechanical drawings
Mental activities	41	Numerical computation
		Verbal comprehension
Work behavior	267	Cutting by sawing (nonpowered)
		Copying/recording

Category	No.	Examples of Work Elements
Work goals	112	Mechanical devices installed or assembled Verbal material transcribed
Work context	77	Electrical hazards Dirty environment
Total	622	

These five categories correspond to the five components of the information process model shown in Figure 6–6. The work elements are generally rated on three standard scales as follows:

Significance to the job	6-point scale: 0, 1, 2, 3, 4, 5, 6
Extent of occurrence	6-point scale: 0, 1, 2, 3, 4, 5, 6
Applicability	Dichotomous: does apply and does not apply

Certain work elements have special rating scales. Many of the work elements are identical or similar to job elements of the PAQ, characterizing jobs in worker-oriented terms. The organization of the two are also similar in that both include elements dealing with information input, mental processes, and work output (paralleling the stimulus—response paradigm commonly used in characterizing human behavior of virtually any type). One feature which differentiates the two is that the OAI incorporates many job-oriented work elements, that is, elements that have some technologically identified associations. Thus, it includes work elements that are associated with medical/veterinary activities (such as Applying medicines), with mechanical and electrical maintenance and repair activities (such as Adjusting/tuning), and with certain specific processes (such as Stitching, Knitting, and Weaving). The second differentiating feature is that the OAI incorporates work elements which deal with work goals (such as Electrical/electronic devices installed or assembled, Plant products harvested or extracted, and Employee relations accomplished).

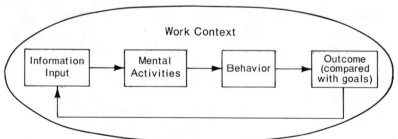

Figure 6-6. Paradigm for the Occupation Analysis Inventory (OAI). (Source: Neeb et al., p. 14)

Attribute Requirements of OAI Work Elements

As a step in the direction of identifying the human requirements of jobs, ratings were obtained of the relevance of 103 human attributes to each of the 622 work elements of the OAI (Cunningham et al.) in much the same fashion as was done with the PAQ. The attributes used with the OAI are incorporated in the Attribute Requirement Inventory (ARI) and include attributes in the following six categories: General vocational capabilities (24), Cognitive abilities (20), Psychomotor abilities (12), Sensory capacities (6), Interests (24), and Needs (17). For each work element, the mean ratings of 9 or 10 raters were used to derive an attribute requirement profile.

These profiles were used later in a series of statistical factor analyses, in order to identify the dimensions of work elements reflected by these attribute requirements. This phase is described and discussed in Chapter 8.

References

Archer, W. B. *Computation of Group Job Descriptions from Occupational Survey Data.* USAF, AMD, Personnel Research Laboratory, PRL-TR-66-12, AD-653, 543. Lackland AFB, Texas: 1966.

Archer, W. B., and Fruchter, D. A. *The Construction, Review, and Administration of Air Force Job Inventories.* USAF, Personnel Research Laboratory, PRL-TR-66-12. Lackland AFB, Texas: 1966.

Birt, J. A. "The Effect of the Consistency of Job Inventory Information upon Simulated Airmen Reassignment." Ph.D. thesis, Purdue University, 1968.

Bouchard, T. J. *A Manual for Job Analysis.* Minneapolis: Minnesota Civil Service Department, 1972.

Burton, B. R., and Driskill, W. E. *Specialty Survey of the Security Police Career Field.* USAF, Occupational Measurement Center. Lackland AFB, Texas: 1969.

Christal, R. E. "Comments by the Chairman." In *Proceedings of Division of Military Psychology Symposium,* 77th annual convention of the American Psychological Association. USAF, AFSC, AFHRL, Personnel Research Division. Lackland AFB, Texas: 1969.

Christal, R. E. *New Directions in the Air Force Occupational Research Program.* USAF, AFHRL, Personnel Research Division. Lackland, AFB, Texas: 1972.

Christal, R. E. *Stability of Consolidated Job Descriptions Based on Task Inventory Survey Information.* USAF, AFSC, Personnel Research Division, AFHRL-TR-71-48. Lackland, AFB, Texas: 1971.

Cragun, J. R., and McCormick, E. J. *Job Inventory Information: Task Reliabilities and Scale Interrelationships.* USAF, Personnel Research Laboratory, PRL-TR-67-15. Lackland, AFB, Texas: 1967.

Cunningham, J. W.; Tuttle, T. C.; Floyd, J. R.; and Bates, J. A. *The Development of the Occupation Analysis Inventory: An "Ergometric" Approach to an Educational Problem.* Center for Occupational Education, Center Research Monograph No. 6. Raleigh, N.C.: North Carolina State U., 1971.

Dictionary of Occupational Titles, 3rd ed. U.S. Department of Labor, Manpower Administration. Washington, D.C.: U.S. Government Printing Office, 1965.

Dictionary of Occupational Titles, 4th ed. U.S. Department of Labor, Employment and Training Administration. Washington, D.C.: U.S. Government Printing Office, 1977.

Dunnette, M. D. *Personnel Selection and Placement.* Belmont, Calif.: Wadsworth, 1966.

Farrell, W. T.; Stone, C. H.; and Yoder, D. *Guidelines for Sampling in Marine Corps Task Analysis.* Evaluation of Marine Corps Task Analysis Program, TR No. 11. Los Angeles: California State University, 1976.

Fine, S. A. *Functional Job Analysis Scales: A Desk Aid.* Kalamazoo, Mich.: W. E. Upjohn Institute for Employment Research, April 1973.

Fine, S. A. "Functional Job Analysis: An Approach to a Technology for Manpower Planning." *Personnel Journal,* November 1974, pp. 813–818.

Fine, S. A., and Wiley, W. W. *An Introduction to Functional Job Analysis.* Kalamazoo, Mich.: W. E. Upjohn Institute for Employment Research, 1971.

Flanagan, J. C. "The Critical Incident Technique." *Psychological Bulletin* 51(1954): 327–358.

Fruchter, B.; Morin, R. E.; and Archer, W. B. *Efficiency of the Open-ended Inventory in Eliciting Task Statements from Job Incumbents.* USAF, AMD/AFSC, Personnel Research Laboratory. Lackland, AFB, Texas: 1963.

Guilford, J. P. *Psychometric Methods.* New York: McGraw-Hill, 1954.

Hemphill, J. K. "Job Descriptions for Executives." *Harvard Business Review* 37(1959): 55–67.

Jeanneret, P. R., and McCormick, E. J. *The Job Dimensions of "Worker Oriented" Job Variables and of Their Attribute Profiles as Based on Data from the Position Analysis Questionnaire.* Occupational Research Center, Department of Psychological Sciences, Report No. 2. West Lafayette, Ind.: Purdue University, 1969.

Kershner, A. M. *A Report on Job Analysis.* USN, ONR Report ACR-5. Washington, D.C.: 1955.

McCormick, E. J., and Ammerman, H. L. *Development of Worker Activity Checklists for Use in Occupational Analysis.* USAF, WADD, Personnel Laboratory, WADD-TR-60-77. Lackland AFB, Texas: 1960.

McCormick, E. J.; Jeanneret, P. R.; and Mecham, R. C. "A Study of Job Characteristics and Job Dimensions as Based on the Position Analysis Questionnaire (PAQ)." *Journal of Applied Psychology* 56(1972): 347–368.

Marquardt, L. D., and McCormick, E. J. *Attribute Ratings and Profiles of the Job Elements of the Position Analysis Questionnaire (PAQ).* Department of Psychological Sciences, Report No. 1. West Lafayette, Ind.: Purdue University, 1972.

Mecham, R. C., and McCormick, E. J. *The Rated Attribute Requirements of Job Elements of the Position Analysis Questionnaire.* Department of Psychological Sciences, Report No. 1. West Lafayette, Ind.: Purdue University, Occupational Research Center, 1969.

Melching, W. H., and Borcher, S. D. *Procedures for Constructing and Using Task Inventories.* Center for Vocational and Technical Education, Research and Development Series No. 91. Columbus, Ohio: The Ohio State University, 1973.

Moore, B. E. *Occupational Analysis for Human Resource Development.* Department of the Navy, Office of Civilian Manpower Management, Research Report No. 25. Washington, D.C.: 1976.

Morsh, J. *Computer Analysis of Occupational Survey Data.* USAF, AFHRL, Personnel Research Division. Lackland AFB, Texas: 1969.

Morsh, J. E., and Archer, W. B. *Procedural Guide for Conducting Occupational Surveys in the United States Air Force.* USAF, AMD, Personnel Research Laboratory, PRL-TR-67-11, AD-664-036. Lackland AFB, Texas: 1967.

Morsh, J. E., and Christal, R. E. *Impact of the Computer on Job Analysis in the United States Air Force.* USAF, Personnel Research Laboratory, TR-66-19. Lackland AFB, Texas: 1966.

Murphy, W. F. "The Application of Readability Principles to the Writing of Task Statements." Ph.D. thesis, Purdue University, 1966.

Mussio, S. J., and Smith, M. K. *Content Validity: A Procedural Manual.* City of Minneapolis Civil Service Commission, Division of Personnel Research, undated.

Neeb, R. W.; Cunningham, J. W.; and Pass, J. J. *Human Attribute Requirements of Work Elements: Further Development of the Occupation Analysis Inventory.* Center for Occupational Education, Center Research Monograph No. 7. Raleigh, N.C.: University of North Carolina, 1971.

Primoff, E. S. *Test Selection by Job Analysis: The J-Coefficient, What It Is, How It Works,* 2nd ed. Test Technical Series No. 20. Washington, D.C.: U.S. Civil Service Commission, 1955.

Primoff, E. S. *Preliminary Draft: The J-Coefficient Procedure.* Washington, D.C.: U.S. Civil Service Commission, 1972.

Primoff, E. S. *Introduction to J-Coefficient Analysis.* Washington, D.C.: U.S. Civil Service Commission, 1973.

Primoff, E. S. *How to Prepare and Conduct Job-Element Examinations.* U.S. Civil Service Commission, Technical Study 75-1. Washington, D.C.: U.S. Government Printing Office, 1975.

Stone, C. H., and Yoder, D. *Job Analysis, 1970.* Long Beach: California State College, 1970.

Task Analysis Inventories. U.S. Department of Labor, Manpower Administration. Washington, D.C.: U.S. Government Printing Office (Stock No. 2900-00163), 1973.

Thorndike, E. L., and Lorge, I. *The Teacher's Word Book of 30,000 Words.* New York: Teachers College Press, Columbia University, 1944.

Yoder, D., and Heneman, H. G., Jr., eds. *ASPA Handbook of Personnel and Industrial Relations.* Washington, D.C.: Bureau of National Affairs, 1979.

PART THREE

Job Interrelationships and Classifications

7

Job Interrelationships and Classifications: Bases and Methods

WE are all familiar with the variability in the forms of the natural features of our environment (plant and animal life, geological materials and features, and the like), and in the personal characteristics and behavior of people. Scientific investigation of these and other classes of objects, events, or phenomena is in part directed toward the following three objectives: (1) the identification and usually the measurement of the characteristics or features of the objects, events, or phenomena in question; (2) the determination of the interrelationships between and among the individual cases in terms of such characteristics or features; and (3) the discovery of whatever order, or system, or structure may be inherent in the area of investigation, including in some instances the development of classification systems into which the objects, events, or phenomena may form themselves.

The area of human work is a domain that lends itself to systematic investigation and classification. Depending on the purpose, one might be interested in determining the interrelationships between and among occupations, jobs, positions, or perhaps tasks or other levels of job-related activities, or, at a more integrated level, in the development of relevant classification systems. In discussing the purposes of classification in general, Sokal sets forth the principal purposes. First, classification can help to achieve *economy of memory*. By characterizing any single case in terms of a given classification category (be it a plant, an animal, a language, a tool, or even a job) it is not necessary to describe the specific features of the case in question. Second, classification allows for ease of *manipulation*, as in data handling, or ease of retrieval. The third (and probably paramount) purpose of a classification is to *describe the structure and relationship* of the constituent objects to each other and to similar objects, and to simplify these relationships in such a way that general statements can be made about classes of objects.

Within this frame of reference of the purposes of classification, there are numerous practical purposes that have been or could be served by the availability of relevant classification systems relating to jobs and job characteristics. Some of these are illustrated and discussed in later chapters.

In this chapter we discuss various principles of classifications and approaches to them, including particular reference to those most relevant to the domain of human work. In addition, we discuss some of the many types of *descriptors,* or characteristics of jobs and occupations, that might be relevant to the development of classification systems, and certain statistical procedures that can play a role in such processes. Chapter 8 includes examples of a number of studies dealing with the analysis of job interrelationships and classification systems.

Definitions of Terms

In considering classification in general terms, we should first differentiate between and among certain terms that are involved. In this regard, Sokal defines classification as *the ordering or arrangement of objects into groups or sets on the basis of their relationships*. Such relationships can be based on observable or inferred properties. The result of classification is best referred to as a *classification system* (although such systems are commonly called simply *classifications*). The assignment of additional objects to their appropriate classes in an already established classification system is most accurately referred to as *identification* although some individuals also refer to this (inappropriately) as *classification.*

Sokal uses the term *taxonomy* to refer to the theoretical study of classification including its bases, principles, procedures, and rules. In turn, the term *taxon* (plural: *taxa*) is used to designate a set of objects of any rank recognized as a group in a classification system.

Basic Considerations in Classification

It has been emphasized by Theologus that the organization of any domain (such as tasks or subject matter) into groups requires (or should require) the previous development of a sound logic and rationale for the organization. Thus, he emphasizes the need for a rigorous taxonomic approach to the development of classification systems. The discussions on classification by Theologus and Wheaton are focused primarily on the classification of *tasks* rather than of *jobs* or *positions.* However, the discussion is as relevant to the classification of jobs or positions as to tasks as such.

In arguing for such an approach, Theologus emphasizes the need for a rationale for classification that requires consideration of the following questions: (1) Why do you want to classify? (2) What do you classify? and (3) How will you classify? Further, he points out that it is essential to consider these questions in the order in which they are presented, since the answers to the second and third questions depend upon the answer to the first.

Basic Types of Classifications

Consideration of the purpose of classification leads into the topic of different types of classification systems which, as Theologus points out, have their own attributes, uses, and limitations. Drawing largely from the field of biology (which has dealt with taxonomic and classification matters more than any other field), he characterizes three general types of classification.

Teleological classification. Teleological classification is based on the usefulness to man of the items being classified, such as the classification of animals into domestic and wild categories. As related to human tasks, he refers to the distinction between *nonsense* tasks (such as carried out in laboratories) as contrasted with *real world* tasks. Teleological classifications have little relevance to the study of human work.

Cosociative classification. What Theologus refers to as *cosociative* classification (in biology referred to as *ecological* classification) is based on variables of interest which are associated with what is being classified, but are not inherent attributes or characteristics of the items being classified. As applied to tasks, for example, such a classification might be based on the abilities of operators or the behavior requirements of the tasks rather than on inherent features of the tasks themselves. As revealed by Wheaton's review, by far the majority of classifications of tasks are of this type. Although such task classifications have some uses, their value is limited to the scope and degree of applicability of the variables which constitute the subject matter base of the classifications. As an example, Theologus states that a classification of tasks in terms of learning principles might be of great value in developing training methods, but would not provide any real guidance in the areas of personnel selection or systems design.

Theoretical classification. The third type of classification, *theoretical* classification, provides for categorizing the items in terms of their inherent attributes and characteristics. In discussing theoretical classification, Theologus refers to three schools of thought regarding taxonomic approaches which have been dominant, particularly in the field of biology, namely, Linnaean, Darwinian, and numerical. *Linnaean* taxonomy is historically the oldest, and is predicated on the classification of individual entities of some broad class in terms of their "essence." Theologus makes the point that the primary criticism of this approach lies in the fact that a priori judgments are required to define the "essential nature" of the objects or events to be classified. He also points out that some task classification systems of a cosociative type have some Linnaean classification features and are subject to the same criticism, namely, that they depend upon the subjective judgments of a priori weights, which means that the classifier (say, of tasks) makes a judgment of the tasks in categorizing them.

Darwinian taxonomy, of course, emerges from Darwin's theory of evolution. The biological classifications are established on the basis of the use of deductive theory concerning the phylogenetic origins of organisms. As applied to biological systems, Darwinian classification has been raked over the coals on the grounds that it is founded on hypothesized relationships or speculations rather than on verifiable facts, and that its use requires subjective judgments, just as Linnaean classifications do. These criticisms probably would also be applicable in the possible use of Darwinian classification as applied to human work. In addition, it seems doubtful that the basic formulation of Darwinian classification—founded on phylo-genetic origins—would have conceptual applicability to the domain of human work. Any such applicability would in any event be very strained, as it would be restricted to depicting human work in an evolutionary frame of reference.

This brings us to the third major school of taxonomic thought, that of *numerical* classification, which has repeatability and objectiv-ity as its cornerstones. The numerical taxonomists feel that classifi-cations must be established on stable, objectively derived data bases, rather than on hypothesized relationships. A couple of central ax-ioms of numerical classification are that the classifications be based on as many characteristics or features of the entities to be classified as possible, and that each such characteristic be given equal weight (to avoid injecting subjective bias into the structure).

Monothetic and Polythetic Classification

In discussing classification, a further distinction should be made be-tween *monothetic* and *polythetic* classification. According to Wheaton, in monothetic classification the taxonomist defines each and every type of category in terms of a unique and usually small set of at-tributes such that the possession of these is both necessary and suf-ficient for membership in the group so defined. Polythetic classifi-cation is based more on the overall pattern of the attributes which can be associated with the individual cases to be classified. As Sokal expresses it, the taxa are groups of individual items or objects that share a large proportion of their properties but do not necessarily agree on any one property. No single attribute or combination of attributes is essential to group membership, nor is it sufficient to make a particular case a member of the group.

The polythetic classification principle is most compatible with the basic precept of numerical classification in that it does not de-pend upon any a priori determination of what variables should be considered as necessary and sufficient for determining group mem-bership of individual cases. At the same time, the polythetic ap-proach can still leave dangling the question of criteria for forming groups. To illustrate this let us look at Wheaton's hypothetical ex-ample (Table 7–1), representing six tasks which are characterized in terms of the presence or absence of four descriptors. The pro-files of tasks 1 and 2 are identical, thus placing them together with-out any question; and in this sample task 6 is clearly an isolate. But, as Wheaton asks, what can be inferred from the remaining tasks and configurations of attributes associated with them? With many

TABLE 7-1. Hypothetical examples of six tasks characterized in terms of the presence (+) or absence (0) of four descriptors, to illustrate task classification issues.

	Task					
Descriptor	1	2	3	4	5	6
A	+	+	+	+	+	0
B	0	0	+	+	+	0
C	+	+	+	0	+	0
D	0	0	0	+	+	0

descriptors (instead of only four) the possible number of combinations and configurations increases tremendously (for n attributes there are 2^n possible configurations). In the absurd situation each task could be in a group by itself. Further, the problem becomes amplified if one deals with quantitative values of the attributes instead of simply categorical description (the presence or absence of each attribute).

Classification of Job-Related Variables

Let us now turn to the implications of classification systems for job-related variables. After reviewing the research related to the classification of tasks, Wheaton came to the dismal conclusion that behavioral taxonomy is still in its infancy and that, in spite of ten years of thought and effort, relatively little had been accomplished. It is probable that the same conclusions would still be applicable.

Looking ahead toward the development of classification systems of tasks (and presumably of other types of job-related data), Theologus argues strongly for the numerical approach on the grounds that it emphasizes repeatability and objectivity in classification, and that it eliminates the arbitrary, subjective preselection of the characteristics or attributes on which the classification is to be based. Granting the desirability of such an approach toward this objective, it is probable that any significant breakthroughs are still years away. In the meantime, however, one should capitalize on whatever data and methods are now available, realizing full well whatever limitations may be implied. Even though much of the work involved in developing job-related classification systems has been based on human judgments (rather than on rigorous numerical classification principles), some of these efforts have had positive, useful results, and those who are concerned with this domain should be familiar with some of the research in the field.

Job-related classification systems fall into two general types. On the one hand, one can develop classification systems of the *descriptors* used in characterizing work entities (such as tasks and jobs), and on the other hand one can use such descriptors as the basis for classification systems of the *work entities*. Much of the taxonomic research regarding job-related variables has dealt with classification systems of descriptors.

The classification of work entities as such can be pitched at a *micro* level (typically at the task level) or at the *macro* level (in which one deals with the classification of positions, jobs, or occupations as complete entities); for semantic simplicity the macro level will be referred to as dealing with jobs. In discussing the classification of tasks (the micro level) Wheaton makes the point that there are four conceptual bases for establishing task classification systems, as follows:

1. A behavior descriptive approach.
2. A behavior requirements approach.
3. An ability requirements approach.
4. A task characteristics approach.

Job Descriptors

Some of the types of job-related information that can be developed or obtained were mentioned in Chapter 3. There are, of course, other facets or attributes by which jobs might also be characterized. Although we can consider virtually any type of job-related information as job descriptors, the types covered by the four conceptual bases listed above probably represent a reasonably appropriate framework for discussing job interrelationships and classification systems (illustrated in Chapter 8). However, for our purposes, we make certain changes in this framework, such as, in the behavior-descriptive approach, distinguishing between work-oriented and behavior-oriented activities (what we have previously referred to as job-oriented and worker-oriented); broadening the categories to cover classification systems of jobs and positions in addition to classification systems of tasks (as they were proposed by Wheaton); changing the titles; and adding an "other" category. The coverage in Chapter 8 will then be treated under the following "expanded" and re-labeled headings:

Work-oriented bases
Behavior-oriented bases
Behavior requirements bases
Attribute requirements bases
Work characteristics bases
Other descriptive bases

Although the next chapter will include examples of classification systems of those types, for the moment let us discuss certain basic distinctions in the nature of job descriptors that might be used for classification purposes.

Subjective Versus Objective Job Descriptors

What differentiates some job descriptors from others is whether the descriptors are based on *subjective* responses or on *objective measurements*. On the one hand, one can elicit subjective responses about many features or aspects of jobs, such as level of responsibility, difficulty, experience required, or job satisfaction. On the other hand, some descriptors are based on objective measurements, such as measurements of energy requirements, time to make certain motions (as in industrial engineering practice), or average number of words typed per minute. In some instances, subjective responses may be elicited from people about job characteristics that "exist" in some objective form, for example, in obtaining estimates of time devoted to specific activities (the additional precision obtained by objective measurement of some such variables may not warrant the effort required to do so).

Categorical Versus Quantitative Job Descriptors

A second way of distinguishing types of job descriptors is to classify them as either *categorical* or *quantitative*. True categorical descriptors are those which can be considered as either applying or not applying to individual jobs, whereas quantitative descriptors are expressed in numerical (that is, quantitative) form. Categorical descriptors represent nominal scales, as discussed earlier (Chapter 6), and can be considered as a form of measurement, just as quantitative descriptors can, but it serves some purposes to express this distinction.

Some categorical job descriptors reflect rather specific distinctions between jobs, such as whether they do, or do not, involve work out-of-doors, the use of handtools, or operating a vehicle. At a grosser level of categorical description, jobs can be classed in any one of several major categories, such as supervision, clerical, professional, and the like. (Such grouping, however, typically is predicated on syndromes of more specific descriptors).

Quantitative descriptors, on the other hand, are those in which jobs are characterized in terms of degree, such as the amount of time involved in personal contact, or the judged level of occupational hazard. Although true categorical descriptors represent dichotomies, in some instances what is essentially a quantitative job variable (varying along some quantitative scale) may be expressed in categorical terms, such as above and below average in judged difficulty, or above and below a specified amount of time devoted to a specific job activity. When such distinctions are made, the data are treated as categorical descriptors in the same fashion as true dichotomies.

Special Types of Job Descriptors

Although most types of job descriptors fall under one or another of the rubrics suggested by Wheaton, there are other types that perhaps do not fall neatly into such classes. Although we will not here attempt to present any inventory of such possible descriptors, there are certain other types that probably warrant special comment at this point.

Job evaluation factors. Job evaluation systems are used as the basis for establishing compensation rates for jobs (a discussion of such systems is covered in Chapter 12). The most common systems provide for the evaluation of jobs in terms of such factors as education required, experience required, mental demands, physical requirements, responsibility, hazards, and working conditions. The totals of the point values assigned to given jobs for the various individual factors are then used in establishing compensation rates. The factors used in typical systems tend to be of different types, some representing work characteristics, some attribute requirements, and so on. In any event, such factors can be considered as job descriptors.

Task and job difficulty. Another rather special type of job descriptor is the construct of job difficulty. For various purposes, measures of the difficulty of tasks or jobs are useful. Perhaps the most common use is in job evaluation systems in which it is sometimes the practice to obtain ratings on the difficulty of jobs as complete entities. However, measures of difficulty of jobs can also be used in establishing job requirements. For those and other possible purposes, measures of task or job difficulty can be considered as descriptors, to relate tasks or jobs to each other.

The most typical scheme in rating difficulty (used in many job evaluation systems) is a simple scale, such as a 5-point or 7-point scale. For our purposes in this discussion, however, we will discuss a unique study directed toward deriving a job difficulty measure by another route, one in which measures of task difficulty are used "to build up" measures of total job difficulty (Mead and Christal, 1970). The primary data for the study consisted of ratings of difficulty of the tasks in the task inventories of three Air Force career fields, namely Medical Material, Vehicle Maintenance, and Accounting and Finance. In the rating process, task difficulty was defined as the time required to learn to perform the task satisfactorily. The ratings were obtained from upper-level noncommissioned officers using a 7-point scale ranging from 1 (the least learning time) to 7 (the longest learning time).

Separately, within each of the three career fields, 250 jobs were rated by noncommissioned officers on relative difficulty. The jobs were represented by job descriptions based on a listing of the tasks performed and the relative time spent on each. The ratings were obtained by the rank order method, each rater having only 25 jobs to rank. The averaged rankings were converted into a difficulty index measure for each job, which served as a criterion of its difficulty.

In turn, various predictor variable indexes were derived for each job on the basis of the task-rating data for the tasks which were part of each of these jobs. A few of these predictor variables were number of tasks performed, mean task difficulty ratings, average task difficulty per unit time spent, and range of task difficulty.

In addition, various combinations of these predictor variables were used, such as the sum of two variables, products of two variables, and the squared values of certain variables.

Subsequently, these predictor variables were used in a regression analysis (discussed below) to identify the variables which best predicted the job difficulty criterion values. The result (based on data from all three career fields) was the derivation of a set of weights for the three variables which best predicted the job difficulty criterion values, as follows:

	Weight
Variable	*(based on standard scores)*
Number of tasks performed	1.33406509
Average task difficulty	
per unit time spent	.45368767
Number of tasks performed,	
squared	− .72012963

Using an equation based on these weights, a predicted job difficulty index was computed for each job, and these were then correlated with the criterion job difficulty values, the correlations for the three career fields being .95, .92, and .95.

With all this statistical manipulation, one might wonder if the game is worth the candle — why not simply use ratings of total job difficulty? In many circumstances this would be the most expeditious method, but in dealing with many different jobs within some occupational area, one can use difficulty ratings for tasks (which are fairly easy to obtain) to build up job difficulty indexes for any and all jobs — regardless of the many varied combinations of tasks performed — if one has a task inventory description of each such job.

Occupational Keywords of United States Employment Service. A unique type of job descriptor has been developed for possible use by the public employment offices operated by the states in collaboration with the United States Employment Service. (At the time of publication of this book, the system was still in the experimental stage.) The system generally provides for the experiences and qualifications of applicants to be described in terms of certain *keywords,* and for job openings also to be characterized in terms of the keywords, in order to facilitate the matching of applicants to jobs. Such matching, in turn, might be done either by the use of computers or by examination of records of individual applicants and job openings. The types of descriptors used in the system fall into two classes. One of these consists of *primary terms* that are classified into 39 occupational units, such as the following: Artwork; Biological Sciences; Construction; Farming/Fishing/Hunting; Health Arts; Insurance; Metal Benchwork; Sales; Services; Transportation; and Woodworking. Each of these occupational units branches out into the form of a tree with subdivisions and, in some instances, one or two more levels of divisions representing various levels of specialization within the occupational unit in question. The primary terms at the various levels are identified with alphabetical tree codes that reflect their relative levels. A partial example, given below, is for the occupational unit of Construction. It is taken from the *Handbook of Occupational Keywords*.

Tree Code	Primary Term
EX	Construction Work
EXA	Building Wrecking
EXB	Carpentry
EXBA	Finish Carpentry
EXBB	Framing
EXBBA	Forms Building
EXC	Carpet Laying Work
EXP	Masonry Work
EXPA	Bricklaying
EXPB	Cement and Concrete Masonry
EXPC	Stone Masonry
EXPD	Tile Setting

The second type of descriptor consists of *complementary terms,* which provide for the description of applicants or job openings in more specific job-related terms that add to, or supplement, the information provided by the primary terms. These include descriptors of various types, including those that deal with education (such as Business Administration); language (such as Italian); environment (such as Hospitals); materials (such as Solvents); products (such as Men's Shoes); specialties (such as Wheel Balancing); machines and equipment (such as Drill Presses and Respirators); handtools (such as Soldering Iron); and processes (such as Forging and Food Freezing). There are other types of complementary term descriptors as well, but whatever their particular nature, they are intended to provide for characterizing applicants and job openings in terms that presumably would be relevant for matching applicants to job openings. The complementary terms are also organized into trees in much the same fashion as the primary terms, with up to five letters used to reflect the various levels of specificity within a comprehensive classification system in which they are organized. Numerical identifications of both the primary and complementary terms are used for computer processing.

In addition to the primary and complementary keywords described above, there are certain *special output keywords* that are used:

Prefixes: Experience In; Education In; Experience/Education In; Skill In; and Knowledge Of.

Mid-fix: One of the Following.
Suffixes: Required; and Desired.

Applicants and job orders can both be described by any of the prefixes, which have code numbers. Job orders can be similarly coded in terms of the mid-fix or the suffixes; thus, an employer can indicate what keyword qualifications are required and what are desired (that is, preferred but not required).

The complete keyword system is, of course, quite comprehensive, and represents a very major effort to provide descriptors for use in the very practical objective of matching applicants and job openings in the public employment offices. Although it is intended primarily for operational uses rather than to serve as the basis for an occupational classification system, the system itself represents a classification of job descriptors.

Discussion

Many job descriptors characterize rather specific and restricted features or aspects of jobs, such as tasks performed, the numerical operations involved, or finger dexterity required. However, in some circumstances groupings of such specific features are developed and used as the basis for broader job descriptors. The development of such groups frequently is done by the use of any one of several statistical methods which are discussed in the next section, especially factor analysis.

The use of job descriptors for determining the relationships between and among jobs is typically facilitated if the descriptors are expressed in categorical or quantitative form, since the data can then be dealt with statistically. This is especially important if the analyses to be carried out involve a large number of jobs.

Statistical Analysis of Job Interrelationships

A major concern of this book can be expressed as having two related facets: (1) the analysis of jobs in such a fashion that the job descriptors used express job-related data in quantitative (or categorical) form, and (2) the statistical analysis of such data.

In discussing statistical analyses of job-related data we cannot avoid reference to at least certain statistical methods used in such analyses, in order to give an impression of the potential uses of such methods, and to provide a basis for greater understanding of the results of some studies to be reported later.

Factor Analysis

Factor analysis (and one of its variants, principal components analysis) is carried out with sets of data that consist of quantitative values for each of several or many *variables* as related to each of several or many *cases*. In the factor analysis of job-related information, the original data might be represented as in Table 7–2, which shows, for each of nine hypothetical jobs (that is, cases), values on each of eight job descriptors (that is, variables). The job descriptors could be of virtually any type. For our present purposes, however, let us consider these as tasks, with the values representing the number of hours in a 40-hour week devoted to the individual tasks.

A conventional factor analysis applied to such a set of data would be directed toward identifying the factors inherent in the relationships between and among the eight job descriptors across the nine jobs. In this instance a factor would be characterized primarily by a combination of tasks which tend to occur in common across the jobs. This is reflected by relatively similar values (across the jobs in question) for certain tasks, whether that value is high, average, or low. In Table 7–2 such relationships are shown as hours spent on the various tasks. Tasks which hang together are those which, across jobs, have relatively similar numbers of hours spent—high, average, or low, as the case may be. Such tasks would then tend to have high correlations with each other, and would likely emerge as a factor in a factor-analysis, which can be characterized primarily by a combination of tasks which tend to occur in common across the jobs. In other words, if a few tasks generally

TABLE 7–2. Matrix of hypothetical data showing values on each of eight job descriptors for each of nine jobs.*

	Job Descriptors							
Job	1	2	3	4	5	6	7	8
A	10	9	8	3	1	3	2	4
B	7	10	9	3	4	1	3	3
C	11	9	6	2	2	1	4	5
D	0	2	1	9	8	9	5	6
E	2	3	0	10	8	11	4	4
F	2	1	3	6	6	5	8	9
G	4	2	1	5	7	6	7	8
H	6	6	5	0	1	0	12	10
I	7	5	4	0	0	2	9	13

*One could consider the job descriptors as tasks, with the data in the table representing hours worked per 40-hour week on the individual tasks.

tend to have high indexes of relative times spent on some jobs, average indexes on other jobs, and low indexes on still other jobs, they would likely emerge as a factor in a factor analysis. Such tasks would then tend to have high correlations, one with another.

The example in Table 7–2 has been rigged to accentuate the factor structure. This was done by assigning the hypothetical values to form three rather clear-cut groupings of the eight variables (that is, the job descriptors). Further, in this example the variables that form each factor are intentionally placed in juxtaposition to each other. A scanning of Table 7–2 shows that variables form three groups (1, 2, and 3; 4, 5, and 6; and 7 and 8); within each group the variables have approximately the same values across the nine jobs. The correlation matrix shown in Figure 7–1 gives the correlation of each variable with every other variable. (For our purposes let us consider these variables as tasks, and the values as indices of "relative time spent.") These three groupings are apparent in that figure, although (as indicated above) this example represents factors more clear-cut than those that typically emerge from factor analyses. Note that there are a number of negative correlations. These indicate that, in general, where one variable is relatively important in jobs, the other variable tends *not* to be important. The number and magnitude of the negative correlations in this example are not typical of real data, but rather are the result of rigging the data in Table 7–2 to make the relationships more clear-cut.

Figure 7-1. Correlation matrix of data presented in Table 7-2, showing the correlation of each of the eight variables with each other.

Job Descriptors

		1	2	3	4	5	6	7
Job Descriptors	2	.87						
	3	.79	.91					
	4	−.76	−.60	−.69				
	5	−.86	−.68	−.71	.93			
	6	−.77	−.60	−.70	.96	.90		
	7	−.23	−.41	−.28	−.40	−.23	−.37	
	8	−.13	−.42	−.27	−.45	−.34	−.38	.88

With a given factor analysis procedure, each factor is *identified* statistically, and its nature is reflected by a set of *loadings* for the variables, the loading for each variable indicating its importance to the factor. The loadings can be considered as the equivalent of the correlations of the individual variables with the factor. A factor is interpreted, and named, on the basis of the variables that have the highest loadings on the factor, usually .30 or higher.

Regression Analysis

Regression analysis is a statistical procedure that provides for combining values on each of several variables (as applicable to individual cases such as jobs) to produce a single estimated or predicted value on some parameter. In this procedure each of the variables ends up with a statistically determined weight that reflects its importance in the composite value that is derived. A very common use of this procedure is in the combining of scores in various personnel tests as predictors of a criterion of job performance.

This procedure has various possible applications in the domain of human work. For example, regression analysis is sometimes used with job evaluation systems as the basis for combining job evaluation ratings on various factors to derive the total point values for individual jobs. In our present context regression analysis is used as the basis for deriving scores on the different factors that are identified by factor analysis procedures. Such a factor score is based on the sum of the values on the individual variable weighted by a statistically derived weight for each (this weight being based on the loading of each variable on the factor in question). In the case of a principal components analysis (a variant of factor analysis) these scores are technically referred to as *principal component scores* rather than as factor scores. But for some purposes, either factor or principal components are simply referred to as *job dimensions*, and scores thereof are referred to as *job dimension scores*.

By whatever name one might wish to use, such scores can be used as job descriptors and can therefore be used in analyzing job interrelationships and in job classification processes.

Cluster Analysis

Although various types of cluster analysis bear considerable similarity to factor analysis, each procedure has its unique features and lends itself to somewhat different applications. Conventional factor analysis procedures can be useful in identifying the basic factors or dimensions that characterize some domain of variables (such as the groupings of tasks which tend to occur in combination across jobs).

On the other hand, cluster analysis procedures tend to identify groupings of cases of some class (such as jobs) that have somewhat similar patterns or profiles across several or many variables. (Although there is this general difference between the two types of procedures, there are circumstances in which one could use either procedure.)

Virtually all cluster analysis methods require some index that reflects the degree of similarity between every *pair* of cases, the index for any pair of cases being based on the similarity of the values on the several variables that are used to characterize the cases at hand (such as jobs). One such index is the D^2 index (D stands for difference). It is based on the numerical differences of the index values of the several variables for the pair of cases in question, these differences being squared and added together. Table 7–3 shows data for two of the hypothetical jobs from Table 7–2, specifically jobs A and B, showing how the D^2 index is derived. In Table 7–3 the sum (Σ) of the D^2 values (ΣD^2) is 26. In the case of Jobs A and D (in Table 7–2) the $\Sigma D^2 = 328$. Again, the data for the jobs in Table 7–2 have been chosen to accentuate the possible similarities between and among the jobs. Further, in that table the nine jobs have been arranged so jobs with similar patterns of values on the eight variables are adjacent to each other. It can be seen at a glance that nine jobs form four rather clear-cut groups or clusters, namely: A, B, and C; D and E; F and G; and H and I. The D^2 values for the pairs of jobs *within* each of these three groups would be low, whereas those for pairs *across* these groups would be higher.

Given the D^2 index of similarity between all pairs of cases (or some other index) it is then possible to use any one of several cluster analysis techniques to identify the clusters which the cases tend to form, such as the four clusters represented in Table 7–2. (Again, it should be kept in mind that the clusters in that table are much more clear-cut than in most actual analyses of job data, the data in

TABLE 7–3. Data showing how the D^2 index is derived, based on Jobs A and B from Table 7–2.

	Job Descriptor							
	1	2	3	4	5	6	7	8
Job A	10	9	8	3	1	3	2	4
Job B	7	10	9	3	4	1	3	3
Difference *(D)*	3	1	1	0	3	2	1	1
D^2	9	1	1	0	9	4	1	1

that table having been accentuated and organized for illustrative purposes.)

One cluster analysis technique that has been used rather commonly with job-based data is the *hierarchical grouping* technique developed by Ward and by Ward and Hook. The computer program used with this procedure begins with task inventory data for n individuals, typically using the estimated percentage of work time as an indication of each incumbent's involvement with each task he performs. (For convenience in this discussion, individuals are sometimes referred to as groups. One can think of starting out with n groups, with one individual in each group.) The computer begins by locating the two most similar cases (the pair of individuals with the lowest D^2 value), forming them into a single cluster, thus reducing the number of groups from n to n-1. The percentages of time of the two cases in the first cluster are then averaged, and a D^2 value is computed between it and every remaining individual. In the next stage the computer locates and clusters the two most similar of the remaining groups (n-1), either by adding another individual to the already formed group or by combining two individuals to form a new group. The total number of groups is then reduced to n-2. In successive stages the computer continues to combine individuals, to add individuals to groups, and to merge existing groups, in order of the similarity index used. The process is repeated in an iterative manner until all individuals are merged into a single group. Using this procedure it is necessary to make judgment regarding the stage in the iterative process that produces the optimum number of clusters. (This issue is discussed further at the end of this section.)

Another cluster analysis technique has been developed by Silverman (1966) for use in the clustering of naval jobs. The procedure, called the Systematic Approach to Multidimensional Occupational Analysis (SAMOA), incorporates the use of a *coefficient of compositional similarity* (CCS) that is computed by the following formula:

$$CCS = \frac{Id}{Id + Un_1 + Un_2}$$

where Id = number of tasks identical between man 1 and man 2
        Un_1 = number of tasks unique to man 1
        Un_2 = number of tasks unique to man 2

This particular procedure has been used by the navy with data from task inventories. The results of one study using it are reported in Chapter 8.

In the application of clustering procedures to job data, the typical outcome consists of various clusters of jobs or positions, or job types, each of which is comprised of jobs which have reasonable homogeneity as reflected by the index that measures the similarity between and among jobs as based on the job descriptors used to characterize the jobs in question.

Discussion. Cluster analysis procedures are applicable to the development of classification systems that are predicated on the numerical approach to taxonomy in that the categories established are formed from similarities in their profiles as represented by the values on the various descriptors used. This approach represents a polythetic (as contrasted with a monothetic) basis for establishing classification systems since it is based on the overall pattern of the descriptors, and since no single descriptor or combination thereof is essential for group membership.

In connection with clustering procedures, however, there is a central issue that is raised by Thorndike in an entertaining (as well as thought-provoking) paper, called "Who Belongs in the Family?" This issue deals with the number of clusters to be formed. Going back to the discussion of cluster analysis procedures, it will be recalled that the scheme consists of an iterative approach in which one starts with n clusters (one job in each group), then forming n-1 groups, and sequentially n-2, n-3, etc., to the point where all jobs are grouped into a single cluster. With decreasing numbers of groups, the homogeneity of the individual clusters increases, and the problem for the taxonomist is to decide at what point in the iterative process one settles upon an optimum number of clusters. It should be added that there are certain statistical indexes that show reduction in the differences between and among the clusters as the numbers of clusters is reduced. In some instances noticeable drops in such indexes can suggest possible stopping points in the iterative process. However, there are no really objective bases for deciding how many clusters to select. Basically, this determination needs to be made by the taxonomist, whose decision should be based on his judgment regarding the number of clusters that would best serve the purposes he has in mind for the classification system.

References

Handbook of Occupational Keywords. U.S. Department of Labor, Manpower Administration. Washington, D.C.: U.S. Government Printing Office, **1975.**

Mead, D. F., and Christal, R. E. *Development of a Constant Standard Weight Equation for Evaluating Job Difficulty.* USAF, AFSC, AFHRL-TR-70-44. Brooks AFB, Texas: 1970.

Silverman, J. *A Computer Program for Clustering Jobs.* U.S. Naval Personnel Research Activity, Technical Bulletin STB 66-23. San Diego, Calif.: 1966.

Sokal, R. R. "Classification: Purposes, Principles, Progress, Prospects." *Science* 185(1974): 1115–1123.

Theologus, G. C. *Development of a Taxonomy of Human Performance: A Review of Biologic Taxonomy and Classification.* Washington, D.C.: American Institutes for Research, TR 3, 1969.

Thorndike, R. L. "Who Belongs in the Family?" *Psychometrika* 18(1953): 267–276.

Ward, J. H., Jr. "Hierarchical Grouping to Optimize an Objective Function." *Journal of the American Statistical Association* 58(1963): 236–244.

Ward, J. H., Jr., and Hook, M. E. "Applications of a Hierarchical Grouping Procedure to a Problem of Grouping Profiles. *Educational and Psychological Measurement* 23(1963): 69–82.

Wheaton, G. R. *A Review of Classificatory Systems Relating to Tasks and Performance.* Washington, D.C.: American Institutes for Research, TR No. 1, 1968.

8

Job Interrelationships and Classifications: Examples

CHAPTER 7 dealt with some of the general considerations that are relevant to the analysis of job interrelationships and to the development of job-related classification systems. That chapter included discussions of taxonomies, of job descriptors, and of certain methods of statistical analysis relevant to the investigation of the interrelationships between and among jobs and job-related variables. To illustrate the discussions in the previous chapters, this chapter draws on various studies of job interrelationships and of classification systems dealing with jobs and job-related variables.

As we noted in Chapter 7, the basic units of analysis in the study of job interrelationships can be of two types, either *descriptors* of job-related variables, or what we call *work entities* (such as tasks, other units of work, or complete jobs). There are, for example, classifications and lists of job descriptors (of various types) that can be used in characterizing jobs, tasks, or other work entities; and on the other hand, there are classifications and lists of jobs, tasks, or other work entities as such. The following section includes some examples of both of these.

The dividing line between interrelationships and classifications (that is, classification systems) is quite fuzzy. The analysis of the relationships between and among jobs does not necessarily result in a formal classification system (although in some cases it does). But let us not get hung up too much on semantics.

In this chapter we take an overview of various systematic analyses of job interrelationships, primarily through examples that reflect the use of a variety of types of job descriptors and analyses, and the use of different methods and approaches. The chapter is organized according to certain classes of *descriptive bases* used in the analysis of job-related variables:

Work-oriented bases
Behavior-oriented bases
Behavior requirements bases
Attribute requirements bases
Work characteristics bases
Other descriptive bases

These descriptive bases parallel Wheaton's four conceptual bases for classification, but with certain variations and elaborations and with modified labels, which seem useful in dealing with the broad spectrum of job-related variables (contrasted with the focus on tasks as such, as discussed by Wheaton). In effect, these bases differ in the nature of the descriptors used in analyzing jobs or job-related variables. As indicated in Chapter 7, the analysis of job inter-relationships and the development of job-related classification systems preferably should involve the measurement of the descriptors used. Thus, this chapter will deal largely with instances where this has been the case.

Work-Oriented Bases

Perhaps the most commonly used types of job descriptors for characterizing jobs are those that tend to describe the *job content,* with particular emphasis on the work activities and related nonactivity aspects of job situations (such as the equipment, machines, and tools used, and the work environment). Such descriptors are essentially the same as the job-oriented variables referred to earlier in that the content is expressed primarily in terms of the end result of work activities (that is, what is accomplished as the result of work activities).

Work-Oriented Descriptors

The most typical descriptors of a work-oriented nature describe *units of work* at some predetermined level of specificity. At a very basic level, any of the various sets of action verb lists can be used. One of the purposes of such lists is to standardize job analysis terminology, which was the objective, for example, in the development of the list of work fields and the associated methods verbs used by the USES. As indicated in Chapter 4, this list includes such work fields (with definitions) as Weaving and Stock checking, each with a list of methods verbs that relate to the work field. Examples of some of the methods verbs, from various work fields, are: calibrating, annealing, kneading, demonstrating, fumigating, and copying. To the extent that such lists of action verbs are complete and are reasonably mutually exclusive, they can serve as a classification system. Both Reed and Oller have developed a glossary of 130 action verbs, each defined with reasonable precision. Their system also incorporates cross-reference synonyms.*

In addition to standardizing terminology, listings of tasks or duties in an occupational area can serve as descriptors of a work-oriented nature. In the most straightforward form such descriptors are incorporated in structured job analysis questionnaires, such as task inventories. If such descriptors have been used directly in the analysis of jobs, the analysis of job interrelationships may well be based on the results of job analyses (which usually have been expressed in quantitative terms, or at least in categorical terms). In some circumstances, however, the original data may be consolidated in some fashion, such as by deriving a summated score based on the descriptors which fall within some rationally established group (such as the tasks which are formed into clusters of duties in a task inventory). Alternatively, the data may be reduced to broader categories, such as the factors resulting from a factor analysis.

---

*Examples of action verbs of work activities developed by Reed and Oller: activate, align, calibrate, checkout, decode, disengage, fill, handle, identify, inspect, interrogate, operate, place, record, replace, rotate, setup, transmit, and walk. Definitions of these clarify ambiguities that might exist from the words by themselves.

Job Factors or Dimensions Based on Job Content

In connection with the use of factor analysis in this context, there are a number of examples that can be presented. (The factors resulting from such analyses sometimes are referred to as *job dimensions*.)

Clerical job activities. In one example of the application of factor analysis methods to job data, Chalupsky developed and used a structured job analysis questionnaire that consisted of 33 clerical operations such as: analyzes, compiles, plans, and translates. The items in the questionnaire were essentially of a job content nature. The questionnaire was used in the analysis of 192 jobs for which job descriptions were available from the USES. A factor analysis of the data resulted in the identification of five factors, as follows: Inventory and stockkeeping, Supervision, Computation and bookkeeping, Communication and public relations, and Stenographer-typing and general clerical. Each of these can be viewed as representing a reasonably stable cluster of the more specific clerical functions which, in the world of work, typically tend to occur in combination. (It might be added that a parallel analysis of the same jobs using a checklist of 58 clerical knowledge items resulted in the identification of factors that corresponded very closely with these, except that the last factor was broken down into two: stenography-typing, and filing and general clerical.) In this study the descriptors of job content can be viewed at two levels, namely, at the level of the 33 clerical operations and at the level of the several factors.

Another example of the factor analysis of data from a structured job analysis questionnaire in the clerical area is reported by Prien. He developed a clerical Position Description Questionnaire that provided for the analysis of clerical jobs in terms of various clerical tasks. This questionnaire was used to analyze a sample of clerical positions, and the resulting data were subjected to factor analysis; the titles of the factors that resulted are listed below:

Typing, processing, and distribution of written material
Supervision of clerical accounting
Bookkeeping and clerical accounting
Filing and retrieval of material
Operation of data-processing equipment
Analysis and reporting of business data
Cash operating accounts
Manpower records maintenance

Secretarial (executive) assistance
Mailing
Communicating and public relations
Receptionist

Most of these types of clerical activity are recognizable in and around most offices and thus tend to confirm our common-sense observations. But even when factor analysis in effect confirms "common sense," there is an additional advantage of such an analysis that permits one to derive factor scores for individual positions or jobs on the basis of specific combinations of tasks as related to each position or job and the statistically determined weight of each task as related to each factor. Thus, any position or job can be described by a profile of factor scores. Further, the structure of jobs in many occupational areas is not as apparent as it is in the case of clerical jobs; in such instances factor analysis permits the statistical identification of factors that could not be otherwise "recognized" or identified. It should be added that there are other statistical techniques such as various cluster analysis procedures that serve a somewhat similar purpose to that of factor analysis.

Prien's study differs in some factors from Chalupsky's. It should be pointed out that the results of factor analysis procedures are very much dependent upon the specific nature of the initial variables used in the data collection phase. Prien's questionnaire consisted of more specific job activities than Chalupsky's, which may in part account for the differences. However, certain of Prien's factors correspond with Chalupsky's and certain others represent essentially finer breakdowns of the job activities (perhaps because of the greater specificity of the original job activity categories).

Work performance factors of health officers. As another illustration of the use of factor analysis of job content data, Brumback and Vincent describe a fairly large-scale survey of commissioned officers of the Public Health Service in which 3,719 officers used a task inventory to report their own work activities. The resulting responses were subjected to factor analysis in order to identify the different functional areas of work represented by the sample. A total of 26 such functional work areas (that is, factors) were identified, a few of which were these: performing public health inspection and control activities; conducting surveys (such as epidemiological investigations); and preparing and testing samples for contaminants or disease agents.

In large part, this analysis was made with the possible objective in mind of providing a more appropriate basis for personnel-appraisal, one that is more job-oriented than person-oriented.

Job factors of high-level positions. Still another example of the use of factor analysis to identify relevant job factors is a study carried out by Baehr. The job analysis questionnaire that she used, the Work Elements Inventory, included 122 generic job elements that are relevant to supervisory, management, sales, and other higher-level positions. The questionnaire was used by 600 job incumbents in describing their own positions. A factor analysis of the data on the 600 positions produced the following 12 factors, here grouped into four categories:

ORGANIZATION
1. Setting organizational objectives
2. Improving work procedures and practices
3. Promoting safety attitudes and practices
4. Developing and implementing technical ideas

LEADERSHIP
5. Judgment and decision-making
6. Developing group cooperation and teamwork
7. Coping with difficulties and emergencies

PERSONNEL
8. Developing employee potential
9. Supervisory practices
10. Self-development and improvement

COMMUNITY
11. Promoting community-organization relations
12. Handling outside contacts

Job Types and Clusters

In many organizations it is the practice to establish job classification systems in which each job category includes similar positions. When various positions are, for practical purposes, identical in content, there usually is no particular problem in identifying those which go together. To take a simple case, there might be several book-keepers, each performing the same tasks, but each responsible for different accounts (such as those identified by names from different sections of the alphabet). But when there are some differences be-tween and among related positions, the establishment of separate job categories, and the allocation of positions to them, can present

a problem. Although the grouping of positions by judgment undoubtedly has served the intended purposes adequately in many
circumstances, it is probable that in other circumstances the use of
appropriate statistical methods would result in the formation of
more satisfactory job categories.

Even in the case of already established job categories, some statistical analysis of data about the positions in the individual categories may serve useful purposes. The categories of related positions can reflect marked differences in the degree of homogeneity
(or of heterogeneity), depending very much upon the level of homogeneity that would best serve the purposes in question. They
may consist of positions that are virtually identical, those that vary
from each other by differing degrees, or even groupings or clusters
of what are related jobs. In the Air Force, positions are grouped
into what are called *job types*. In effect, the distinctions between jobs,
job types, and what are sometimes called job clusters or job families
are essentially differences in degree rather than in kind.

Job descriptions based on task inventories. To begin with, let us illustrate how data from task inventories can be used to develop job descriptions of an already established job classification. This procedure has been developed and used primarily by what is now called
The Manpower and Occupational Research Division of the USAF
Human Resources Laboratory in its occupational research activities.
The task inventories used in the USAF typically are completed by
job incumbents to report "relative time spent" on various tasks
within a career field. The data on relative time spent is converted
to an estimate of actual time, and it is such data that are used primarily in their analyses of task inventory responses.

In the case of data from incumbents in a given, existing job
group, the pooled data from many incumbents can be summarized
in the fashion shown in Table 8–1, which presents information on
(1) the percent of individuals in the total group who perform each
task; (2) the average percent of time devoted to the task by those
who do perform it; (3) the average percent of time spent on the
task by all members collectively; and (4) the cumulative sum of that
average. The tasks typically are arranged in decreasing order of
item 3. Data such as that given in the table can provide management with some indication of the number of incumbents within a
given group who perform various tasks, and of the time devoted to
the various tasks.

Identification of job types from task inventories. Aside from the use
of task inventory data to develop job descriptions of members of

some already identified, existing job group, it is possible to use data from task inventories to identify what the USAF calls job types within a career field. The individual job types consist of groups of positions with relatively similar combinations of tasks. In the USAF the identification of the job types is carried out by the cluster analysis procedures described in Chapter 7.

The results of such a procedure are illustrated in Table 8–2, which shows parts of the computer-generated job descriptions for two types of USAF electronics engineers. Altogether, 17 job types were identified, each one consisting of positions with relatively similar combination of tasks. (Table 8–2 shows only a few of the tasks that charac-

TABLE 8–1. Portion of a group job description: U.S. Air Force Disbursement Accounting Specialist. (Source: *Proceedings of Division of Military Psychology Symposium*)

Task Title	(1)	(2)	(3)	(4)
Answer inquiries concerning military pay or allowances	51.32	7.08	3.63	3.63
Provide counter service for military pay section	37.59	7.39	2.78	6.41
Write correspondence about military pay matters	28.01	4.91	1.38	26.28
Maintain files of travel documents and records	18.80	7.16	1.35	27.63
Review travel vouchers	17.48	7.63	1.33	28.96
Edit travel documents	15.41	7.07	1.09	41.04
Estimate costs of travel and transportation	13.91	5.65	0.79	52.23
Key punch travel documents	6.95	6.98	0.49	65.59
Prepare U.S. Treasury checks	6.39	6.71	0.43	67.44
Conduct on-the-job training	11.28	3.31	0.37	73.05
Plan methods for organizing and filing records	8.83	2.87	0.25	81.78
Prepare statement of accountability	4.51	5.17	0.23	83.99
Audit U.S. Treasury checks against vouchers	4.89	4.77	0.23	84.22
Prepare monthly payroll	3.95	4.34	0.17	89.94

Note: The lines between tasks indicate tasks that are not listed in this table. Column headings are:
(1) Percent of members performing
(2) Average percent time spent by members performing
(3) Average percent time spent by all members
(4) Cumulative sum of average percent time spent by all members

terized each job type.) Since such data reflect the manner in which work in a given career field actually is organized into job entities, these data have been used by the USAF in formally establishing new job classifications or in modifying existing classifications.

Another illustration of the use of task inventories for identifying job categories comes from a study in the navy by Carr deal-

TABLE 8–2.   Parts of job type descriptions for two job types of Air Force electronics engineers. (Source: Morsh)

Job type: electronics system evaluator	*(1)*	*(2)*	*(3)*	*(4)*
Monitor the testing of systems and subsystems	100.00	5.72	5.72	5.72
Review and evaluate functional test data	62.50	7.03	4.40	24.47
Maintain liaison with contractors	87.50	3.93	3.44	43.49
Supervise the testing of systems, subsystems, and equipment	62.50	5.13	3.21	49.99
Establish acceptance criteria for equipment	37.50	6.24	2.34	63.73
Prepare test program documentation	75.00	3.07	2.30	66.03
Analyze system or component defects and make recommendations for corrective action	37.50	3.73	1.40	74.29
Analyze reliability data	37.50	2.86	1.07	80.50
Job type: project supervisor				
Counsel engineers and technicians in the performance of their duties	100.00	3.43	3.43	3.43
Supervise the testing of systems, subsystems, and equipment	100.00	3.32	3.32	6.74
Supervise office, technical, and administrative personnel	88.89	3.20	2.84	12.48
Establish work priorities	88.89	2.83	2.52	28.19
Develop procedures to conserve manpower and material	77.78	2.87	2.23	35.13
Establish quality control procedures and charts	44.44	4.44	1.97	41.37
Develop standards or instrumentation to determine performance of equipment	77.78	2.47	1.92	45.26
Develop practical applications of basic designs, ideas, or discoveries	77.78	2.32	1.81	52.63
Direct test force efforts	55.56	2.78	1.55	60.95
Perform engineering flight or operational tests	66.67	2.27	1.51	62.46

Note: These job types have been identified by a computer program that groups together task inventories of incumbents who perform essentially the same combinations of tasks. The descriptions are based on a partial listing of tasks resulting from responses to the task inventory. Column headings are:
(1) Percent of members performing
(2) Average percent time spent by members performing
(3) Average percent time spent by all members
(4) Cumulative sum of average percent time spent by all members

ing with positions in the engineering department of naval destroy-
ers. A job inventory consisting of 135 tasks was completed by 350
personnel, and the resulting data were subjected to cluster analysis
using the SAMOA method described in Chapter 7. Five basic job
categories (referred to as job clusters) were identified. As a further
elaboration of this study, each cluster was characterized in terms of
a statistically derived index on each of three TOC dimensions
(T = Technical; O = Organizational; C = Communicational). The
five clusters and their indices on these dimensions are:

Cluster	*T*	*O*	*C*
1. Propulsion and auxiliary	4	3	3
2. Apprentice	1	2	2
3. Assistant	2	1	2
4. General	4	3	3
5. Refrigeration and air conditioning	2	4	3

Although the development of the dimension values will not be given,
they were derived in a reasonably objective manner. With such dimensions then quantified, it was possible to represent the five clusters
in a three-dimensional manner, as shown in Figure 8–1.

Management job types. The problems involved in the analysis of
management positions and the systematic investigation of the relationships between and among them have haunted job analysts and
researchers for years. One investigation that has shed some light on
this area was carried out by Mahoney et al. The investigators used
two sets of descriptors (or dimensions) in the analysis of the positions of 452 managers in 13 companies. One of the sets consisted
of eight functional dimensions: planning, investigating, coordinating, evaluating, supervising, staffing, negotiating, and representing.
The other set dealt with six areas of technical competence or
knowledge required in job performance: employees, finances, materials and goods, purchases and sales, methods and procedures, and
facilities and equipment. The managers were asked to estimate
their "usual allocation of time" among the two sets of dimensions so
the sum of time estimates for each set would total 100 percent.

The profiles of the individual managers were then grouped
(with the help of certain guidelines) into reasonably homogeneous
job types on the basis of relative concentration of time in specific
functions. Eight job types were identified. In addition, all the positions were categorized in terms of organizational level (low, middle,
and high). The results are presented in Figure 8–2, which shows
the percent of those in each of the three levels who had been cate-

Figure 8-1. Illustration of five categories (clusters) of a naval engineering department positions in terms of their values on three dimensions. (Source: Carr)

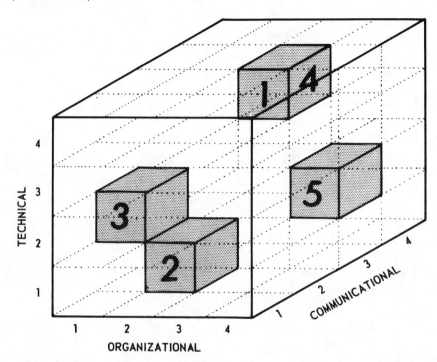

gorized in various job types on the basis of their work activities. The results of the study demonstrate that the generally amorphous domain of management positions can be characterized in a reasonably systematic, quantitative manner.

Another study dealing with the analysis of management positions was carried out by Hemphill. To collect data, he used a questionnaire of 575 elements that might be relevant to the work of executives. A few examples are:

Instruct employees in proper procedures
Review plans with outside agencies.
Estimate the life of new construction.
Adjust customer complaints.
Be active in community affairs.
Be away from home at least 60 days a year.

Figure 8-2. Distribution of estimates of time devoted to various job dimensions by managers at three organizational levels (Source: Mahoney et al., p. 109)

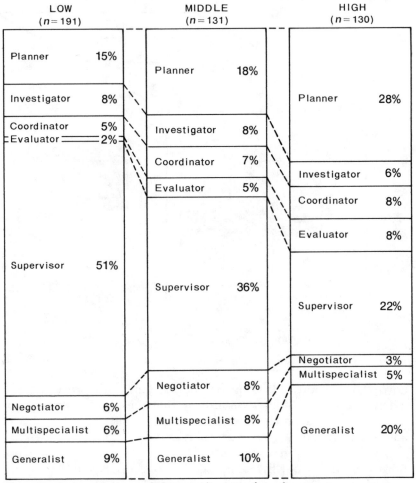

LOW (n = 191)	MIDDLE (n = 131)	HIGH (n = 130)
Planner 15%	Planner 18%	Planner 28%
Investigator 8%	Investigator 8%	Investigator 6%
Coordinator 5%	Coordinator 7%	Coordinator 8%
Evaluator 2%	Evaluator 5%	Evaluator 8%
Supervisor 51%	Supervisor 36%	Supervisor 22%
Negotiator 6%	Negotiator 8%	Negotiator 3%
Multispecialist 6%	Multispecialist 8%	Multispecialist 5%
Generalist 9%	Generalist 10%	Generalist 20%

Note: Totals do not add up to 100 percent because of rounding.

A sample of 93 executives completed the questionnaire, responding to each element using a 7-point scale to indicate how much a part of the respondent's position each element comprised. (This scale was illustrated in Chapter 7.)

A unique feature of this study was its use of an inverse-factor analysis as its statistical procedure. By means of this procedure each of the 93 positions was correlated with every other one across the 575 elements. The resulting correlations were used in the factor analysis.

The factors then were characterized by groups of positions (rather than by groups of variables, which in this instance were the elements.) Ten groupings (or dimensions) were identified, as follows:

Providing a staff service in nonoperational areas.
Supervision of work.
Internal business control.
Technical aspects of products and markets.
Human, community, and social affairs.
Long-range planning.
Exercise of broad power and authority.
Business reputation.
Personal demands.
Preservation of assets.

Actually, most positions had some involvement with each of the ten dimensions (the level of this involvement was reflected by the factor loadings of the positions on the various factors). However, each dimension (technically, each factor) is characterized by those positions which measure high on the dimensions. In addition, Hemphill included, for each dimension, a listing of the items in the questionnaire that were characteristic of those positions having high loadings in the dimensions.

Job and Occupation Classification Systems

Job and occupation classification systems (based on work-oriented descriptions) fall into two general classes: systems that are developed and used within individual organizations, and comprehensive systems that are intended to encompass virtually all jobs and occupations in the labor force.

Classification systems of specific organizations. Many organizations have job classification systems that consist of separate classifications for each job. In some organizations such systems may be very informally recognized, whereas in other organizations there may be some formal recognition of the systems. This is the case, for example, in some unionized organizations in which there is management-labor recognition of the various job classifications, frequently with specifications of the types of duties and activities that fall within each class.

Other formally recognized classification systems are those of the United States Civil Service Commission, and those of the military services. In the United States Air Force, for example, each separate job type, referred to as an Air Force Specialty (AFS), has an officially established title and code. In turn, these are organized into *career ladders* for each of a number of occupational fields, and these career ladders reflect the specialties (that is, the AFS classifications) at various levels, and the typical progressions from lower to higher classifications.

It is probable that the classification systems of most organizations have been based on rational or logical considerations rather than on systematic research. Further, in most such systems the classification of individual jobs or occupations in specific categories is essentially subjective. Such classification typically is based on the job or occupation as a total entity rather than on data on certain descriptors related to the job or occupation. In certain organizations, however, the classification systems have benefited somewhat from more systematic analyses of job data. This has been the case, for example, with the career ladders of the United States Air Force, which have at least been modified on the basis of data from task inventories.

Comprehensive job and occupation classification systems. Certain job and occupation classification systems are intended to encompass virtually all jobs and occupations. The major systems of this type are those established by government agencies to serve certain specific purposes, such as the classification system of the United States Bureau of the Census and that of the United States Employment Service. A few comprehensive systems are intended primarily to reflect the psychological and sociological implications of occupation affiliation and would thus serve various research and theoretical objectives, and could be of use in connection with vocational counseling. One such classification system is that of Anne Roe.

The occupational classification of the Bureau of the Census is used for classifying people in the labor force by their present or past occupation. This system contains 10 major occupational categories, each with many specific occupations. The major categories are:

Professional, technical, and kindred workers
Farmers and farm managers
Clerical and kindred workers
Sales workers
Craftsmen, foremen, and kindred workers
Operatives and kindred workers
Private household workers
Service workers, except private household
Farm laborers and foremen
Laborers, except farm or mine

In its operations the United States Employment Service provides for the classification and coding of applicants and of available positions by the use of an occupational classification system that is incorporated in the *Dictionary of Occupational Titles* (DOT). The major occupational categories are:

Professional, technical, and managerial occupations
Clerical and sales occupations
Service occupations
Agricultural, fishery, forestry, and related occupations
Processing occupations
Machine trades occupations
Benchwork occupations
Structural work occupations
Miscellaneous occupations

Within these occupational categories are fewer than a hundred occupational divisions (such as occupations in life sciences, computing and accounting-recording occupations, printing occupations, and packaging and materials handling occupations); these are identified by a two-digit code. At the next level (a three-digit code) are about 560 more specific occupational groups (such as physicians and surgeons, mail carriers, hoisting and conveying occupations, and tailors and dressmakers). The basis for the occupational groups is essentially job content as judged by analysts. The fourth, fifth, and sixth digits are the worker function codes for data, people, and things (shown in Figure 4–2, Chapter 4). The seventh, eighth, and ninth digits identify specific occupations within the six digit code groups. For example, let's decode the number 629261010 according to the USES occupational classification system:

	Digit	What Digit Codes for	Code No.	Meaning of Code No.
	1	Occupational category	**6**	Machine trades occupations
	2	Occupational division	**62**	Mechanics and machine repairers
	3	Occupational group	**629**	Special industry machinery mechanics
Worker functions	4	Data	6292	Analyzing
	5	People	62926	Speaking-signaling
	6	Things	629261	Precision working
	7, 8, 9	Specific occupation	629261**010**	Laundry machine mechanic

   The jobs in the *Dictionary of Occupational Titles* are also characterized in terms of other variables, in particular the worker traits mentioned in Chapter 4 (including training time, aptitudes, interests, temperaments, physical demands, and working conditions).

   The classification of occupations by Roe was developed primarily
for use by vocational counselors as an aid to them in providing vocational guidance to individuals. Therefore, the system classifies occupations in such a fashion as to reflect something about the personality,
intellectual, and social characteristics of persons in different occupations. In this system occupations are classified into eight general
groups at six different levels (Table 8–3). The groups reflect the function in society of the occupations, and the levels reflect the degree of
skill or training required. Table 8–3 gives examples of some of the
occupations that have been classified in this way.

Behavior-Oriented Bases

The behavior-oriented classification of job-related variables is based
on categories that describe what people actually do when performing some job activity. Such categories, essentially worker-oriented, are characterized by basic human behaviors, including not
only those of an overt, physical nature but also those of a sensory-
input and meditation nature.

   Behavior-oriented classification systems can be viewed both at
the level of descriptors used in characterizing jobs and at the level
of job entities.

Classifications of Behavioral Descriptors

Several classifications of behavioral descriptors have been developed; some of these are discussed below.

   Behavioral classification of Berliner et al. The classification system
of behavioral descriptors developed by Berliner et al. was intended
primarily for use with jobs in military systems. It is a hierarchical
classification structure aimed at establishing a bridge between types
of behaviors and conditions of training. The structure contains
three levels — processes, activities, and specific behavior, as shown in
Figure 8–3. The system is based on 47 specific behaviors, represented by action verbs which were considered to be well recognized
and relatively distinct from one another. In the development of the
system judges were asked to group the specific behaviors into the
larger process categories. In its final form the system includes those
behaviors which had been grouped in the process categories by at
least six of eight judges. In its complete form the system provides

TABLE 8–3. The classification of occupations developed by Ann Roe, showing the two-way basis for classification by group and by level, with examples. (Source: Roe)

Level	I. Service	II. Business Contact	III. Organization	IV. Technology	V. Outdoor	VII. Science	VII. General Cultural	VIII. Arts and Entertainment
1	Personal therapists; Social work supervisors; Counselors	Promoters	United States President and Cabinet officers; Industrial tycoons; International bankers	Inventive geniuses; Consulting or chief engineers; Ships' commanders	Consulting specialists	Research scientists; University, college faculties; Medical specialists; Museum curators	Supreme Court justices; University, college faculties; Prophets; Scholars	Creative artists; Performers, great; Teachers, university equivalent; Museum curators
2	Social workers; Occupational therapists; Probation, truant officers (with training)	Promoters; Public relations counselors	Certified public accountants; Business and government executives; Union officials; Brokers, average	Applied scientists; Factory managers; Ships' officers; Engineers	Applied scientists; Landowners and operators, large; Landscape architects	Scientists, semi-independent; Nurses; Pharmacists; Veterinarians	Editors; Teachers, high school and elementary	Athletes; Art critics; Designers; Music arrangers
3	YMCA officials; Detectives, police sergeants; Welfare workers; City inspectors	Salesmen: auto, bond, insurance, etc.; Dealers, retail and wholesale; Confidence men	Accountants, average; Employment managers; Owners, catering, dry-cleaning, etc.	Aviators; Contractors; Foremen (DOT I); Radio operators	County agents; Farm owners; Forest rangers; Fish, game wardens	Technicians, medical, X-ray, museum; Weather observers; Chiropractors	Justices of the Peace; Radio announcers; Reporters; Librarians	Ad writers; Designers; Interior decorators; Showmen
4	Barbers; Chefs; Practical nurses; Policemen	Auctioneers; Buyers (DOT I); House canvassers; Interviewers, poll	Cashiers; Clerks, credit, express, etc.; Foremen, warehouse; Salesclerks	Blacksmiths; Electricians; Foremen (DOT II); Mechanics, average	Laboratory testers, dairy products, etc.; Miners; Oil well drillers	Technical assistants	Law clerks	Advertising artists; Decorators, window, etc.; Photographers; Racing car drivers
5	Taxi drivers; General houseworkers; Waiters; City firemen	Peddlers	Clerks, file, stock, etc.; Notaries; Runners; Typists	Bulldozer operators; Deliverymen; Smelter workers; Truck drivers	Gardeners; Farm tenants; Teamsters, cow-punchers; Miners' helpers	Veterinary hospital attendants		Illustrators, greeting cards; Showcard writers; Stagehands
6	Chambermaids; Hospital attendants; Elevator operators; Watchmen		Messenger boys	Helpers; Laborers; Wrappers; Yardmen	Dairy hands; Farm laborers; Lumberjacks	Nontechnical helpers in scientific organization		

Group

quantifiable measures of the various behaviors in terms of such criteria as time errors, use-frequency data, workload data, and motion dynamics.

Functional job analysis (FJA). Functional job analysis is another example of a classification system of behavioral job descriptors. This approach, described in Chapter 6, characterizes activities in terms of the level on each of three hierarchies, namely, the involvement with data, people, and things (see Figure 6–1). The USES takes this approach to classify total jobs in terms of their involvement, whereas Fine proposes to relate it to individual tasks. In either case, each work entity (task or job) is characterized by the judged level of involvement with each of the hierarchies.

Job elements of the PAQ. Although the Position Analysis Questionnaire (PAQ) is essentially a structured job analysis questionnaire, it can also be viewed as a classification system of behavioral descriptors. The individual job elements characterize human behaviors directly, or at least infer the human behaviors involved. The complete assortment of job elements covers most types of such behaviors.

Job dimensions based on the PAQ job data. Aside from the use of the PAQ job elements as job descriptors of a behavior-oriented nature (and serving in effect as a classification scheme), job dimensions based on the PAQ job elements can represent descriptors at a broader level and as a broader classification system of behavior-oriented descriptors. In this regard, two types of principal components analyses (a particular variant of factor analysis) have been carried out with two sets of job-related data based on the PAQ. One set of data was based on *job data,* that is, the data from the analysis of jobs with the PAQ. These analyses are described below. The other set, based on *attribute data,* is discussed later in this chapter.

Actually, three series of principal components analyses have been carried out with the PAQ, one based on Form A and the other two based on Form B (a slightly modified form). The analyses with Form A were based on data for a sample of 536 jobs as carried out by Jeanneret and McCormick and reported in McCormick et al. (1972). The analyses with Form B included one series based on a sample of 3,700 jobs (Marquardt and McCormick 1974) and another series based on a sample of 2,200 jobs (Mecham). For various reasons (including the representativeness of the sample) the results based on the sample of 2,200 jobs are reported here.

In this study, separate principal components analyses were carried out for the job elements within each of the six divisions of the

Figure 8-3. Hierarchical classification of behaviors developed by Berliner et al. (Source: Berliner et al., pp. 30-31)

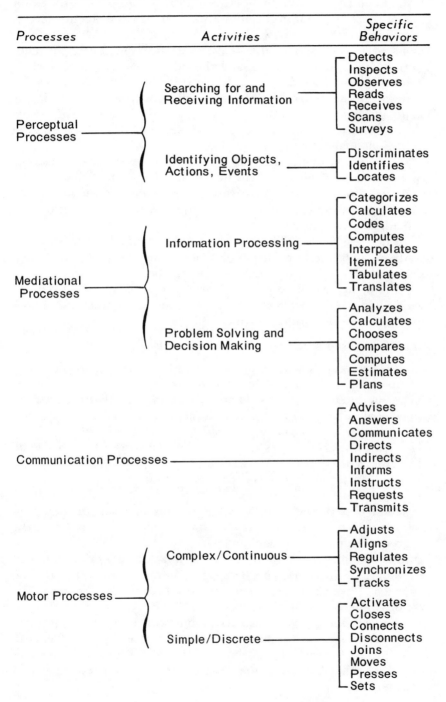

Processes	Activities	Specific Behaviors
Perceptual Processes	Searching for and Receiving Information	Detects Inspects Observes Reads Receives Scans Surveys
	Identifying Objects, Actions, Events	Discriminates Identifies Locates
Mediational Processes	Information Processing	Categorizes Calculates Codes Computes Interpolates Itemizes Tabulates Translates
	Problem Solving and Decision Making	Analyzes Calculates Chooses Compares Computes Estimates Plans
Communication Processes		Advises Answers Communicates Directs Indirects Informs Instructs Requests Transmits
Motor Processes	Complex/Continuous	Adjusts Aligns Regulates Synchronizes Tracks
	Simple/Discrete	Activates Closes Connects Disconnects Joins Moves Presses Sets

PAQ. (The elements in division 5 were divided into two groups for this purpose. Division 5 includes a number of job elements, largely concerned with certain working conditions, for which a dichotomous scale was used in the analysis of the jobs. These elements were included in one group, and the other elements, for which 6-point scales were used, were included in the second group; this was done to avoid having data based on different types of scales in the same analysis.) In addition, a separate principal components analysis was carried out with 150 of the job elements pooled together, as an overall analysis.

The results of the analyses by Mecham are summarized in the first column of Table 8–4. This shows the division and principal components referred to as job dimensions. (Reference to the job dimensions in the second column, from Marquardt and McCormick, 1973, is made later in this chapter.)

Since it is not feasible to present the voluminous data on factor loadings, only the titles of job dimensions are given. These dimensions, based on data from 2,200 jobs, can be interpreted as reflecting the structure of human job behaviors—that is, the extent to which basic job behaviors tend to be grouped together in the jobs that comprise the world of work.

Classifications of Jobs Using Behavior-oriented Descriptors

There are very few examples of classification systems in which groupings of tasks or jobs have been developed on the basis of behavior-oriented descriptors. One such example is that reported by Shaw et al. The study in question dealt with a reasonably representative sample of 746 jobs which had been analyzed with the PAQ. The job dimension scores used for these jobs were the 13 overall dimensions developed by Mecham.

The cluster analysis was carried out using a hierarchical clustering procedure similar to that described by Ward, with a slight variation that provides for weighting items in terms of their contributions to the clusters. The D^2 value was used as the index of the degree of similarity of job dimension scores for pairs of jobs or groups of jobs. One iteration resulted in 60 clusters or job families. Examples of three clusters from this iteration are illustrated in Figure 8–4, which shows the percentile values of mean scores in the various dimensions for each cluster.

This cluster analysis was carried out with the view of possibly using the clusters as the basis for establishing an aptitude requirement profile for each cluster that, in turn, might be applied to individual jobs that fall within the cluster. (This is discussed further in Chapter 10.)

Behavior Requirements Bases

The behavior requirements approach to the classification of job-related variables places emphasis on the cataloging of behaviors which, as Wheaton puts it, *should* be emitted or which are assumed to be *required* in order to achieve an acceptable level of work performance. The primary concern of most of the schemes of this type has been with possible descriptors of *operator* types of tasks and jobs.

An example of this approach is the one worked out by Folley principally to aid in the development of training devices and programs for certain types of military jobs. His procedure provides for analyzing work activities in terms of five behavioral descriptors:

1. Procedure following (PF). Performing a sequence of discrete steps, each of which has an identifiable beginning and ending.
2. Continuous perceptual motor activity (CPMA). Observing displays and operating controls continuously to maintain a specified relationship between an object under the operator's control and other objects not under his control.
3. Monitoring (M). Observing a display, or displays, or a portion of the environment to detect a specified kind of change.
4. Communicating (C). Receiving information and/or sending information in words or other symbols.
5. Decision making or problem solving (DM). Piecing together facts, opinions, and other information and arriving at a conclusion about what action to take.

The distinction between the behavioral requirements base and the behavior-oriented base is not entirely clear-cut, since both provide for characterizing activities in terms of general classes of human behaviors. However, the behavior requirements approach tends to be more specifically focused on those behaviors as they are operationally required. For example, Folley's procedure provides for the more specific analysis of work activities within each of the classes listed above in terms of specific operational aspects, such as (in the case of monitoring) specifying the nature of the change in a display that should be detected).

Attribute Requirements Bases

Another method for analyzing job interrelationships and for developing classification systems of job-related variables is based on specified human attributes required by individuals to perform given work activities, either at the micro (such as task) level or at the macro (job) level. This method is predicated upon three assumptions:

TABLE 8–4. Job dimensions resulting from principal components analyses of data based on the Position Analysis Questionnaire (PAQ). (Sources: Mecham; Marquardt and McCormick, 1973)

Job Dimensions Based on Job Analysis Data	*Job Dimensions Based on Attribute Profiles of Job Elements*
DIMENSIONS OF INFORMATION INPUT	
1. Interpreting what is sensed	A1-1 Visual input from devices/materials
2. Using various sources of information	A1-2 Evaluation of visual input
3. Watching devices/materials for information	A1-3 Perceptual input from processes/events
4. Evaluating/judging what is sensed	A1-4 Verbal/auditory input/interpretation
5. Being aware of environmental conditions	A1-5 Nonvisual input
6. Using various senses	
DIMENSIONS OF MENTAL PROCESSES	
7. Making decisions	A2-6 Use of job-related knowledge
8. Processing information	A2-7 Information processing
DIMENSIONS OF WORK OUTPUT	
9. Using machines/tools/equipment	A3-8 Manual control/coordination activities
10. Performing activities requiring general body movements	A3-9 Control/equipment operation
11. Controlling machines/processes	A3-10 General body/handling activities
12. Performing skilled/technical activities	A3-11 Use of foot controls
13. Performing controlled manual/related activities	
14. Using miscellaneous equipment/devices	
15. Performing handling/related manual activities	
16. General physical coordination	
DIMENSIONS OF RELATIONSHIPS WITH OTHER PERSONS	
17. Communicating judgments/related information	A4-12 Interpersonal communications
18. Engaging in general personal contact	A4-13 Signal/code communications
19. Performing supervisory/coordination/related activities	A4-14 Serving/entertaining
20. Exchanging job-related information	
21. Public/related personal contacts	

Table 8–4 (cont.)

Job Dimensions Based on Job Analysis Data	*Job Dimensions Based on Attribute Profiles of Job Elements*
DIMENSIONS OF JOB CONTEXT	
22. Being in a stressful/unpleasant environment	A5-15 Unpleasant physical environment
23. Engaging in personally demanding situations	A5-16 Personally demanding situations
24. Being in hazardous job situations	A5-17 Hazardous physical environment
DIMENSIONS OF OTHER JOB CHARACTERISTICS	
25. Working non-typical vs. day schedule	A6-18 Work schedule I
26. Working in businesslike situations	A6-19 Job responsibility
27. Wearing optional vs. specified apparel	A6-20 Routine/repetitive work activities
28. Being paid on a variable vs. salary basis	A6-21 Attentive/discriminating work demands
29. Working on a regular vs. irregular schedule	A6-22 Work attire
30. Working under job-demanding circumstances	A6-23 Work schedule II
31. Performing structured vs. unstructured work	
32. Being alert to change	
OVERALL DIMENSIONS	
33. Having decision, communicating, and general responsibilities	AG-1 Cognitive and interpersonal skills
34. Operating machines/equipment	AG-2 General physical skills
35. Performing clerical/related activities	AG-3 Sensory/judgmental/memory demands
36. Performing technical/related activities	AG-4 Visual discrimination/perception
37. Performing service/related activities	AG-5 Quantitative/technical demands
38. Working regular day vs. other work schedule	AG-6 Psychomotor skills
39. Performing routine activities	AG-7 Aesthetic judgment/originality versus perceptual/response demands
40. Being aware of work environment	AG-8 Chemical senses
41. Engaging in physical activities	AG-9 Work pressures/risks
42. Supervising other personnel	
43. Public/customer/related contacts	
44. Working in an unpleasant/hazardous/demanding environment	
45. Unnamed	

1. There are different *kinds* of basic human attributes.
2. People vary in the level of each such attribute.
3. Variation in the level of individual attributes is associated with some aspect of job-related behavior on certain tasks or jobs.

Classifications of Attribute Descriptors

Psychologists for years have been concerned with identifying broad classes of what one might consider basic human attributes. These broad classes have variously been viewed as including sensory skills, perceptual skills, psychomotor skills, physical abilities, cognitive (mental) abilities, and affective attributes (that is, interests, motivation, personality, and the like). At a grosser level these classes can be viewed as falling within two groups, namely, *abilities,* and *affective attributes.* Although many psychologists have hypothesized the existence of specific attributes from the observed behaviors of people, inferences about the existence of intrinsic attributes from such observations are not proof that such attributes are reasonably distinct basic human qualities.

Since the nature of basic human abilities cannot be determined directly by observation, one needs to use some other approach, like the factor analysis of combinations of tests. Given the results of a factor analysis of several or many cognitive tests, for example, one can infer the existence of various attributes from the factor analysis

Figure 8-4. Examples of three clusters or job families resulting from a hierarchical clustering of 746 jobs. The profile for each cluster represents percentiles of the mean scores on the various dimensions of the jobs in the cluster. (Adapted from Shaw et al.)

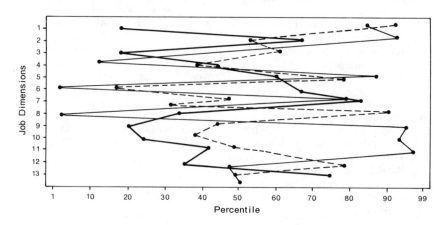

data. Given the several tests which have high statistical loadings on a given factor, the investigator examines the content of those tests to make what is admittedly a judgment about the common denominator that runs through those tests, and names the factor accordingly. The underlying basis for the emergence of a given factor lies in the intercorrelations of the tests that characterize it. These intercorrelations presumably reflect the extent to which a given attribute (such as numerical ability) is required by the various tests.

However, in conceptualizing the variety of human attributes, one should assiduously avoid the trap of viewing human attributes as being completely independent of one another, as in hermetically sealed compartments. As Carroll puts it, there probably are no such things as truly "pure" factors of human abilities. At the same time there is reasonable evidence to justify the acceptance of the notion that the patterns of human behavior and responses reflect the existence of some underlying structure of attributes which can serve certain practical purposes, even if the individual attributes are not entirely independent entities.

Let us now turn to a review of a few research programs that have been directed toward the identification of such attributes.

Guilford's structure of intellect (SI) model. Numerous investigators—Binet, Terman, Spearman, and Thorndike—habe been concerned with the nature of human cognitive abilities. The most current research in this area is the work of Guilford, who has developed the concept called the *structure of intellect* (SI). His model of intellectual abilities is organized along three dimensions:

1. Operations (the major kinds of intellectual activities or processes; what the organism does with the raw materials of information which is defined as *that which the organism discriminates*).

2. Products (the forms that information takes in the organism's processing of it).

3. Contents (the broad classes or types of information discriminable by the organism).

Each of these dimensions is in turn subdivided into several subcategories, as shown in Figure 8–5. The various possible combinations of these subcategories form 120 cells, each of which is hypothesized to represent a reasonably discrete, unitary type of intellectual ability. Many of those hypothesized abilities have been identified by factor analysis procedure and have been defined. For example, the factor MMU represents the combination of M–Memory (an operation), M–Semantic (a content), and U–Units (a

Figure 8-5. The structure of intellect (SI) developed by Guilford to represent the three basic classes of intellectual abilities and their respective subcategories. (Source: Guildford, p. 53)

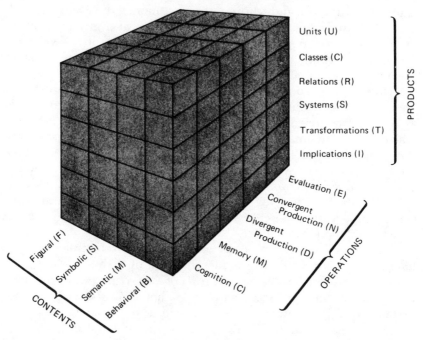

product), and is defined as *the ability to remember isolated words or word meanings.*

Although Guilford's SI has received considerable attention and is viewed by many as a very promising formulation of intellectual abilities, it has also been criticized. Carroll, for example, considers it to be too pat and rigid and not sufficiently well supported either by theoretical considerations or empirical facts to stand for all time as a final model for the structure of intellect or of cognition. Thus, it probably needs to be viewed at the present time with at least some reservations.

Fleishman's ability dimensions. A major research effort carried out by Fleishman and his associates at the American Institutes for Research was specifically directed toward the development of a taxonomy of human performance that might be used as ability dimensions for classifying human tasks (Theologus et al.; Theologus and Fleishman). Such a task-descriptive language would lend itself to various purposes, such as relating human performance in one task to that observed in other tasks, or applying the results of task-related research to operational tasks. In this regard, Fleishman differentiates between what he refers to as an *ability* (a general trait of the individual which has been inferred from certain response tendencies) and a *skill* (the level of proficiency on a specific task or group of tasks). He postulates the notion that the development of proficiency (that is, skill) on any given task is predicated in part on the possession of relevant basic abilities.

As an initial phase of the research program, Theologus et al. crystallized at least a tentative listing of human abilities that have relevance to human task performance and developed scales for use in classifying tasks in terms of such abilities. An initial listing of 50 such abilities was used, based primarily on previous factor analyses of human performance in the sensory, perceptual, cognitive, psychomotor, and physical areas. These 50 abilities were used experimentally in a couple of pilot studies and were then reduced to 37.*

Each ability is rated on a 7-point scale, with three examples of tasks used as benchmarks to indicate specific positions along the scale. The scale positions of these three benchmarks were derived by the use of a scaling procedure. The first step in this procedure, which consisted of developing a list of everyday occupational or laboratory tasks, was done by asking a sample of staff members of the Institute and of graduate psychology students to generate examples of such tasks that might serve to represent each of the 37 abilities. Some of these examples are as follows: Reach for the control lever on a drill press; design an aircraft wing using the principles of aerodynamics; and load five full 50-gallon drums into a truck. Eighteen graduate student raters then rated each of the example tasks on the particular ability scale it was intended to reflect. The mean values of these ratings and their standard deviations were computed. Three tasks were then selected to represent scale positions for each ability, those being tasks which had, respectively, high, moderate, and low scale values, and which had low standard deviations (indicating considerable rater agreement). An example of one such scale is shown in Figure 8–6.

As one phase of the study, two groups of raters rated the degree to which each of the 37 abilities was judged to be required in each of 6 hypothetical tasks. Although the reliability of the individ-

*The 37 abilities are listed and defined in Appendix C.

Figure 8-6. Example of the scale of one of the 37 abilities resulting from the study by Theologus et al. The three examples are benchmarks that indicate the position of actual tasks along the 7-point scale. (Source: Theologus et al., p. 191)

34. MANUAL DEXTERITY

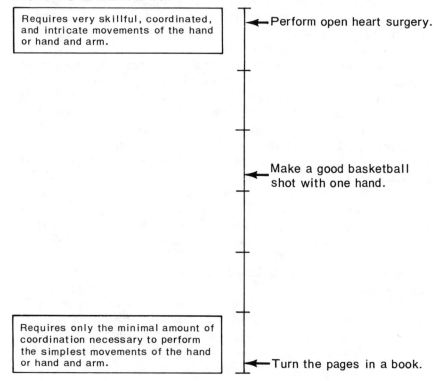

Requires very skillful, coordinated, and intricate movements of the hand or hand and arm.

←Perform open heart surgery.

Make a good basketball shot with one hand.

Requires only the minimal amount of coordination necessary to perform the simplest movements of the hand or hand and arm.

←Turn the pages in a book.

ual raters was relatively modest, the pooled reliability of the ratings of the groups of raters (10 and 20) was very respectable, being about .90 and .91.

ETS ability and temperament factors. The Educational Testing Service (ETS) has been involved in an extensive research program directed toward the identification of tests and other instruments that can serve as markers for well-established cognitive and temperament factors (Harman). A major facet of this research was the review and analysis of many studies dealing with such factors, resulting in the identification of factors within these classes which seemed to be well established on the basis of the studies in question. (The research program also resulted in the identification of certain tests which measured these factors.) The titles of the factors in the two sets are given in Table 8–5.

Discussion. There is probably no single set of factors which can be considered as representing a reasonably complete inventory of human attributes or qualities. However, the combination of Fleishman's listing and that of ETS probably represents the best available approximation to such an inventory. Fleishman's list of abilities includes sensory, psychomotor, and physical factors (which are not

TABLE 8–5. Cognitive and temperament factors identified as a phase of a research project of the Educational Testing Service. (Source: Harman)

Cognitive Factors	Temperament Factors
1. CF Closure, flexibility of	24. Ac General activity
2. DS Closure, speed of	25. Ag Agreeableness
3. CV Closure, verbal	26. Al Alertness
4. FA Fluency, associational	27. Au Autistic tendency
5. FE Fluency, expressional	28. Ca Calmness vs. anxiety
6. FF Fluency, figural	29. Co Concentration
7. FI Fluency, ideational	30. De Dependability
8. FW Fluency, word	31. Do Dominance
9. I Induction	32. Em Emotional maturity
10. IP Integrative processes	33. Es Emotional stability
11. M Memory, associative	34. Gs Gregariousness
12. MS Memory span	35. In Individualism
13. MV Memory, visual	36. Me Meticulousness
14. N Number	37. Mo Morality
15. P Perceptual speed	38. Na Need for achievement
16. RG Reasoning, general	39. Ob Objectivity vs.
17. RL Reasoning, logical	paranoid tendency
18. S Spatial orientation	40. Om Open-mindedness vs.
19. SS Spatial scanning	dogmatism
20. V Verbal comprehension	41. Pe Persistence
21. VZ Visualization	42. Po Poise vs. self-
22. XF Flexibility, figural	consciousness
23. XU Flexibility of use	43. Rt Restraint vs.
	rhathymia
	44. Sc Self-confidence
	45. Se Sensitive attitude
	46. So Sociability
	47. Ss Self-sufficiency
	48. Su Surgency
	49. Th Thoughtfulness
	50. To Tolerance of human
	nature vs. cynicism
	51. Wb Well-being vs.
	depression

included in the ETS list), and the ETS list includes temperament factors (which are not included in Fleishman's). The two sets have in common cognitive (including perceptual) factors, and although there are certain differences (including some of content and some of terminology), the common ground between them is very substantial, thus suggesting considerable agreement regarding such factors.

Job Factors or Dimensions of Human Trait Requirements

Previous examples have been given of job factors or dimensions based on data from structured job analysis questionnaires that provide for the analysis of jobs in terms of job content. Other analyses have been based on data that characterize the human attributes or traits (that is, the aptitudes, physical abilities, personality characteristics, and the like) presumably required for satisfactory job performance. The factors or dimensions that emerge from such analyses can then be viewed as reflecting something about the patterns or structure of the attribute requirements of jobs.

Job dimensions based on PAQ attribute data. One of the few examples of this type of analysis is based on the Position Analysis Questionnaire (PAQ). Previous mention was made in Chapter 6 of the development of the attribute profiles of the job elements of the PAQ, which were based on the ratings of the relevance of each of 76 human attributes to each of the job elements of the PAQ. The matrix of 71 of these profiles (values on 71 attributes for 182 job elements) served as the data for two types of principal components analyses (Marquardt and McCormick, 1972). The one of particular interest to our present discussion is a principal components analysis of the profiles in the 71 attributes of the PAQ job elements within each of the 6 divisions of the PAQ. These analyses produced dimensions characterized primarily by the combination of job elements which had reasonably similar attribute profiles.

The results of this analysis are given in the second column of Table 8–4. The first column of that table gives the titles of the job dimensions resulting from the principal components analysis of job data from 2,200 jobs. In viewing these two sets of job dimensions it can be seen that there is at least a moderate degree of similarity between the dimensions, although they result from two analyses based on entirely different types of data. In other words, there is at least a moderate degree of similarity between the combinations of job elements that occur in jobs in the world of work and the combinations of job elements derived on the basis of their attribute profiles.

(Although Table 8–4 lists the two sets of dimensions in parallel columns, the listing of the individual dimensions across from each other is not intended to imply that such pairs of dimensions are considered to be comparable.)

The other type of analysis of the data in the matrix of attribute profiles of the PAQ job elements was directed toward identifying the dimensions formed by the attribute values across the 182 job elements. Actually, two analyses were carried out, one using the 49 attributes of an *aptitude* nature, and the other using the 22 attributes of a *situational* nature (those that implied the personality, temperament, or interest qualities that presumably were required to adapt to different work situations). In each instance the values for the attributes (49 or 22) were correlated with each other, and the analyses were based on these correlations. These dimensions are listed below:

Dimensions based on aptitudinal attributes
1. General physical skills
2. Cognitive skills
3. Visual perception/interpretation
4. Psychomotor skills
5. Physical response/coordination versus imaginative orientation
6. Quantitative skills
7. Chemical senses

Dimensions based on situational attributes
1. Social/intellectual orientation
2. Sensory/judgmental demands
3. Structured work situations
4. Work pressures/risks

Job dimensions based on OAI attribute requirements. Mention was made in Chapter 6 of the Occupation Analysis Inventory (OAI) and of the attribute profiles that were based on the ratings of the relevance of 102 attributes of the 622 work elements of the OAI developed by Cunningham (Neeb et al.). As indicated in that discussion, some of the OAI work elements are more job-oriented than those of the PAQ, and the collection of attributes used in the development of the OAI attribute requirement profiles included certain classes (such as general vocational capabilities and needs) that were not included in the PAQ attribute profile data.

The attribute requirement profiles of the OAI work elements

were subjected to principal components analyses in the same manner as the PAQ attribute profiles. Separate analyses were carried out with the work elements within each of the six sections of the OAI, and these analyses resulted in the generation of 77 factors (dimensions). The data from these principal components analyses were used, in turn, in what is called a *higher-order analysis*. This was done in order to reduce the redundancy among the dimensions, to reduce the dimensions to a more manageable number, and possibly to aid in the interpretation of the dimensions. The first stage in this analysis was to consolidate the 622 work elements into the 77 first-order dimensions, thus producing a matrix of attribute requirement profiles across the 102 attributes for the 77 dimensions. These were then subjected to a principal components analysis, producing 21 higher-order dimensions, which are given in Table 8–6.

These dimensions have the unique feature of characterizing 21 broad groups of work elements of both a behavior-oriented and a work-oriented nature, each of which has a relatively comparable set of attribute requirements.

TABLE 8–6. Higher-order job dimensions (factors) of attribute requirement profiles of the work elements of the Occupation Analysis Inventory (OAI). (Source: Neeb et al., p. 94)

Dimension	Title of Work Dimension
H-1	Machine operation, maintenance, and repair
H-2	Behavior modification and control
H-3	Mathematical/symbolic activities
H-4	Health related activities
H-5	Figural arrangements and relationships
H-6	Personal service activities
H-7	Agricultural activities
H-8	Clerical activities
H-9	Verbal activities
H-10	Art/decorative activities
H-11	Material processing and modification
H-12	Business/sales activities
H-13	Work activities requiring balance and body coordination
H-14	Medically related responsibility
H-15	Construction and assembly activities
H-16	Planning and innovation
H-17	Direct interpersonal communication
H-18	Electrical/electronic maintenance and repair
H-19	Inspecting, measuring, and testing
H-20	General tool usage
H-21	General physical labor

Classification of Work Entities Using Attribute Descriptors

There have been at least a few efforts to develop classification systems of work entities using attribute descriptors, although most of these have dealt with jobs as the work entities rather than with tasks. Such a classification system groups jobs which have relatively comparable combinations of attribute requirements. A few examples of such classifications are described below.

Job families of attribute requirement patterns. In Chapter 7 several examples were given of the use of cluster analysis procedures to identify job types or clusters, each comprising jobs which are reasonably homogeneous in terms of the descriptors used. At a broader level one can group jobs into what might be called job families, which can be done with almost any type of descriptor. An example of the development of such job families using patterns of attribute requirements is based on a factor analysis of worker trait requirements carried out by Finn and reported by McCormick et al. (1957). This study was based on data on 48 worker trait variables used by the USES in rating 4,000 jobs defined in the *Dictionary of Occupational Titles* (DOT). In connection with preparing a revised edition of the DOT, the USES carried out an intensive study which included the rating by job analysts of the requirements of the 4,000 jobs in terms of 48 traits of the following classes: education, aptitudes, temperaments, interests, physical capacities, and working conditions. The factor analysis resulted in the identification of seven factors (listed below). Three of the factors (1, 6 and 7) are bipolar in that certain of the variables were negatively correlated with others and represented, in each instance, completely opposite ends of the basic underlying continuum.

Barker carried out a somewhat similar study with a sample of 764 of the 4,000 jobs. Although there were some differences between the factor structures of Barker and Finn, there was a substantial degree of correspondence between the two sets of factors. (The differences that did emerge tended to consist of the splitting of a couple of Finn's factors into two or three more specific factors.)

McCormick et al. derived, for each job, a score on each of the seven factors, and used these scores for forming job families. This was done by categorizing each job as *high* on each factor (above average) or *low* (below average), except that on factor one (the dominant factor) jobs were divided into three categories (high, average, and low). The factors, with an example of a job in each factor score level, are:

1. Mental and educational development vs. Adaptability to routine
    High (1) Metallurgist, physical
    Average (2) Boilermaker, maintenance
    Low (3) Laborer, warehouse
2. Adaptability to precision operations
    High (1) Wheel alignment mechanic
    Low (2) County agricultural agent
3. Body agility
    High (2) Plumber
    Low (1) Pay station attendant
4. Artistic ability and esthetic appreciation
    High (1) Photographer, commercial
    Low (2) Teamster
5. Manual art ability
    High (2) Precision lens grinder
    Low (1) Airways observer
6. Personal contact ability vs. Adaptability to routine
    High (2) Cashier, front office
    Low (1) Rag sorter
7. Heavy manual work vs. Clerical ability
    High (1) Laborer, wharf
    Low (2) Auditor

These categories (two for six factors and three for one factor) could be combined into 192 possible combinations ($2 \times 2 \times 2 \times 2 \times 2 \times 2 \times 3 = 192$). In turn, each of these unique combinations can be considered as a separate job family, and in fact the individual jobs were classified in their appropriate job families on the basis of their own combinations of factor score levels.

In effect, the mutually exclusive job families resulting from this study can be viewed as a classification system, each family consisting of jobs with reasonably similar patterns of attribute requirements as the jobs are characterized by the profiles of the factor scores which were used as descriptors.

Occupational classification based on personality factors. Another example of a classification system for classifying jobs in terms of certain attributes is the system developed over the years by Holland. This system is based on a theory of personality types. The underlying rationale is that vocational choice, and presumably vocational success, are a function of personality factors, and that personality types are in fact reflected by vocational choice. Holland's classification system is discussed more fully in Chapter 9.

Clusters of related jobs. Still another example of a clustering of related jobs is reported by Thorndike in his paper entitled "Who Belongs in the Family?" In brief, he dealt with 12 Air Force specialties that had been rated in terms of their requirements on each of 19 attributes (such as strength, familiarity with tools, and manipulative ability). Subjecting these to a cluster analysis resulted in a final grouping of the 12 jobs into 3 clusters, as shown in Table 8–7, which shows the *centroids* of the individual jobs with respect to all the jobs that form each of the clusters. *Low* centroid values reflect closer similarity to a cluster than do *high* values. The asterisk beside a centroid value shows the cluster to which a job was assigned. Although not revealed by this table, cluster A is made up of jobs which call for relatively high amounts of familiarity with tools, manipulative ability, spatial judgment, and facility in manipulating multiple controls. Cluster B emphasizes social adaptability and ability to take responsibility for work of others. The jobs in cluster C are high on requirements for clerical perception, arithmetic computation, and fluency of expression, and low in strength, coordination, and similar physical attributes.

Work Characteristics Bases

Another basis for the analysis of job interrelationships is characterization of tasks or jobs in terms of aspects of the work itself, rather than in terms of behaviors of incumbents or their attributes. In effect, this approach is predicated on the assumption that tasks or jobs can be described and differentiated in terms of intrinsic properties. Wheaton suggests that these properties may pertain to the goals toward which a person works, relevant stimuli, instructions, procedures, the characteristics of the responses to be made, or the content of the activity.

Classifications of Work Characteristics Descriptors

There have been relatively few efforts to develop classifications of work characteristics descriptors, and those systems which have been developed have dealt largely with descriptors for tasks.

Task characteristics for performance prediction. One such example has been developed as part of the research program of the American Institutes for Research referred to earlier. This particular phase, re-

TABLE 8–7. Final grouping of 12 Air Force jobs into 3 clusters based on their ratings on each of 19 attributes. (Source: Thorndike, p. 273)

	Clusters		
	A	B	C
Job	Jobs 1, 2, 5	Jobs 3, 4, 11, 12	Jobs 6, 7, 8, 9, 10
1 Radio mechanic	83*	96	131
2 Aircraft mechanic	70*	74	117
3 Cook	89	62*	94
4 Supply technician	90	62*	73
5 Petroleum supply technician	91*	84	155
6 Clerk	124	94	52*
7 Career guidance specialist	130	99	54*
8 Personnel specialist	143	108	52*
9 General instructor	132	88	86*
10 Budget & fiscal clerk	146	121	69*
11 Medical corpsman	68	62*	114
12 Air policeman	93	78*	127

*Asterisk indicates cluster to which each job is assigned.
†Job 5 (Petroleum supply technician) is assigned to Cluster A rather than Cluster B because, owing to the small size of the cluster, it has less effect on the overall average distance in that cluster than it would in the larger Cluster B.

ported by Farina and Wheaton, was directed toward the development of a task descriptive system which would provide a basis for classifying tasks in terms of their observed similarities and dissimilarities, and which could also be utilized to relate variations in the characteristics of tasks to variations in performance. The task domain that was considered embraced primarily operator types of tasks.

In the formulation of the system, a task was considered as having five components with each component possessing certain salient characteristics. The components are as follows: (1) an *explicit goal* (a specification of the state or condition to be achieved by the operator; a statement of the means by which the goal was to be attained, consisting of (2) *procedures* specifying the (3) *stimulus-response relationships* to be formed and their sequencing; a specification of the relevant (4) *input stimuli* attended to by the operator; and a statement of the (5) *set of responses* contributing to goal attainment. Within each component, the task is to be further specified in terms of a number of specific characteristics. The formulation is represented in Figure 8–7.

As an important facet of the system, there is provision for rating any given task on each of the 19 task characteristics, using rating scales such as the one shown in Figure 8–8. Thus, any given task would have a value on each of those 19 descriptors.

Other Descriptive Bases

In discussing job interrelationships and classification systems, we have touched particularly on two aspects, namely, the identification of job descriptors of various types, and the grouping of discriptors or jobs into clusters or classification systems. There are, however,

Figure 8-7. Task characteristics classification system developed by Farina and Wheaton for use in describing operator tasks. (Source: Farina and Wheaton, p. 12)

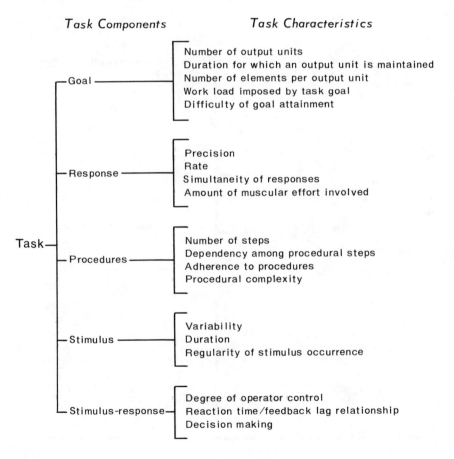

Task Components   *Task Characteristics*

Goal
- Number of output units
- Duration for which an output unit is maintained
- Number of elements per output unit
- Work load imposed by task goal
- Difficulty of goal attainment

Response
- Precision
- Rate
- Simultaneity of responses
- Amount of muscular effort involved

Procedures
- Number of steps
- Dependency among procedural steps
- Adherence to procedures
- Procedural complexity

Stimulus
- Variability
- Duration
- Regularity of stimulus occurrence

Stimulus-response
- Degree of operator control
- Reaction time/feedback lag relationship
- Decision making

various other approaches to the analysis of the relationships between and among jobs, given the initial analysis of individual jobs in terms of some relevant descriptor. An example of one such approach is discussed below.

McCormick and Asquith reported on one phase of a study

Figure 8-8. Sample of one of the task characteristics rating scales used in the task classification system of Farina and Wheaton. (Source: Farina and Wheaton, p. 46)

VARIABILITY OF STIMULUS LOCATION

Judge the degree to which the physical location of the stimulus or stimulus complex is predictable over task time.

Definitions		Examples
High predictability— stimulus location remains basically unchanged.	7	• Stimulus is a red light located on a display panel.
	6	
	5	
Medium predictability— location changes but in a known manner or pattern.	4	• Visually following an arrow in flight toward a target.
	3	
	2	
Low predictability— location changes in an almost random fashion.	1	• Predicting which leaf will fall from a tree next.

dealing with manning guidelines for naval vessels. This phase of the study consisted of analyzing the relationships, for each of six groups of officers and enlisted personnel, of the job activities for each of the several individuals in each group from day to day *across time* (over a period of about two weeks), as contrasted with the activities *between individuals* of each work group for the same day. The data used consisted of the time reported by the incumbents for each of about two dozen specified job activities. At the end of each day, each incumbent reported the number of minutes (to the closest five minutes) devoted to each activity for each day. This structured questionnaire was used essentially as a diary. An average intercorrelation of these times was computed for each individual *across time* for the several days, and also for each day *between individuals* within each work group. Although our interest here is more in methodology than in results as such, the results are summarized briefly below. The data given are *means* of the average intercorrelations of individuals across time and of those between individuals of each work group for the separate days.

	Range	Mean
Across time (for individuals)	.03 to .92	.42
Between individuals (within each group for same day)	−.12 to .73	.21

These correlations can be interpreted as follows: on the average, the similarity of the work activities of individuals from day to day (across time) is represented by a mean coefficient of about .42, whereas on the average, the similarity of the work activities of the several individuals within each of the work groups (between individuals) is represented by a coefficient of .21.

Discussion

The analysis of job interrelationships is clearly a complex matter, as reflected by the results of some of the investigations touched on in this chapter. This complexity is attributable in large part to the fact that jobs have different facets that can be used as their descriptors, and in part to the fact that the methods of dealing with masses of job-related data have an inevitable influence upon the nature of the results of any such investigation. However, it should be clear that despite the complexity that pervades this domain of investigation, it is possible to quantify or categorize job-related data and to manipulate it statistically, toward the end of obtaining greater insight into the structure, or order, underlying this important aspect of human life. Because there are so many different characteristics of jobs that can be dealt with, however, it behooves the investigator to choose those which most appropriately will serve his end purpose, and to apply the statistical methods that will be most suitable in the analysis of the data for the purpose in mind.

References

Baehr, M. E. *A Factorial Framework for Job Description.* Chicago: The University of Chicago, Industrial Relations Center, 1967.

Barker, D. G. "Factor Analysis of Worker Trait Requirements." *Journal of Employment Counseling,* December 1969, 162–168.

Berliner, D. C.; Angell, D.; and Shearer, J. "Behaviors, Measures, and Instruments for Performance Evaluation in Simulated Environments." In *Proceedings of the Symposium and Workshop on the Quantification of Human Performance.* Albuquerque: The University of New Mexico, 1964.

Brumback, G. B., and Vincent, J. W. "Factor Analysis of Work-performed Data for a Sample of Administrative, Professional, and Scientific Positions." *Personnel Psychology* 23(1970): 101–107.

Carr, M. J. *The SAMOA Method of Determining Technical Organizational and Communicational Dimensions of Task Clusters.* U.S. Naval Personnel and Training Research Laboratory, Technical Bulletin STB-68-5. San Diego, Calif.: 1967.

Carroll, J. B. *Psychometric Tests as Cognitive Tasks: A New "Structure of Intellect."* Princeton, N.J.: Educational Testing Service, RB-74-16, 1974.

Chalupsky, A. B. "Comparative Factor Analysis of Clerical Jobs." *Journal of Applied Psychology* 46(1962): 62–67.

Dictionary of Occupational Titles, 4th ed. U.S. Department of Labor, Employment and Training Administration. Washington, D.C.: U.S. Government Printing Office, 1977.

Farina, A. J., and Wheaton, G. R. *The Task Characteristics Approach to Performance Prediction.* Washington, D.C.: American Institutes for Research, TR No. 7, 1971.

Fine, S. A. *Functional Job Analysis: A Desk Aid.* Kalamazoo, Mich.: The W. E. Upjohn Institute for Employment Research, 1973.

Finn, R. H. "A Factor Analysis of Selected Job Characteristics." Ph.D. Thesis, Purdue University, 1954.

Folley, J. D. *Development of Improved Method of Task Analysis and Beginnings of a Theory of Training.* U.S. Naval Training Devices Center, NAVTRADEVCEN 1 218-1. Port Washington, N.Y.: 1964.

Guilford, J. P. *The Nature of Human Intelligence.* New York: McGraw-Hill, 1967.

Handbook for Analyzing Jobs. U.S. Department of Labor, Manpower Administration. Washington, D.C.: U.S. Government Printing Office (Stock No. 2900–0131), 1972.

Harman, H. H. *Final Report of Research on Assessing Human Abilities.* Princeton, N.J.: Educational Testing Service, PR-75-20, 1975.

Hemphill, J. K. "Job Descriptions for Executives." *Harvard Business Review* September–October, 1959, pp. 55–67.

Holland, J. L. *Making Vocational Choices: A Theory of Careers.* Englewood Cliffs, N.J.: Prentice-Hall, 1973.

McCormick, E. J., and Asquith, R. H. *An Analysis of Work Patterns of CIC Personnel for CVA-59 Class Ships.* Washington, D.C.: The Clifton Corporation, 1960.

McCormick, E. J., Finn, R. H., and Scheips, C. D. "Patterns of Job Requirements." *Journal of Applied Psychology* 41(1957): 358–364.

McCormick, E. J.; Jeanneret, P. R.; and Mecham, R. "A Study of Job Characteristics and Job Dimensions as Based on the Position Analysis Questionnaire (PAQ)." *Journal of Applied Psychology* 56(1972): 347–368.

Mahoney, T. A.; Jerdee, T. H.; and Carroll S. J. "The Jobs of Management." *Industrial Relations,* February 1965, pp. 97–110.

Marquardt, L. D., and McCormick, E. J. *Attribute Ratings and Profiles of the Job Elements of the Position Analysis Questionnaire (PAQ).* Department of Psychological Sciences, Report No. 1. West Lafayette, Ind.: Purdue University, 1972.

Marquardt, L. D., and McCormick, E. J. *Component Analyses of the Attribute Data Based on the Position Analysis Questionnaire (PAQ).* Department of Psychological Sciences, Report No. 2. West Lafayette, Ind.: Purdue University, 1973.

Marquardt, L. D., and McCormick, E. J. *The Job Dimensions Underlying the Job Elements of the Position Analysis Questionnaire (PAQ) (Form B).* Department of Psychological Sciences, Report No. 4. West Lafayette, Ind.: Purdue University, 1974.

Mecham, R. C. Personal communication. February 1977.

Morsh, J. E. *Job Types Identified with an Inventory Constructed by Electronics Engineers.* USAF, TR No. 66–6, Personnel Research Laboratory. Lackland AFB, Texas, 1966.

Neeb, R. W.; Cunningham, J.W.; and Pass, J. J. *Human Attribute Requirements of Worker Elements: Further Development of the Occupation Analysis Inventory.* Center for Vocational Education, Research Monograph No. 7. Raleigh, N.C.: University of North Carolina, 1971.

Oller, R. G. *Human Factors Data Thesaurus.* AMRL-TR-67-211. Wright Patterson AFB, Ohio: 1968.

Prien, E. P. "Development of a Clerical Position Description Questionnaire." *Personnel Psychology* 18(1965): 91–98.

Proceedings of Division of Military Psychology Symposium. 77th annual convention of the American Psychological Association. Personnel Research Division, USAF, AFPTRC. Lackland AFB, Texas: 1969.

Reed, L. E. *Advances in the Use of Computers for Handling Human Factors Task Data.* AMRL-TR-67-16. Wright Patterson AFB, Ohio: 1967.

Roe, A. *The Psychology of Occupations.* New York: Wiley, 1956.

Shaw, J. B.; Denisi, A. S.; and McCormick, E. J. *Cluster Analysis of Jobs Based on a Revised Set of Job Dimensions From the Position Analysis Questionnaire (PAQ).* Department of Psychological Sciences, Report No. 3. West Lafayette, Ind.: Purdue University, 1977.

Theologus, G. C., and Fleishman, E. A. *Validation Study of Ability Scales for Classifying Human Tasks.* Washington, D.C.: American Institutes for Research, TR No. 10, 1976.

Theologus, G. C.; Romashko, T.; and Fleishman, E. A. *A Feasibility Study of Ability Dimensions for Classifying Human Tasks.* Washington, D.C.: American Institutes for Research, TR No. 5, 1970.

Thorndike, R. L. "Who Belongs in the Family?" *Psychometrika* 18(1953) 267–276.

Ward, J. H., Jr. "Hierarchical Grouping to Optimize an Objective Function." *Journal of the American Statistical Association* 58(1963): 236–247.

Wheaton, G. *A Review of Classificatory Systems Relating to Tasks and Performances.* Washington, D.C.: American Institutes for Research, TR No. 1, 1968.

PART FOUR

Applications of Job-Related Information

9

Vocational Choice and Work Adjustment

MORE than a third of the waking hours of most employed individuals is spent on their jobs. Because of the importance of jobs to the labor force (and to their families) one would hope that the types of vocations which individuals have would be compatible with their abilities and interests and would provide the opportunity for reasonable personal adjustment and job satisfaction. Although many people have achieved such occupational matching, such matching is far from universal, and it is doubtful if such matching is a reasonable possibility on virtually an across-the-board basis within the foreseeable future.

This somewhat pessimistic point of view stems from such considerations as the following: the belief that the numbers of available jobs of different types do not correspond with the numbers of people who would voluntarily choose them (perhaps many jobs would go unfilled if jobs were filled strictly on the basis of vocational choice, and not economic necessity); the belief that the processes of occupational change are, and will continue to be, slow;

and the suspicion that some individuals (hopefully not many) are psychologically averse to virtually any kind of gainful employment.

Although it is not likely that circumstances within the foreseeable future will enable the vast majority of people to have jobs optimally compatible with their abilities and interests, this does not mean, however, that one should declare a moratorium on the efforts to achieve this objective. Such efforts primarily should be directed along two general routes. On the one hand, the processes of facilitating such matching certainly should be continued — and in fact expanded — to help people make realistic choices of vocations and jobs which, in the light of employment opportunities, are at least moderately compatible with their abilities and interests. Such processes can cover formal vocational counseling, dissemination of information about vocations and jobs (for example, through high school vocational counseling services, and other public and private organizations), and the responsible and efficient operation of both public and private services. On the other hand, efforts should be made in the design of jobs to create work situations which, in the long run, would increase the odds of achieving reasonable job compatibility for most people in the labor force.

It is not within the scope of this book to deal extensively with factors that influence the choices of vocations and jobs that people make, or the processes (systematic or fortuitous) that lead up to such decisions, but we discuss a couple of theoretical formulations that are relevant to matching people with vocations.

The Theory of Work Adjustment

One of the most extensive research programs with substantial relevance to vocational choice is the Work Adjustment Project carried out by the Industrial Relations Center of the University of Minnesota. A major result of this research program is the formulation of a theory of work adjustment that provides an appropriate frame of reference in discussing vocational choice. The theory of work adjustment resulting from the Work Adjustment Project has been set forth by Dawis et al.

The Basic Theory*

The theory of work adjustment is based on the concept of *correspondence between the individual and the environment,* which implies

*This description of the theory of work adjustment is drawn largely from Dawis et al. Quoted material is from that source.

conditions that can be described as a harmonious relationship between the individual and the environment, the suitability of the individual and the environment to each other, consonance or agreement between the individual and the environment, and a reciprocal and complementary relationship between them.

It is a basic assumption of the theory that "each individual seeks to achieve and maintain correspondence with his environment." Achieving and maintaining such correspondence are considered to be basic motives of human behavior.

There are several aspects of a person's total environment to which he must relate, such as home, school, and work. "Work represents a major environment to which most individuals must relate."

The individual brings certain skills to the work environment. The work environment imposes certain requirements upon the individual, but also provides certain rewards (such as wages, prestige, personal relationships) to the individual, which enable it to "respond" to the individual. "Correspondence can be described in terms of the individual fulfilling the requirements of the work environment, and the work environment fulfilling the requirements of the individual."

If the individual finds a correspondent relationship between himself and the work environment, he seeks to maintain it. If he does not, he seeks to establish such correspondence, or failing in this, to leave the work environment. "The continuous and dynamic process by which the individual seeks to achieve and maintain correspondence with his work environment is called work adjustment."

As correspondence increases, the probability of tenure (remaining on the job) increases, and the projected length of tenure increases. Conversely, as correspondence decreases, both the probability of remaining on the job and the projected length of tenure decrease. In effect, tenure is the most basic indicator or criterion of correspondence. It can therefore be said that "tenure is a function of correspondence between the individual and his work environment."

The basic concepts of correspondence and tenure lead to the concepts of *satisfactoriness* and *satisfaction*. If the individual fulfills the requirements of the work environment, he is defined as a satisfactory worker. In turn, if the work environment fulfills the requirements of the individual, he is defined as a satisfied worker. "Satisfactoriness and satisfaction indicate the correspondence between the individual and his work environment."

In turn, various characteristics of the individual (the *work personality*) and of the job (the *work environment*) influence the correspondence between the individual and the work environment and, in sequential fashion, the level of satisfactoriness (on the job) and satisfaction (of the individual).

The Theory in Operational Terms

With this theoretical backdrop let us now see how the theory of work adjustment relates in operational terms to the adjustment of individuals to jobs. Figure 9–1 illustrates certain of the concepts and relationships discussed above, plus other, more specific aspects. The individual may be characterized by his work personality, which is made up of his *abilities* and *needs*. "Abilities are the basic dimensions of response capability generally utilized by the individual. In turn, needs are preferences for responding in certain stimulus conditions which have been experienced to be reinforcing." In other words, abilities are what people can do, and needs are the things people want to fulfill (as in their jobs).

The job. The job is the dominant feature of the work environment and may be described in work personality terms, in particular in terms of the *ability requirements* and the *reinforcer systems.* The ability requirements may be determined from a study of satisfactory workers with substantial tenure, and the reinforcer systems from a study of satisfied workers with substantial tenure.

Figure 9-1. Basic model of the theory of work adjustment. (Source: Dawis et al., p. 12)

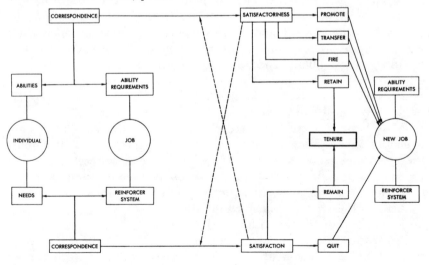

Correspondence between the individual and the job. The correspondence between the individual and the job depends essentially on the match between the abilities of the individual and the ability requirements of the job, and between the needs of the individual and the reinforcer system of the job. These two aspects of correspondence contribute to the levels of satisfactoriness (based primarily on the abilities — ability requirements match), and of satisfaction (based primarily on the needs–reinforcer system match). (Actually these different variables are postulated to have an interactive effect.)

Specific aspects of tenure. Satisfactoriness and satisfaction are postulated to influence the tenure of individuals on their jobs. As shown in Figure 9-1, the level of satisfactoriness can lead to any of four possible actions (those being decisions of the employing organization), namely: promote, transfer, fire, and retain. In turn, the level of satisfaction on the part of the employees can lead to their decisions to remain on the job or to quit. In the case of those employees who are promoted, transferred, or fired, or who quit, the cycle usually would being anew with a new job.

Measurement of Work Adjustment Components

For testing or implementing the theory of work adjustment, there need to be measurements of the various components of the model that represents the theory. Such measurements have been selected or developed as part of the Work Adjustment Project of the Minnesota Industrial Relations Center and these, shown in Figure 9-2, are discussed briefly below.

Abilities: GATB. The tests used as measures of abilities of individuals in the research project are those of the General Aptitude Test Battery (GATB) of the USES.

Needs: MIQ. The Minnesota Importance Questionnaire (MIQ) is used for measuring the needs of individuals. The original format, which provided for measuring vocational needs, consisted of a scale that provided for individuals to indicate the importance of each of 20 statements dealing with such variables as achievement and recognition. This format was found to be somewhat unsatisfactory and was replaced by a paired-comparison format in which the respondents rated such statements in pairs, indicating which was the more important to them. As with the original format, the paired-comparison format resulted in scores on 20 different needs. An additional need category was added later, making a total of 21.

Ability requirements: WTR. The ability requirements of jobs were derived with the use of the Worker Trait Requirements (WTR)

Figure 9-2. Measurement instruments used to measure the various components of the theory of work adjustment. (Source: Dawis et al., p.14)

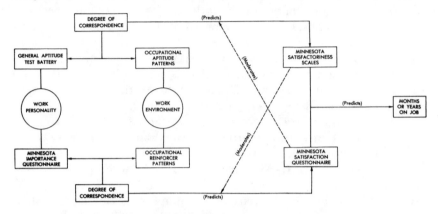

procedures of the USES. To derive an index of the correspondence between abilities of individuals and the ability requirements of jobs, the GATB scores of individuals were converted to the same scale as the WTR ratings.

Reinforcer System: ORPs. The reinforcer systems of jobs were presented in the form of Occupational Reinforcer Patterns (ORP). Figure 9–3 illustrates an ORP for the occupation of key-punch operator. The profile shows, for each need listed at the left, how the job in question was rated in comparison with other jobs. ORPs were developed by the use of the Minnesota Job Description Questionnaire (MJDQ). This is essentially a variation of the MIQ, adapted for use by raters in rating the extent to which each of the 21 needs would be expected to be fulfilled on any given job.

ORPs like the one shown in Figure 9–3 have been developed for 148 occupations. The ORPs for the 148 occupations were formed into 12 clusters on the basis of the similarity of the profiles of the 21 reinforcers which characterized the ORPs. Some of the occupations that had similar ORPs and thus fell into the same clusters (from Rosen et al.) include:

Accountant, certified public
Instructor, vocational school
Interior designer and decorator
Newspaper publisher
Occupational therapist

Optometrist
Salesman, life insurance
Salesman, securities

The common denominators of descriptive reinforcers that serve as the basis for this cluster are listed below.
Workers in these occupations:

"Make use of their individual abilities" (Ability utilization).
"Get a feeling of accomplishment" (Achievement).
"Have work where they do things for other people" (Social service).
"Make decisions on their own" (Responsibility).
"Try out their own ideas" (Creativity).
"Receive recognition for the work they do" (Recognition).
"Plan their work with little supervision" (Autonomy)

The ORP profile for this cluster is shown in Figure 9–4. It can be seen in that figure that the reinforcers listed above are the ones that stand out in the profile. The other eleven clusters were similarly depicted, with their own unique profiles.

Satisfactoriness: Special scale. On the basis of considerable research, a questionnaire of 19 items was developed for use in rating the satisfactoriness of individuals. A few illustrative items are given below:
Compared to others in his work group, how well does he
— follow company policies and practices?
— adapt to changes in procedures or methods?
— accept the responsibility of his job?

Satisfaction: MSQ. For the measurement of satisfaction of individuals a short form of the Minnesota Satisfaction Questionnaire (MSQ) was developed. It included 20 items dealing with the same variables used in the MIQ, except that the MSQ provided for the individual to indicate how he feels about the variable (such as Achievement or Responsibility) using a 5-point scale ranging from Very Dissatisfied to Very Satisfied.

Implications of Theory of Work Adjustment

A number of investigations have been carried out that can be viewed as tests of the theory of work adjustment (Betz et al.; 1966; Lofquist and Dawis; 1972; Weiss et al., 1965 and 1966). The results

Figure 9-3. An Occupational Reinforcer Pattern (ORP) for the occupation of key-punch operator. The scale used represents standard deviation units above and below the means of the ratings for the needs. (Source: Rosen et al., p. 80)

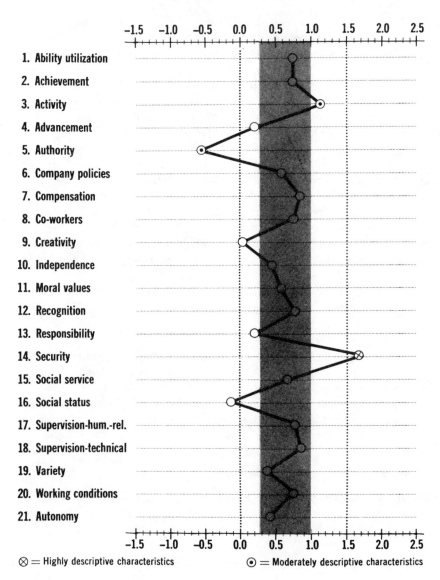

Key-Punch Operator

(*n* = 33 Raters)

	-1.5	-1.0	-0.5	0.0	0.5	1.0	1.5	2.0	2.5

1. Ability utilization
2. Achievement
3. Activity
4. Advancement
5. Authority
6. Company policies
7. Compensation
8. Co-workers
9. Creativity
10. Independence
11. Moral values
12. Recognition
13. Responsibility
14. Security
15. Social service
16. Social status
17. Supervision-hum.-rel.
18. Supervision-technical
19. Variety
20. Working conditions
21. Autonomy

⊗ = Highly descriptive characteristics   ⊙ = Moderately descriptive characteristics

Figure 9-4. The Occupational Reinforcer Pattern (ORP) of a cluster formed from the ORPs of nine occupations. (Source: Rosen et al., p. 176)

Cluster XII: Achievement-Autonomy-Social Service-Recognition-Variety

n = 311 Raters

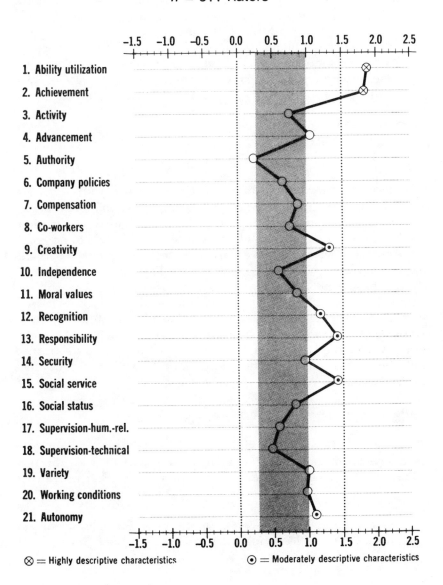

⊗ = Highly descriptive characteristics   ⊙ = Moderately descriptive characteristics

of these studies tend to support the theory and lead to the following conclusions: There are indications that the theory may be more relevant for people in some occupations than in others; there is more consistent evidence of the relevance of need-reinforcer relationships as predictors of satisfaction than there is of the relevance of ability–ability-requirements relationships as predictors of satisfactoriness; there are reasonably stable differential reinforcement patterns for some occupations; there is reason to believe that the factors of sex, job tenure, and full-time versus part-time employment may affect the reinforcement pattern that operates in a given work environment; the abilities of people and their needs seem to be reasonably independent of each other; satisfaction and satisfactoriness should be considered as two independent sets of variables; and the theory seems to have particularly practical applications in connection with the rehabilitation and counseling of handicapped persons.

Although the theory probably cannot be viewed as a fully confirmed theory that has virtually universal applicability, it nonetheless seems to have sufficient support to serve as a general frame of reference in considering the variables associated with work adjustment. In particular, it focuses our attention to the fact that human abilities and needs are relatively independent of each other, which implies that the work adjustment of people tends to be greatest when both of these have correspondence with the ability requirements and reinforcer systems of jobs. Further, the theory crystallizes the fact that satisfactoriness (performance on the job) and satisfaction (the reaction of the individual to the job) are relatively independent criteria. The optimum combination of these would of course be characterized by individuals who are high in both criteria, that is, they are good job performers and are also satisfied with their work environment (presumably because it fulfills their needs reasonably well).

Holland's Theory of Vocational Choice

Over a period of a couple of decades, Holland and his associates have developed and refined a theory of vocational choice that has achieved substantial prominence in vocational counseling circles.

The Basis of the Theory

The basic features of the theory are reflected by a number of key statements in one of Holland's early works (1966), as follows:

1. The choice of a vocation is an expression of personality. Pre-

viously, vocational choice was considered to be largely a function of the individual's *interests,* which were viewed as distinct from *personality.* Holland expresses the opinion that vocational choice is an implementation of self-concept, and that self-concept is an integral part of personality. According to his theory, it therefore follows that vocational interests are a facet of personality.

2. Interest inventories, then, are personality inventories. In discussing the rationale behind the development of interest inventories Holland makes the following statement (1966, p. 4):

> The choice of an occupation is an expressive act which reflects the person's motivation, knowledge, personality, and ability. Occupations represent a way of life, an environment rather than a set of isolated work functions or skills. To work as a carpenter means not only to use tools but also to have a certain status, community role, and a special pattern of living. In this sense, the choice of an occupational title represents several kinds of information: the [subject's] motivation, his knowledge of the occupation in question, his insight and understanding of himself, and his abilities. In short, item response may be thought of as limited but useful expressive or projective protocols.

3. Vocational stereotypes have reliable and important psychological and sociological meanings. People of various ages, races, and socioeconomic backgrounds view individual occupations in much the same way.

4. Members of specific vocations tend to have somewhat similar personalities and to have had somewhat similar histories of personal development. In other words, specific vocations do tend to attract and retain somewhat similar types of people.

5. Because people in specific vocational groups tend to have similar personalities, they tend to respond to many situations and problems in similar ways, and they tend to create characteristic personal environments.

6. Vocational satisfaction, stability, and achievement depend upon congruence between personality and the environment in which the individual works.

The concept of congruence bears a similarity to the theory of work adjustment discussed earlier, but there are certain differences between the two theories. The theory of work adjustment is predicated on two bases of congruence as follows:

Individual	*Job*
Ability	Ability reinforcements
Needs	Reinforcer systems

Holland focuses essentially on the second of these forms of congruence (albeit with some important differences), which he refers to as the congruence between the personality and the environment. He emphasizes the fact that both personalities and environments can be characterized in terms of certain common denominators. In particular, he postulates the existence of six personality types, and the possibility of characterizing individual jobs in terms of these personality types.

Basic Personality Types

The six personality types are referred to as Realistic, Investigative (originally called Intellectual), Artistic, Social, Enterprising, and Conventional. Below are abbreviated descriptions of these types, in particular the kinds of behaviors toward which the individual types are predisposed, along with examples of occupations for which each type of individual presumably would be best suited (Holland, 1973).

REALISTIC TYPE

1. Prefer realistic occupations or situations (for example, crafts) in which they can engage in preferred activities and avoid the activities demanded by social occupations or situations.
2. Use realistic competencies to solve problems at work and in other settings.
3. Perceive themselves as having mechanical and athletic ability and lacking ability in human relations.
4. Value things or tangible personal characteristics: money, power, status.

Examples of occupations: electrician, tool and die maker, baker, mechanical engineer, plumber, nurseryman, printer, barber, cattle rancher.

INVESTIGATIVE TYPE

1. Prefer investigative occupations or situations in which they can engage in preferred activities and competencies and avoid the activities demanded by enterprising occupations or situations.
2. Uses investigative competencies to solve problems at work and in other settings.
3. Perceive themselves as scholarly, intellectually self-confident,

having mathematical and scientific ability, and lacking in leadership ability.
  4. Value science.

Examples of occupations: economist, physician, computer operator, geologist, oceanographer, tool designer.

ARTISTIC TYPE

  1. Prefer artistic occupations or situations in which they can engage in preferred activities and competencies and avoid the activities demanded by conventional occupations or situations.
  2. Use artistic competencies to solve problems at work and in other settings.
  3. Perceive themselves as expressive, original, intuitive, feminine, nonconforming, introspective, independent, disorderly, and having artistic and musical ability (acting, writing, speaking).
  4. Value esthetic qualities.

Examples of occupations: philosopher, art teacher, writer, dancer, interior decorator, photographer.

SOCIAL TYPE

  1. Prefer social occupations and situations in which they can engage in preferred activities and competencies and avoid the activities demanded by realistic occupations and situations.
  2. Use social competencies to solve problems at work and in other settings.
  3. Perceive themselves as liking to help others, understanding of others, having teaching ability, and lacking mechanical and scientific ability.
  4. Value social and ethical activities and problems.

Examples of occupations: interviewer, host or hostess, bartender, recreation director, housekeeper, social worker, personnel director, YMCA secretary.

ENTERPRISING TYPE

  1. Prefer enterprising occupations or situations in which they can engage in preferred activities and avoid the activities demanded by investigative occupations or situations.

2. Use enterprising competencies to solve problems at work and in other situations.
3. Perceive themselves as aggressive, popular, self-confident, sociable, possessing leadership and speaking abilities, and lacking scientific ability.
4. Value political and economic achievement.

Examples of occupations: banker, furniture dealer, restaurant manager, sales manager, salesman, retail merchant.

CONVENTIONAL TYPE

1. Prefer conventional occupations or situations in which they can engage in preferred activities and avoid the activities demanded by artistic occupations or situations.
2. Use conventional competencies to solve problems at work and in other situations.
3. Perceive themselves as conforming, orderly, and as having clerical and numerical ability.
4. Value business and economic achievement.

Examples of occupations: keypunch operator, file clerk, teller, typist, office machine operator, reservation agent, cashier, sewing machine operator, accountant.

In the early formation of the theory, people and environments were characterized in terms of one or another of these six personality types. Later, however, it became evident that people and environments could be characterized by combinations of types. In practice, any environment can be coded for two, three, or more types, so that the first letter of the code represents the dominant classification and the other letters represent other types in order of decreasing relevance. Some examples from Holland et al. (1972) are given below, the codes R, I, A, S, E, and C representing the six classifications.

Code	Occupation
RIA	Painter
RIE	Mechanical engineer; machinist
RSC	Collector
RCI	Motion picture projectionist
IAR	Physicist
AIR	Architect, photoengraver
AIS	Commercial artist
SRI	Guide

SAC	Hairdresser
ESR	Routeman
ESI	Manager of retail store
CIR	Computing machine operator
CSE	Secretary

The personalities of individuals can be characterized by the three categories which, in terms of their interests, are found to be most dominant. The interests of individuals are measured by the Vocational Preference Inventory (VPI). The responses of individuals can be represented by the letter symbols for the six categories, and the profile for any individual is usually represented by the letters of three of the categories in descending order of importance.

The Hexagonal Model

The use of the codes to represent specific occupations makes it possible to determine the relationships between these six categories and the interests of people as measured by the Vocational Preference Index. For a sample of about 20,000 people, the correlations between all possible pairs of the six categories gave rise to the development of Holland's hexagonal model, shown in Figure 9–5, where the values by the lines between the various pairs are the correlations between them. The six categories are so ordered that those with the highest correlations are adjacent to each other; the correlations of the pairs of categories opposite each other are generally the lowest.

Research Relating to the Theory

Several studies relating to Holland's theory have been carried out with the view toward collecting data to either support or reject the theory. The primary thrust of these studies has been toward determining if the six constructs represented by Holland's categories (which are rooted in personality theory) can also be used to characterize jobs. A number of these studies tend to support the theory.

One example of such studies is an analysis of the relationship between data from the Position Analysis Questionnaire (PAQ) and Holland's categories. Holland was provided data from Purdue University on PAQ analyses for 879 jobs, these data consisting of job dimension scores (technically, principal component scores) for 32 job dimensions. These jobs were then classified by raters into the six Holland categories. Of the 879 jobs, 832 were classified by rater agreement in one or another of the categories that were used; 47

Figure 9-5. Holland's hexagonal model of six personality types. (Source: Holland et al., p. 272)

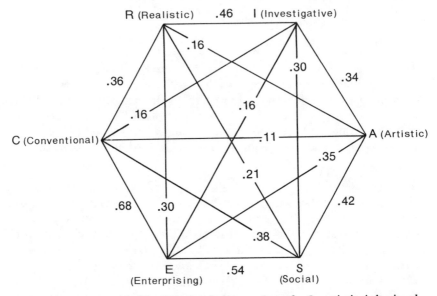

jobs were unclassifiable. (Since there were only 2 artistic jobs in the sample, this category was not used in the analyses.)

A statistical analysis of variance was carried out that reflected a statistically significant relationship between job dimension scores for the jobs and their classification into the five Holland categories. The results demonstrated distinct patterns of PAQ job dimension scores for jobs, and Holland's classifications, thus indicating that jobs do lend themselves to being classified into categories that are predicated on personality types. This relationship provides the basis for using PAQ data for classifying jobs into the five Holland categories.

However, other research evidence is not entirely supportive of Holland's theory, as indicated, for example, by the results of investigations by Smart, Fishburn and Walsh, and Hughes. One inkling that has emerged from certain such studies is that the theory may be less relevant in the case of non-college-degreed workers than those with college degrees. (The theory had been developed initially with college students as the principal subjects.)

Discussion

Research relating to various theories that deal with different aspects of human behavior frequently provides partial—but not complete—

support for the theories in question. This seems to be the case with Holland's theory of vocational choice. Although one might wish for clearly defined formulations about human behavior to serve as the basis for developing practical policies and practices, the complexities of human behavior frequently preclude such clear-cut answers. Continued research efforts sometimes can bring about some great insight. Although some theories have to be accepted with reservations, they may still provide useful frames of reference, until the time when modifications of theories, or alternative and more definitive theories, are supported with further research.

Another Approach to Congruence

A relatively recent development relating to vocational choice is based on the use of the Job Activity Preference Questionnaire (JAPQ).* The JAPQ is an interest inventory that basically parallels the Position Analysis Questionnaire (PAQ) in that it includes most of the job elements of the PAQ. It provides for individuals to indicate the extent to which they would be interested in the job activities or situations characterized by the PAQ job elements as a part of a job they might have.

On the basis of the responses of an individual, it is possible to carry out the following statistical operations: (1) derive job dimension scores of the individual's interests in terms of the same job dimensions for which jobs can be scored from the PAQ; (2) compare the job dimension profile of the individual's interests with the job dimension scores of jobs, and derive a statistical index of the degree of correspondence with any given job; and (3) order jobs in sequence of the degree of match between the individual's interests and the individual jobs in any given sample of jobs. An example of such an ordering is given in Figure 9–6.

The JAPQ is, in effect, another manifestation of the concept of congruence between people's interests and jobs. Although the procedure is in the experimental stage at the time this book is being written, it seems to offer reasonable promise of providing a direct bridge between expressed interests in job activities and jobs.

Bases of Vocational Choice

The conscious choice of a vocation probably can be viewed essentially as a decision that the individual perceives as being reasonably

*For information about the Job Activity Preference Questionnaire (JAPQ), write to PAQ Services, Inc., P.O. Box 3337, Logan, Utah, 84321.

Figure 9-6. A listing of jobs in the order in which the job dimension interest profile of an individual (based on the JAPQ) matches the job dimension profiles of various jobs (based on the PAQ). (Source: Mecham)

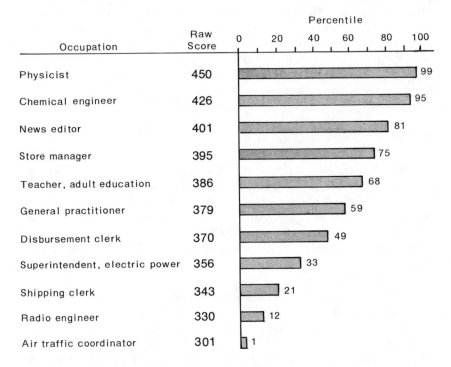

Note: The raw score for any occupation is an arbitrary index of the degree of match. The percentile shows the percent of jobs (in a sample of 778) for which the match for the job in question is better. Thus a percentile of 95 indicates that the match for that job is better than the matches for 95 percent of the sample jobs.

congruent with his personality makeup. However, it is probably true that many people do not go through any intentional process of choosing a vocation, but rather tend to drift into whatever types of jobs happen to be available. Further, the inexorable laws of supply and demand in the labor market undoubtedly operate to prevent some people from getting into the types of jobs that are most congruent for them.

Granting that the objective of congruence is a desirable one, but one that in fact is often not achieved, there probably is still some question as to the basis of the congruence that would generally be viewed as optimum. For example, the theory of work adjustment is predicated in part on congruence between the needs of people and the reinforcer systems of jobs (these being based on 21 identified needs), whereas Holland's theory is predicated on congruence in terms of six personality types. In spite of these differences, however, these two formulations have in common the concept of congruence between some type of personality characteristics (which embody personal value systems) and the characteristics of jobs which correspond to, or reinforce, those characteristics. In general, we probably can assume that there are certain combinations of personal factors and job characteristics that are more congruent than others. Further, we probably can assume that, insofar as individuals are able to be selective in choosing the types of vocations they get into, they tend to make such choices on the basis of the types of jobs which they feel would be reasonably congruent for them.

Although the consideration of congruence with one's needs or personality is undoubtedly an important factor in vocational choice (especially for some people), economic considerations undoubtedly serve as important counterbalances to induce some people to seek out, and to remain on, jobs which are not to their liking but which give them the means to provide basic food, shelter, and clothing, or to provide these in greater quantity and quality (and possibly more luxuries) than would be possible from other vocational pursuits which might in the long run be more personally satisfying.

We should also allude again to the concept of congruence between the abilities of people and the ability requirements of jobs, as expressed in the theory of work adjustment. Although the research relating to that theory is rooted in the notions of congruence between abilities of people and ability requirements of jobs, and congruence between personal needs and reinforcer systems of jobs, it must be accepted that the optimum circumstance is one in which both types of congruence exist. The representatives of the labor market (that is, prospective employers) typically are primarily concerned with the criteria of satisfactoriness (which stems primarily from the ability–ability-requirements match), whereas the individuals in the labor market probably tend to think more in terms of personal variables, usually with greater emphasis on the satisfaction criterion.

However, it is postulated that in the long run there is (or at least should be) no intrinsic conflict between the points of view of prospective employers and those of job candidates in the mutual decisions relating to personnel employment. This notion of mutuality seems to be supported by the expectation that the goals of each (the prospective employer and the job candidate) could better be fulfilled if the goals of the other were likewise fulfilled. The theory of work adjustment postulates that the ultimate criterion of tenure would be influenced by both how well individuals do their jobs (satisfactoriness) and how well the needs of individuals are fulfilled (satisfaction). Thus, it seems that management should be concerned about the satisfaction of employees, and conversely, employees (in addition to being satisfied with their jobs) should be concerned about the quality of their own performance, since in the long haul a person's vocational success (and therefore economic success) is in part a function of how well he fulfills the operational requirements of his vocation.

The notion of everyone being both happy and successful in his work is, of course, an impossible goal, and the turbulent, and at times bloody, history of management-labor conflict reflects some of the practical problems of achieving this goal. Although management-labor relations are now more civilized than they used to be (since collective bargaining has tended to replace some of the pitched battles of the past), the achievement of a state of general and widespread mutual compatability in management-labor relations is still elusive.

Although some of the troublesome issues of management-labor relations are tangential to the processes of matching people with jobs, both parties to the bargaining process should nevertheless share the basic objective of providing for reasonable congruence between abilities and needs on the one hand and job requirements on the other hand. Such matching presumably would enhance the possibility of fulfilling the two relevant criteria of satisfactoriness and satisfaction.

References

Betz, E.; Weiss, D. J.; Dawis, R. V.; England, G. W.; and Lofquist, L. H. *Seven Years of Research on Work Adjustment.* Minnesota Studies in Vocational Rehabilitation: XX. Minneapolis: University of Minnesota, 1966.

Borgen, F. H.; Weiss, D. J; Tinsley, H. E. A.; Dawis, R. V.; and Lofquist, L. H. *Occupational Reinforcer Patterns,* Vol. 1. Minnesota Studies in Vocational Rehabilitation: XXIV. Minneapolis: University of Minnesota, 1968(a).

Borgen, F. H.; Weiss, D. J.; and Tinsley, H. E. A.; Dawis, R. V.; and Lofquist, L. H. *The Measurement of Occupational Reinforcer Patterns.* Minnesota Studies in Vocational Rehabilitation: XXV. Minneapolis: University of Minnesota, 1968(b).

Dawis, R. V.; Lofquist, L. H; and Weiss, D. J. *A Theory of Work Adjustment.* Minnesota Studies in Vocational Rehabilitation: XXIII. Minneapolis: University of Minnesota, 1968.

Fishburn, F. J., and Walsh, W. B. "Concurrent Validity of Holland's Theory for Noncollege Degreed Workers." *Journal of Vocational Behavior* 8(1976): 77–84.

Holland, J. L. *Psychology of Vocational Choice.* Waltham, Mass.: Blaisdell, 1966.

Holland, J. L. *Making Vocational Choices: A Theory of Careers.* Englewood Cliffs, N.J.: Prentice-Hall, 1973.

Holland, J. L.; Hollifield, J. H.; Nafziger, D. H.; and Helms, S. T. *A Guide to the Self-directed Career Program: A Practical and Inexpensive Vocational Guidance System.* Center for Social Organization of Schools, Report No. 126. Baltimore, Md.: The Johns Hopkins University, 1972.

Holland, J. L.; Whitney, D. R.; Cole, N. S.; and Richards, J. M., Jr. *An Empirical Occupational Classification Derived from a Theory of Personality and Intended for Practice and Research.* ACT Research Report No. 29. Iowa City, Iowa: American College Testing Program, 1969.

Hughes, H. M. "Vocational Choice Level and Consistency: An Investigation of Holland's Theory on an Employed Sample." *Journal of Vocational Behavior* 2(1972): 377–388.

Lofquist, L. H., and Dawis, R. V. *Application of the Theory of Work Adjustment to Rehabilitation and Counseling.* Minnesota Studies in Vocational Rehabilitation: XXX. Minneapolis: University of Minnesota, 1972.

Mecham, R. C. Personal communication, 1978.

Rosen, S. D.; Weiss, D. L.; Hendel, D. D.; Dawis, R. V.; and Lofquist, L. H. *Occupational Reinforcer Patterns,* Vol. 2. Minnesota Studies in Vocational Rehabilitation: XXIX. University of Minnesota, 1972.

Smart, J. C. "Distinctive Career Orientations of Holland's Personality Types." *Journal of Vocational Behavior* 8(1976): 313–319.

Weiss, D. J.; Dawis, R. V.; England, G. W.; and Lofquist, L. H. *A Theoretical Approach to Occupational Reinforcement.* Minnesota Studies in Vocational Rehabilitation: XIX. Minneapolis: University of Minnesota, 1965.

Weiss, D. J.; Dawis, R. V.; England, G. W.; and Lofquist, L. H. *Instrumentation for the Theory of Work Adjustment.* Minnesota Studies in Vocational Rehabilitation: XXI. Minneapolis: University of Minnesota, 1966.

10

Establishing
Job Requirements

THE selection of candidates for any given job is predicated on two types of data, one type dealing with the requirements of the job itself, and the other dealing with the qualifications of candidates. Presumably the candidate whose qualifications best match the job requirements would be selected. Although this objective appears to be simple enough, the problems inherent in its application have haunted personnel managers over the years and have triggered many personnel research efforts. But the efforts expended have not yet resulted in simple, pat procedures for fulfilling this rather simply stated objective.

In actual situations the job requirements for any given job may be formally set forth, or they may exist only in the minds of the individuals who make personnel decisions. When formally set forth they may include any of a number of types of requirements, such as a minimum score on a given test (for example, a score of 70 on a specified arithmetic test); a statement of minimum experience or training (for example, "three years experience as a bookkeeper," or "completion of

240

machinist apprentice program"); a statement of knowledge required (for example, "comprehensive knowledge of heat treating procedures"); a statement of physical characteristics (for example, "good physical condition"). The qualifications of candidates may also be set down in black and white, for example, in the form of test scores or as descriptions of the length and type of work experience, or they may be in part assessed by a personnel manager or interviewer on the basis of an interview with a candidate.

Although the determination of the qualifications of candidates for jobs is clearly an important function for our current interests we should restrict ourselves to the function of establishing the job requirements, with particular reference to the role of job-related data in this function.

The Concept of Validity

One cardinal principle of establishing job requirements is that they should be valid. This simply means that the requirements as stated should be possessed by job candidates selected for the job in order to provide reasonable assurance that they will become satisfactory workers on the job. Validity, however, is not a clear-cut, unitary concept; rather, there are different varieties of validity (discussed below); it is usually not feasible to refer to any given job requirement as *valid* or *not valid*. Instead, one needs to think in terms of the degree of validity or, perhaps more practically, to view validity in terms of the probabilities that those fulfilling a stated requirement will become satisfactory employees. Even the term *satisfactory* is fairly slippery, since in the case of most jobs the incumbents vary in degree of satisfactoriness.

Types of Validity

These matters of semantics aside, let us now consider the various types of validity. The American Psychological Association, referring specifically to the matter of validity of tests and related forms of measurement, has set forth in *Standards for Educational and Psychological Tests* definitions of three types of validity: content, criterion-related, and construct validity. These are discussed below.

Content validity. The content validity of a test is demonstrated by showing how well the content of the test samples the class of situations or subject matter about which conclusions are to be drawn. Content validity is relevant in particular to tests used in education and training, and to tests used to measure the achievement or skills of people in some area (such as job knowledge tests, and job sample tests). The validity of such tests typically must be based on the judgments of experts regarding the appropriateness or relevance of the test questions or problems (that is, the content) to the subject matter or skills the test is intended to measure.

Criterion-related validity. Criterion-related validity is demonstrated by comparing the test scores of individuals with one or more external variables considered to provide a direct measure of the characteristic or behavior in question.

Criterion-related validity has been used quite extensively in connection with the validation of personnel tests. The typical procedure used, as related to any given job, consists of the following steps:

1. The selection of an experimental battery of tests (tests which one has reason to believe might be relevant for selection of candidates for the job).
2. The administration of the tests to a sample of incumbents now on the job, or candidates for the job.
3. The development of one or more appropriate criteria that would reflect the level of the performance of individuals on the job.
4. The derivation of a criterion value for each individual tested. (If present employees are tested, this value could be obtained immediately. If job candidates are tested, this value would be obtained after the selected candidates have had time to demonstrate their level of performance.)
5. The analysis of the results to determine the relationship between scores on each test and the criterion values of the individuals. Such results usually are reflected by either of two procedures, namely: (1) the computation of a coefficient of correlation between the two variables as the relationship is shown on a scattergram; and (2) the development of an expectancy chart. These two procedures are illustrated in Figures 10–1 and 10–2, respectively.

Construct validity. The construct validity of a test relates to the extent to which the test measures the human attribute or quality (or "construct") that it is intended to measure, such as abstract reasoning, spatial relations, or introversion-extroversion). The determination of the construct validity of a test is a long and difficult process, involving the derivation of correlations of scores on the

Figure 10-1. A scattergram, showing the relationship between employee test scores and job performance ratings. This relationship results in a coefficient of correlation (a validity coefficient) of .94.

Performance Ratings	1	2	3	4	5	6	7	8	9	10	11	12	13	14	15	16	17	18
100																		
99																		
98															I		I	
97																		
96													II					
95										I		II		II	I			
94									I	I		I						
93							I	I		I		I						
92				I		III	I	III										
91										II		I						
90					II		II		I									
89						II	I	I										
88		I					I		I									
87			I	II	II	I												
86		I																
85		II																
84			I															
83																		

Test Scores

test with scores on other tests or variables that one has reason to believe reflect the attribute in question.

Job component validity. In addition to the three types of validity set forth by the American Psychological Association, there is another, namely, job component validity. (This concept has most frequently been referred to as *synthetic validity,* but for various reasons it is believed that the term *job component validity* is a more descriptive one.) It has also been referred to as generalized validity. The concept of job component validity is predicated on the assumption that the human requirements of any given job activity or "component" would be comparable in the case of any job in which that activity or component occurred in equal degree. The development of a procedure for establishing the job-component validity for jobs would consist of the following: (1) some method for identifying or quantifying the various constituent components of jobs; (2) a method for determining, for an experimental sample of jobs, the human attribute(s) required for successful job performance when a given job component is common to several jobs; and (3) some method of combining the estimates of human attributes required for individual job components into an overall estimate of the human attribute requirements for an entire job. Such a procedure would make it possible to build up the aptitude requirements for any given job by: (1) knowing what job components occur in the job in question, (2) knowing what aptitudes are required for each such component, and (3) having a procedure for "summating" the attribute requirements that are relevant to the individual job components.

This basic notion is reflected in Table 10–1, in which certain hypothetical job components are listed (A, B, C, D, . . . , N), along with

Figure 10-2. An expectancy chart, showing the relationship between employee test scores and job performance evaluation. (Source: McCormick and Tiffin, p. 122. Reprinted with permission)

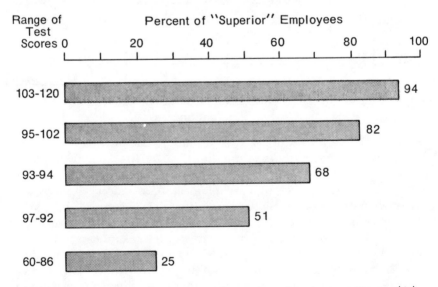

Note: Each bar represents the proportion of cases in each test-score category which are above some specified level on the criterion, such as above average.

TABLE 10-1. **Simplified hypothetical example of application of concept of job-component validity.**

Job Component	Attribute Required for Component	Importance of Component in Given Jobs			Total Attribute Requirements for Jobs		
		Job X	Job Y	Job Z	Job X	Job Y	Job Z
A	a	5	1	0	5a	1a	—
B	b	1	0	5	1b	—	5b
C	c	0	4	1	—	4c	1c
D	d	3	0	2	3d	—	2d
⋮	⋮	⋮	⋮	⋮	⋮	⋮	⋮
N	n	0	3	1	—	3n	1n

the human attribute required to perform each (a, b, c, d, . . . , n). Each of three jobs (X, Y, and Z) is described in terms of the importance of each component to the job. The level of the requirement for each *attribute* for a given job is a function of the importance of the *component* for which the attribute is required. The total job requirement, in turn, is the summation of the requirements thus derived from the individual attributes. This is an oversimplified model; in practice, building up total job requirements is not this straightforward.

The job component validity of a test would be predicated primarily on the content validity of the test if the test of the component measures some specific job content (such as job-related knowledges or skills), or on construct validity if the test of the component measures some basic human attribute (that is, construct).

Discussion of Validity

Since we are dealing essentially with jobs and the world of work, we should be particularly concerned with those types of validity which are relevant to that domain. To begin with, we should differentiate between two rather different types of circumstances in which one would want to predict the suitability (usually performance) of individuals for various jobs. In one type of circumstance the predictions deal with essentially *inexperienced* individuals, for example, in the selection of job candidates to be trained from scratch in a given job, or (looking at the matter from the point of view of individuals) in vocational counseling circumstances. In such instances one is primarily interested in predicting the suitability of individuals for learning and adapting to a job or vocation; this prediction is largely formed on the basis of abilities (that is, aptitudes), personality and interests, and other attributes. Any tests which might be used in this process preferably should have substantial construct validity, that is, they should measure with reasonable fidelity the basic attributes (the constructs) which they are intended to measure. However, although a test may have substantial construct validity (in the case of a test of spatial relations), that construct (spatial relations) may have no relevance at all to performance on a given job. Thus, one would need to have evidence that the test would be relevant for a particular job before using it. Such evidence can be based on criterion-related validity or can be inferred from a sound job analysis.

In the second type of circumstance, one is dealing essentially with *experienced* individuals, that is, those who have had (or claim to have had) the type of experience (including training) required for satisfactory job performance. Thus, one is interested in measures or indications of the specific job-related knowledges and/or skills which the job requires. For this type of circumstance the content validity of the tests would be particularly appropriate, since the content of the tests should match the corresponding content of the job. The tests which are most relevant in such cases are achievement tests and job-sample tests. However, even when one might use achievement or job-sample tests which are judged to have substantial content validity, it is also good practice to determine their criterion-related validity if that is feasible.

Although criterion-related validity is always desirable when feasible, the selection of inexperienced job candidates has its roots primarily in construct validity (associated with basic human attributes, or constructs), whereas the selection of experienced job candidates has its roots more in content validity (associated with job-related knowledges and skills). In practice, this distinction between inexperienced and experienced job candidates (with the respective references to construct and content validity) becomes very blurred.

In recent years in the United States, much greater emphasis has been placed on the need for evidence of the validity of personnel selection procedures, following the *Uniform Guidelines on Employee Selection* promulgated by the federal government (1978). These guidelines generally require reasonable evidence of the validity (sometimes referred to as the *job-relatedness* of tests and other procedures used in personnel selection, in order to minimize the possibility of unfair discrimination in such selection. Those guidelines then make it particularly important for employing organizations to develop appropriate evidence of the validity of their selection procedures.

Methods for Establishing Job Requirements

As discussed above, it is usually desirable (when feasible) to determine the validity of tests and other predictors by the use of criterion-related validity, even when there is reasonable evidence of content validity. However, when it is not feasible to determine the criterion-related validity of tests or other predictors (as when there are too few job incumbents), one would need to rely upon other evidence of validity, such evidence stemming primarily from job-related data. It must be stated that in the past (and probably even today), the requirements for some jobs probably have been based on little more than guesses or unsupported judgments (such as the belief that a given test would be valid for selection for a given job). But both the EEOC guidelines and good professional practice argue against such an approach and focus attention on the potential utility of sound job-related data as the most justifiable basis for establishing statements of job requirements.

This is essentially an inferential process, since the requirement (typically some ability) must be inferred from the work activity. Such inferences are fairly straightforward in some instances. For example, the requirement for a reasonable level of arithmetic computation ability can be inferred with considerable confidence in the case of an account clerk who needs to add and subtract numbers. The inferences of the requirements for many types of job activities, however, are not at all manifest, such as the requirements for learning to perform a complicated chemical laboratory test. At the same time, inferences frequently must be made in such circumstances.

To aid in making such inferences, the job analyses preferably should be as analytical and specific as possible, and the important work aspects of jobs should be identified in such a fashion that inferences can be made about their job requirements. The specific work units can be identified as a part of a conventional job analysis procedure, for example, by identifying the individual work units separately, possibly in some organized, structured arrangement. However, structured job analysis procedures frequently would facilitate the inferential process since they already provide for the analysis of jobs in terms of units of work. In any event, it usually is easier to make inferences about job requirements from specifically identified units or components of jobs than from global descriptions of total jobs or their major subdivisions.

In this regard, Mussio and Smith report that some analysts experience difficulty in using what they refer to as tasks (which represent rather broad job components) as the bases for making inferences about the required knowledges, abilities, etc. They then propose an intermediate step that would involve a listing of the behaviors required to perform a task. These specific behaviors would then be used as the basis for the inferences, rather than the more all-encompassing general tasks. As an illustration they draw from the analysis of the job of Housing Inspector. One of the tasks is described below, along with the behaviors involved in the task.

TASK:
Investigates complaints and makes routine inspections of dwellings, premises, non-dwelling structures, and vacant lands to determine compliance with the Housing Maintenance Code, Zoning Ordinance, and other applicable laws and ordinances.

BEHAVIORS:
1. Drives car to inspection site.
2. Gains entrance.
3. Observes, or looks for, "problems" that don't meet code in those areas: structure; electrical; plumbing; heating; ventilation; fire hazards; health hazards; safety hazards.
4. Records these observations in written form.
5. Based on his findings, in line with the nature and seriousness of the problems, fills out forms, writes tags, or refers elsewhere.
6. Follows up later to see if conditions were improved, by visiting site, telephoning, or writing.

Granting that there are no easy formulas for deriving sound job requirements, we will recap a few approaches that have been developed for using job-related data as the basis for establishing job requirements.

Critical Incident Technique

In discussing the process of inferring job requirements from job-related data, Bouchard urges the use of critical incident technique as the basis for identifying job dimensions, as discussed in Chapter 6. He suggests that such job dimensions be used as the units of job behaviors about which inferences of job requirements can be made. In this regard the rating of the importance of the dimensions can serve as cues about the relative importance of the requirements inferred from them. Table 10–2 illustrates the concept of job dimensions based on critical incidents and the nature of the inferences about the abilities required for satisfactory performance of the behaviors associated with the dimensions, and lists relevant tests to measure those abilities.

Clearly, making inferences about the abilities (or other attributes) required to perform the behaviors associated with any given dimension (or other type of job component) depends upon judgment. It is usually good practice to have two or more well-qualified persons make such judgments, preferably independently.

Judgments about Job Requirements

Although some judgments about job requirements may be no more substantive than thin air, job analysts and personnel officials repeatedly make estimates of the aptitude test requirements of jobs on the basis of reasonable job-related data.

Validity of judgments about job requirements. Even if such judgments are based on job analysis data, however, one would be curious about the validity of such judgments. Oddly enough, there is

TABLE 10–2. Job dimensions for a hypothetical job based on the critical incident technique, and the ability requirements inferred from them. (Adapted from Bouchard)

Job Dimension	Importance Rating*	Abilities Inferred	Relevant Tests
Planning (coordination of information and projection to future)	1.2	Intelligence	WAIS Watson-Glaser Wessman
		Verbal comprehension	Terman Concept Mastery Quick Word Test
Supervision of subordinates	1.6	Leadership	Fleishman Leadership Opinion Questionnarie (LOQ)
		Dominance	California Personality Inventory (CPI)
Communication with higher level personnel and other agencies	2.5	Verbal fluency	SRA Verbal Fluency Guilford Fluency Test
		Self-confidence	California Personality Inventory (CPI)

*The ratings in this table are based on a 5-point scale of importance, where 1 = extremely important and 5 = hardly important at all.

actually little evidence on this point, although Trattner et al. do report the results of one study relating to this. Their study dealt with data for ten jobs. As criteria of the aptitude requirements of the jobs they used the mean test scores of the job incumbents on each of ten tests. One group of eight job analysts estimated the mean aptitudes (for the ten aptitudes) required for each of the ten jobs, these estimates being based on written job descriptions. Another group of eight analysts made similar ratings based on actual observation of the jobs. Correlations of the estimated aptitudes with the mean test scores of the job incumbents were computed for each group of analysts; these correlations are below for two groups of aptitudes:

Aptitudes	*Analysts Using Job Descriptions*	*Analysts Using Observation*
Mental and perceptual	.60	.71
Physical	.01	.27

Although these data need to be interpreted with some reservations, they do suggest that analysts can estimate the level of mental and perceptual requirements of jobs more adequately than they can physical aptitudes.

As another approach to judging job requirements, Parry (1968) compared the estimates of validity coefficients (for three groups of employees and for 14 tests and subtests) with the actual validity coefficients, found only a moderate degree of relationship. However, the study did not comprise a really rigorous analysis, so the results of this study also need to be accepted with reservations.

Some other evidence about the use of judgments in establishing job requirements comes from an investigation in the USAF by Mullins and Usdin. The procedures used were rather intricate and will not be spelled out here, except to say that samples of psychologists and instructors in four technical training schools were asked to rate or rank the relevance of scores on ten tests and of educational level as predictors of final school grades of airmen who were sent to those schools for training. In the case of three of the four schools, the predictions based on these judgments were as valid as those which are generated by typical validation studies (and the predictions in the case of the fourth study were not too far off the mark).

In another USAF study, behavioral scientists were asked to rate the aptitude requirements of work activities at the task level

(Christal). One of the products of this procedure consisted of a statistical equation which was used to derive an estimate of the average aptitude requirement level of tasks performed, per unit time (abbreviated AARPUT). This index was based essentially on the average difficulty values of tasks described earlier in Chapter 7. These AARPUT index values for individual tasks can be used to build up an estimate of the aptitude requirements for any given job, given a task inventory for the job. This scheme also proved to be a reasonably satisfactory one for deriving such estimates.

As a tryout of the procedure, AARPUT index values were derived for the tasks in each of 14 Air Force career fields, and those values were then used to derive estimates of the aptitude requirements for each of a number of jobs in each career field. The results are given in Figure 10–3, which shows, for each career field, the mean estimated aptitude requirement of all the jobs in the sample, and the standard deviation of those values, shown by the bar (the length of that bar covers about two-thirds of all the jobs). The results of this study were used as the basis for the modification of the previously established standards for selection for certain of the career fields.

Ratings of worker traits (USES). The United States Employment Service (USES) provides for the rating of jobs in terms of each of several worker traits, including training time, aptitudes, temperaments, interests, and physical demands. These procedures are summarized in the Appendix.* In general terms, the procedures include definitions of the various traits, and scales to be used in rating them; the various scale values for any given trait are represented by benchmark examples as an aid to the rater. The ratings on the different traits for one job are included in the job analysis schedule shown earlier in Figure 4–1.

Discussion. Using very modest amounts of data and a good deal of subjective judgment, we probably can make the following surmises about job requirements set forth on the basis of judgments: such judgments probably have at least moderate validity, but perhaps more for some kinds of requirements than for others; the level of such requirements can be estimated more adequately than the degree of their validity; such estimates will be enhanced by increased familiarity with the jobs in question; systematic methods for doing this are generally better than catch-as-catch-can methods;

---

*For the detailed procedures, see Appendix B in the USES *Handbook for Analyzing Jobs.*

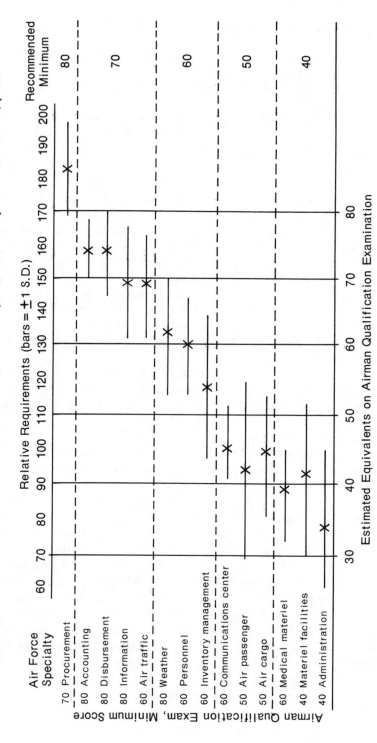

Figure 10-3. Estimated aptitude requirements of jobs in 14 USAF career fields (indicated by an X) and the standard deviation of the requirements of the jobs within each field (represented by the bar). (Adapted from Christal, p. 35)

and pooled group judgments are generally more valid than those of individuals.

Generic Skills Approach

The Training Research and Development Station in Prince Albert, Saskatchewan, Canada, has carried out a unique study under authorization of the Canadian Department of Manpower and Administration which has interesting implications for deriving job requirements (Kawula and Smith). The study was focused on the identification of generic skills that would be relevant in the training of people for various occupations. For this purpose, generic skills are considered to be those behaviors which are fundamental to the performance of many tasks carried out in a wide range of occupations. Five classes of generic skills were covered in the study. They are listed below along with a few examples of specific skills within each class:

Class	*Examples*
1. Mathematics skills	Multiplying whole numbers
	Adding fractions
	Solving single variable algebraic equations
2. Communication skills	Reading to determine job requirements
	Recording data on forms
	Writing technical reports
3. Reasoning skills	Scheduling work
	Diagnosing problems
	Making decisions
4. Interpersonal skills	Giving rewards and discipline
	Using attending behaviors
	Using group maintenance skills
5. Manipulative skills	Using eye-hand coordination
	Using proper body posture for lifting and carrying

A total of 192 such skill items were identified, and these were grouped into two core clusters, one at the nonsupervisory level and the other at the supervisory level.

Although the major focus of the study was toward the development of broad-based occupational training programs, the study has interesting implications in connection with at least a couple of aspects of the process of establishing job requirements. In the first place, it provides a reasonably well-formulated inventory of generic skills which could be considered as units of job requirements. In the second place, the study involved a potentially useful procedure for determining the relevance of such units of job requirements, specifically an interview procedure using employees and supervisors as respondents.

The survey by Kawula and Smith encompassed 76 occupations involving 820 worker interviews and 1,130 supervisor interviews; a major aspect of the interviews dealt with the identification of the specific skills involved in individual positions. Thus, for each occupation it was possible to tally the frequency with which specific skills were actually used. These frequencies were converted to a common metric, specifically the "number of skill users out of 10." If this was 3 (out of 10) or more for a particular skill, that skill was considered to be significant. One of the results of this survey was an occupational matrix that shows, for each occupation, the number of significant skill users (that is, the number of skill users of 3 out of 10, or above). A partial matrix is shown in Figure 10–4.

In a subsequent elaboration of the generic skills concept *(Generic Skills: Key to Job Performance)* workers or supervisors were surveyed in 77 occupations to obtain their opinions regarding the specific generic skills that were used in the occupations. (A comparison of the judgments of a sample of workers and supervisors indicated that their judgments had a correlation of .95.) The survey dealt specifically with generic communications, mathematics, science, and reasoning skills. Some of the results, summarized for 13 occupational families plus foremen/supervisors, are shown in Figure 10–5. This figure shows, for certain illustrative skills, the relative skill need for each; the skill need was reflected by the relative frequency with which each skill had been reported as being required, ranging from nil, to few, to many, to most/all. Figure 10–5 also shows certain skills that were required for virtually all, or many of the occupational families, and still other skills that were required for only very few families.

As a follow-up, the profiles of the occupations were compared on the basis of data such as those in Figure 10–5. A few examples of such comparisons are given in Figure 10–6, which shows several groups of occupations with similar profiles, and a group of occupations with nonsimilar profiles.* An interview procedure such as this, concerned with the generic skills program, probably could be justified only if the ultimate results were to be applied on a fairly

---

*The generic skills program is being carried out by the Occupational and Career Analysis and Development Branch, Canada Employment and Immigration Commission, Ottawa, Ontario, K1A 079.

Figure 10-4. Partial matrix of generic skills for a sample of nonsupervisory occupations (Adapted from Kawula and Smith, 1975, pp. 120-125)

GENERIC SKILLS	Surveyor, helper	Nurse's aide	Secretary	Sales clerk	Policeman	Cook	Salesman, hardware	Meat cutter	Heavy equipment operator	Lineman	Construction laborer
1. Whole numbers											
Add and subtract	10	10	10	10	10	10	10	10	9	4	10
6. Measure											
Weigh	3	3		3	4	8		10	4		
9. Drawings and graphs											
Read scale drawings	10		3		7		5		5	8	
10. Algebra											
Quadratics											
16. Read											
Charts and tables	7	7	6	7	8	5	8	5	4	7	3
18. Write											
Business letters	8	7	9	4	8		9				
20. One-to-one conversation											
Elementary conversation		9	9	9	10	6	6			10	8
23. Instructional communication											
Demonstration		10	7	8	6	4	6		5	9	7

broad scale, but in such instances it would seem to represent a promising method for developing indications of the relative importance of the generic skill types of job requirements provided for in the survey procedures.

The Job Element Method

The job element method of job analysis developed by Primoff is used by the United States Civil Service Commission either for selecting personnel tests, or as the basis for developing job-related tests. The first of these purposes is especially germane to our present discussion.

The job element method for test selection. As indicated earlier, the analysis of a given job by several expert raters results in a total value for each job element as related to the overall job. These ratings are used in combination with a previously developed set of test values that consist of a matrix in which there is a given value for each of several standardized tests for each of the job elements. Some examples of hypothetical values are shown in Figure 10–7. (Note that the vacant cells represent zero values.) The statistical underpinnings of this matrix and of its use are quite intricate, and

Figure 10-5. Requirements of illustrative generic skills for certain occupational families. (Source: *Generic Skills: Keys to Job Performance*)

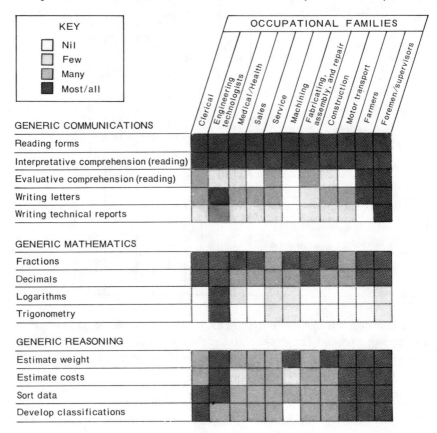

Figure 10-6. Illustrations of occupations with similar and nonsimilar generic skill profiles based on the frequency with which the three types of skills were reported as being required. (Source: *Generic Skills: Keys to Job Performance*)

KEY
- ☐ Few/none
- ▨ Many
- ▩ Most/all

Skill columns (each group): Mathematics, Communications, Science, Reasoning

OCCUPATIONS WITH SIMILAR PROFILES

Occupation (left group)	Occupation (right group)
Stenographer/typist/receptionist	Electrician
Nurse's aide	Medical/laboratory/technician
Construction laborer	Radio/Television repairman
Product assembler, metal	Maintenance man, building
Welder, combination	Painter
Heavy equipment operator	Tractor-trailer driver
Barber	Farmer, general
Cosmetologist	Construction equipment mechanic
Accounting clerk	Motor-vehicle mechanic
Bookkeeper	**OCCUPATIONS WITH NONSIMILAR PROFILES**
Bookkeeping clerk	Salesperson, hardware
Storeman	Nursing assistant
Meat cutter	Sales clerk
Cook	Machinist, general
Janitor	Secretary
Receiving clerk	Commercial traveler
Taxi/bus/truck/driver	Nurse, general duty
	Architectural technologist

will therefore not be discussed.* Given the total values for the individual job elements as derived for a particular job, and the matrix of test values, it is possible to derive a J-coefficient for each test, representing in effect the estimated coefficient of validity of the test as a predictor of potential success of job candidates. The specific arithmetic manipulations are not given here, but an important step in this process is the multiplication of the (total) rating on each job element with the values in the matrix. These cross-products are then added for each test. Although there are other manipulations, one can see that, for any given test, high ratings on those job elements which have high test values in the matrix would result in a

*For discussion of this point see Primoff.

Figure 10-7. Partial matrix of hypothetical test values for use in the derivation of the J-coefficients of tests for personnel selection. (Adapted from Primoff, 1955, p. 5)

Job Element	Matrix of Test Values (hypothetical)			
	Test A	Test B	Test C	Test Z
1	44	47		9
2	2		13	
3	17	27		17
.				
.				
.				
n	40	42	7	

high sum (across all job elements), and this would tend to produce a high J-coefficient.

Primoff states that a J-coefficient of .09 or above is statistically significant, and that the test might therefore be considered for inclusion in a test battery. However, one would ordinarily select the tests with the highest J-coefficients above that value.

Variations in the procedure provide for developing weighting systems for individual tests of specialized knowledges or abilities that might be uniquely relevant to specific jobs or groups of jobs (Primoff, 1972; 1973).

The basic procedure of the job element method is, of course, a form of job component validity (that is, synthetic validity), as discussed earlier in this chapter.

The job element method for test construction. The second major use of the job element method of job analysis is to serve as the basis for the construction of tests whose content tends to match that of specific jobs. For this purpose the job elements used usually would be those which characterize specific job-related knowledges and abilities, such as those in a list for trades and labor occupations or for clerical positions (Primoff, 1975). One aspect of the job analysis procedure used for this purpose consists in rating each job element on the four rating factors referred to in Chapter 6 and shown in Figure 6–5. Three of these ratings (S, T, and P) are used in deriving an item index for each item (see last column of Figure 6–5). These indexes and the ratings on the fourth factor (B) for the individual raters are then summarized for all raters and converted to percentages related to all items. In turn, items with percentages above 50 on both the item index and on factor B (with some exceptions) are used as the basis for construction of test items. In general terms a test developed from this basis would then have items which are relatively representative of the more important elements of the job in question.

The operational use of the job element method by the Civil Service Commission incorporates a couple of additional uses of the job element data derived from the job analysis process. One of these provides for job candidates to rate themselves on the individual job elements using a self-report checklist. Further, the ultimate crediting of individual job candidates (that is, the total official evaluation of candidates for individual jobs) is in part based on assessments of the candidates with respect to the elements which are important to the job.

The Position Analysis Questionnaire (PAQ)

One of the primary uses of the PAQ is for developing estimates of aptitude requirements for individual jobs on the basis of PAQ analyses. Three major studies have been carried out toward this end, one by Mecham and McCormick, another by Marquardt and McCormick, and one by Mecham. The third, which is the most recent, will be summarized here. The approach used represents the job component type of validity, since it resulted in the derivation of estimates of job requirements (specifically of aptitudes) directly from job data (PAQ analyses of jobs.)

Sample of jobs used. In this phase of the study, data for 163 job classifications were used, specifically job classifications identified by the nine-digit codes of the Dictionary of Occupational Titles (DOT) of the USES. These were job classifications for which the USES had published test data for the nine tests of the General Aptitude Test Battery (GATB) for samples of jobs.

Job dimension scores used as predictor. In this study the scores on the 32 division job dimensions, were used as the predictors. In the case of most of the job classifications, there were multiple PAQ analyses. In such instances the job dimension scores of the jobs within a given classification were averaged, and these averaged job dimension scores were used to represent all the PAQ analyses within the individual classifications. When only one PAQ analysis was available for a job classification, the job dimension scores of that one analysis were used.

Criteria. The ultimate test of the validity of a method of developing job requirements based on the concept of job component validity would be to try out the system over a period of time to see if it generally results in the selection of satisfactory personnel for various jobs. For purposes of the present study a more modest approach was undertaken in which aptitude test data available primarily from the USES were used as the basis for the criteria against which (tentative) job component job requirements could be tested.

To illustrate the approach used, first let us consider a single attribute, specifically an attribute for which there is a corresponding test in the General Aptitude Test Battery (GATB) of the USES. Next let us select a sample of jobs for which test scores based on that test are available for samples of job incumbents, and for which job analysis data expressed in terms of a set of job components. One could then correlate the job data on these components for the jobs in the sample with the mean test scores of people on corresponding jobs. This approach would be predicated on the assumption that jobs tend to differ in the level of a given attribute required for successful performance, and that people somehow tend to gravitate into jobs which are commensurate with their own abilities; if these assumptions are reasonably valid, it follows that, for a given attribute, the differences in the mean test scores of people on various jobs would reflect in a very gross way the varying job requirements, on that attribute, of the jobs in question. There are potential loopholes in this chain of reasoning (but there is also some fairly substantial support for it). Recognizing some of the possible loopholes, for purposes of this test of a system of deriving job requirements based on job components, the mean test scores of personnel on each of the several jobs in the sample were used as one set of criterion values.

A variation in the use of the mean test scores of job incumbents as criterion values for jobs is to use some value in the distributions of scores of incumbents other than the mean scores. In this study, the test score one standard deviation below the mean was used. In a reasonably normal distribution this would be a value below which about 16 percent of the cases would fall. This value was used since it might be somewhat more typical of possible cutoff scores used in personnel selection than the mean. (It is recognized, however, that cutoff scores used in employment operations usually are adjusted up or down, according to labor market conditions.) This criterion was also called a potential cutoff score.

Considering the same set of data (that is, a set of job requirements for a sample of jobs derived from their individual components, and test-score data for incumbents on such jobs), there is another possible way of teasing out some indication of the validity of the job requirements so derived. This method involves the coefficients of validity of test scores against appropriate performance criteria for samples of people on those jobs. A validity coefficient, in a sense, is a reflection of the relative importance of a test (or of the attribute that the test measures) in relationship to the criterion. For a given attribute, if one can somehow derive—on the basis of the components present in individual jobs—indexes of the requirements of various jobs for that attribute, these attribute indexes could then be correlated, for a sample of jobs, with the coefficients of validity of a test that presumably measures that attribute. Thus, a third criterion used consisted of the validity coefficients of tests for jobs that corresponded to the jobs used in this phase of the project.

Summary of data used. The basic data used in the job component validity study than consisted of the following:

1. Test data from the USES for incumbents on each of 163 jobs, the tests being the nine tests of the General Aptitude Test Battery (GATB). The criterion values for each of the sample jobs as based on these test data were: (a) the mean test score of job incumbents; (b) a potential cutoff score (specifically the test score in the distribution for each job that was one standard deviation below the mean); and (c) the coefficient of validity. Such criterion values were used for each of the nine tests.

2. PAQ analyses of the 163 job classifications. In the case of most job classifications there were multiple PAQ analyses. In such instances the average job dimension scores of all the individual analyses were used to represent the job classification. If there was only a single PAQ analysis for a particular job classification that analysis was used.

Regression analyses with job dimension scores. A separate build up stepwise regression analysis was carried out for each of the nine GATB tests, using the job dimension scores as the predictors of the three test-related criteria. The results of this analysis are expressed in terms of multiple correlations that reflect the extent to which a selected assortment of job dimensions, with statistically derived weights, can predict where any given job might fall on the scales that represent each of the three criteria. Thus, for example, the predicted mean test score for a given job could be interpreted as an estimate of what the mean test score of a hypothetical sample of incumbents on the job would be.

The primary results of this multiple regression analysis of job dimension scores as predictors of the three criteria are given in Table 10–3.* It can be seen that the mean test scores and the mean minus the standard deviation scores (the potential cutoff scores) are considerably more predictable than the validity coefficients, with multiple correlations for the nine tests ranging from .30 to .83 for the mean test-score criterion, and from .24 to .84 for the mean minus the standard deviation criterion. The predictions were generally higher for the cognitive and perceptual tests (intelligence, verbal, numerical, and so on) than for the last two psychomotor tests (finger dexterity and manual dexterity). The lower predictability associated with validity coefficients is probably, in part, a reflection of their relatively unstable nature; such instability is associated with such factors as small sample sizes and restricted range, unreliable criteria, and the like.

According to the *ASPA Handbook of Personnel and Industrial Relations,* the general level of the correlations indicates that reasonably valid estimates of the derived aptitude requirements for jobs can be derived statistically from quantitative data about job components, in this instance statistically identified combinations of job-dimension scores based on the PAQ. Thus, it seems feasible that in some circumstances one could determine the aptitude requirements of jobs on the basis of job-component validity, thus eliminating the need for conventional test-validation procedures. In this regard, there are, of course, many jobs for which conventional test-validation procedures simply are not possible, as when there are too few incumbents on a job to use for such validation.

These predictions are, of course, in terms of criteria of test-related data from the GATB tests of the USES. Since these tests are not available for general use, a subsequent study was carried out using test data from certain commercially available tests that were considered to measure the same constructs (that is, the same aptitudes) as certain of the GATB tests (McCormick et al., 1977). Such

---

*The multiple correlations shown are "shrunken" by the use of the Wherry shrinkage formula. The formula provides a downward adjustment, based on the number of predictors and the number of cases, to account for chance interrelationships that might produce a spuriously high correlation. In effect, such a correlation can be considered as an estimate of what the correlation would be if the regression equation were applied to another sample.

TABLE 10-3. Multiple correlations of combinations of PAQ job dimension scores with three test-related criteria as measured by the General Aptitude Test Battery (GATB) of the United States Employment Service. (Source: Mecham)

	Criterion		
	Mean	Minus	Coefficient
GATB	Test	Standard	of
Test	Score	Deviation	Validity
G-Intelligence	.79	.78	23
V-Verbal	.83	.84	06
N-Numerical	.77	.73	08
S-Spatial	.69	.70	24
P-Form perception	.61	.60	13
Q-Clerical perception	.78	.75	−.02
K-Motor coordination	.73	.67	−.04
F-Finger dexterity	.41	.41	.15
M-Manual dexterity	.30	.24	.39
Median coefficient	.73	.70	.13

tests were matched with five of the GATB tests. In the case of each such construct the scores of the tests that were considered to measure the construct were converted to a common metric, specifically, a scale with a mean of 100 and a standard deviation of 20 (the same as used with the GATB tests). It should be noted that the conversion of scores to this common metric in some instances left something to be desired since, for certain tests, there were no general working population norms to use. In such instances norms for two or more groups were put together to approximate a general working population sample. Thus, certain of the conversions need to be accepted with reservations.

Recognizing these limitations, we present the results of this study in Table 10-4. Although the multiple correlations from this study are not as high as those based on the GATB tests, they nonetheless support the notion that aptitude requirements for jobs can be derived statistically from data from a structured questionnaire such as the PAQ.

Job Analysis Basis for Content Validity

As indicated in the discussion of various types of validity, content validity is especially relevant in circumstances in which it is desirable to use tests or other measures which cover the specific job-related knowledges and skills (that is, the content) of a given job. In the typical circumstance the contents of jobs for which correspond-

TABLE 10–4. Correlations between predicted and actual criteria for five constructs as measured by various commercial tests. (Source: McCormick et al.)

	Criterion			
Construct	Mean Test Scores	1 S.D. Below the Mean	Validity Coefficients	N †
G: Intelligence	.74***	.66***		33/
V: Verbal	.71***	.71***	.30	50/36
N: Numerical	.67***	.63***	.29**	64/76
S: Spatial	.74***	.76***	.27	26/43
Q: Clerical	.53*	.60**	−.02	15/29
Average	.66***	.68***		

*Significant, $p < .05$
**Significant, $p < .01$
***Significant, $p < .001$
†The N at the left applies to the first two criteria; the N at the right applies to the third. (There were too few jobs with validity coefficients to report for the "G" construct.)

ing tests are used are job-oriented in nature in that they deal with technical aspects of jobs. (The term *test* as used here is intended to embrace any type of measurement of the attribute or quality in question.) Thus, one might use a test of electrical principles and practices for an electrician job, or a test of shorthand for a secretarial job. However, the concept of content validity can also apply to more basic human attributes, such as arithmetic skills, communication skills, and interpersonal skills, which were represented in the list of generic skills discussed earlier in this chapter.

In any event, the content of jobs as it might be relevant to the content validity of tests typically would be predicated on job analysis data. Such an analysis might be used, operationally, for either the selection of already available tests or other measures, or for the development of such tests.

Unlike the Ten Commandments, the optimum procedures for crossing the content validity bridge from the job to the selection or development of tests have not yet been revealed. However, the job element method used by the United States Civil Service Commission (discussed above) represents one approach. Another, more specific, treatment of content validity is that of Mussio and Smith (undated). Their treatment consists essentially of a procedural manual developed for use by the Civil Service Commission of the city of Minneapolis. Although the details of this treatment cannot be given here, a few of the salient features are discussed.

Content validity procedures of Minneapolis. The content validity procedures of the Minneapolis Civil Service Commission are directed in large part toward the development of examinations for use in sorting out candidates for specific jobs. Although we will not go into the development of such examinations as such, the job analysis processes leading up to that development are, of course, relevant to the discussion of content validity. Their procedures are best illustrated by the example Mussio and Smith use in their manual, the position of Housing Inspector. The basic job description is shown in Figure 10-8. It is based on an initial review of materials

Figure 10-8. Job description for the position of Housing Inspector, illustrating the content validity procedures of the Minneapolis Civil Service Commission. (Source: Mussio and Smith, p. 18)

HOUSING INSPECTOR

GENERAL RESPONSIBILITIES

Under supervision to do work of more than ordinary difficulty and complexity in the inspection of existing dwellings, in investigating complaints, and in the enforcement of applicable laws or ordinances; and to do related work as required.

TYPICAL DUTIES

1. Explains the City Housing Code to city property occupants.

2. Makes routine inspections of dwellings, premises, non-dwelling structures and vacant lands to determine compliance with the housing maintenance code. Includes inspecting and re-inspecting as required, public areas basement areas, interior and exterior buildings, and yards checking for condition, cleanliness, safety devices, vermin and rodent infestation, location, size, type, occupancy, window area, and the like; inspects yard areas for improper handling of garbage, rubbish, and junk; inspects for the presence of rodents and vermin or for conditions leading to infestation; inspects and investigates complaints of improper dumping of garbage, rubbish, junk, and other objectionable material.

3. Consults with owners, managers, and others on violations observed in a dwelling and recommends remedial action; consults with other agencies as necessary for the enforcement of applicable ordinances and regulations as they may affect housing; issues verbal and written orders for correction of violations observed during inspections; issues violation tags as appropriate; gathers evidence of violation; makes up charge sheets for the City Attorney as appropriate; and serves as a witness in court cases.

4. Keeps complete and accurate records of all work performed; keeps daily records of all activities and prepares information for monthly reports; may issue permits for trucks, small animals, and fowl; and makes other investigations as assigned.

relating to the position, followed by observation of current employees and meetings with relevant officials. As one phase of the meetings, the individuals were asked to list the knowledges, skills, and personal characteristics they believed were needed to carry out each task. Those lists were then consolidated into a tentative listing by job analysts. The tentative list was submitted for review to the original participants at the meetings, and a final list was developed. The final list is given in Figure 10–9, which includes only the knowledges and skills, not the personal characteristics.

The participants were then asked to respond to the following questions for each item on the list:

1. Is it absolutely essential for newly hired employees to possess this knowledge or skill?
2. Is there a way of measuring this knowledge or skill quantitatively?
3. Would varying amounts of this knowledge or skill cause varying levels of job effectiveness?

Negative answers to these questions were used to eliminate some items, and the respondents were then asked to assign percentage weights of importance to each of the general categories of items, adding up to 100 percent. In addition, they assigned similar percentage weights of the items within each of the general categories. The results of this weighting (based on the judgments of the several participants), are given in Figure 10–10.

In this particular study the resulting percent values in Figure 10–10 were used as guidelines for the development of examinations which would reflect the relative importance of the different content areas of the job. In other circumstances such a procedure could be used to select (and weight) already available tests or other measures.

As indicated before, content validity depends very much upon the judgments of experts about the content of tests as related to the content of, say, a job. This procedure illustrates how such judgments can be elicited using a systematic procedure, thus giving reasonable assurance that the content of the tests is appropriate.

Discussion

The problems associated with many aspects of human life defy easy, off-the-shelf solutions. This is certainly the case with the problems relating to the establishment of job requirements. At the same

Figure 10-9. List of knowledges and skills for the position of Housing Inspector, illustrating the content validity procedures of the Minneapolis Civil Service Commission. (Source: Mussio and Smith, pp. 20-23)

HOUSING INSPECTOR

TASKS

I. Investigates complaints and makes routine inspections of dwellings, premises, non-dwelling structures, and vacant lands to determine compliance with the housing maintenance code, zoning ordinance, and other applicable laws and ordinances.

   A. Knowledges Required

      1. Working knowledge of housing maintenance code.

      2. Familiarity with general construction and environmental factors relating to the housing code.

         a. Structure.
         b. Electrical.
         c. Plumbing.
         d. Heating.
         e. Ventilation.
         f. Fire Protection.
         g. Health.
         h. Safety.

      3. Working knowledge of relevant parts of city zoning ordinance.

         a. Conformance to zoning ordinances on residential property.
         b. Number of dwelling units in the structure.
         c. Number of persons per unit.
         d. Type of unit: dwelling, tenement, rooming.
         e. Other permitted uses. (Number of autos, etc.)

      4. Knowledge of department procedures.

         a. Issuance of orders and tags.
         b. Search warrants.
         c. Placards and condemnations — can be executed only by the Housing Inspector.
         d. Permit process.
         e. Appeals process.
         f. Referral agencies.
            (1) Cooperative inspections with fire inspectors.
            (2) Cooperative inspections with welfare case workers.
            (3) Cooperative inspections with health inspectors.
         g. Departmental forms.
         h. Court procedures.
         i. Functional breakdown of Inspections Department.
            (1) District Inspector
            (2) Paving District Inspector.
            (3) Hotel and Board and Care Inspector.
            (4) Urban renewal Inspector.
            (5) Neighborhood Conservation Area Inspector.
            (6) Model City Area Inspector.
            (7) Weed Inspector.

5. Knowledge of purpose of housing maintenance code and consequences of noncompliance.

    a. Health.
    b. Safety.
    c. Legal.

B. Skills or Abilities

1. Interpret and apply code judiciously.

    a. Applies code consistently in his routine work.
    b. Makes judgments in undefined situations.
    c. Pays attention to details.

2. Reading ability.

    a. Plans; blueprints; specifications; etc.
    b. Ordinances; codes; legal documents; etc.

3. Ability to translate observations into written form.

    a. Orders.
    b. Tag reports.
    c. Letters.

4. Numerical ability.

    a. Addition.
    b. Subtraction.
    c. Multiplication.
    d. Division.
    e. Ratios.
    f. Geometry.

5. Planning and organizational ability.

    a. Schedules daily activities.
    b. Establishes work priorities.
    c. Organizes information for reports.
    d. Lays out strategy for correction of violations.

6. Ability to drive automobile.

II. Consults both in person and on phone with owners, managers, and others on violations observed in a dwelling and recommends remedial action; consults with other agencies as necessary for the enforcement of applicable ordinances and regulations as they may affect housing; issues verbal and written orders and tags for correction of violations observed during inspections.

A. Knowledges Required

1. Socioeconomic composition of his district.
2. Behavioral characteristics of cultural subgroups within district.
3. Past offenders and problem areas within his district.

B. Skills or Abilities

1. Verbal ability to communicate with people from varied socioeconomic and educational levels.
2. Ability to establish rapport with managers, occupants, owners, and others regarding code compliance.
3. Ability to enforce regulatory provisions with firmness, courtesy, and impartiality.
4. Ability to translate language of the code into terminology appropriate to layman.
5. Ability to explain purpose of code and hazardous consequences of non-compliance.

Figure 10-10. Final list of weighted knowledges and skills for the position of Housing Inspector, illustrating the content validity procedures of the Minneapolis Civil Service Commission. (Source: Mussio and Smith, p. 26)

	Weight
1. Familiarity with general construction principles and environmental factors relating to the Housing Code.	20

a) Structure	10	
b) Electrical	10	
c) Plumbing	10	
d) Heating	10	
e) Ventilation	10	
f) Fire Protection	10	
g) Health	20	
h) Safety	20	
Total	100%	

	Weight
2. Ability to translate observations into written form.	30

a) Orders	33
b) Tags	33
c) Letters	33
Total	100%

	Weight
3. Planning and organizational ability.	10

a) Schedules daily activities	15
b) Establishes work priorities	15
c) Organizes information for reports	70
Total	100%

	Weight
4. Verbal ability to communicate with people from varied socioeconomic and educational levels.	20
5. Ability to translate housing code into terminology appropriate to layman.	10
6. Ability to explain purpose of code and hazardous consequences of noncompliance.	10
Total	100%

time, one should not despair of resolving such problems. In this chapter we have discussed briefly several examples of systematic approaches to the processes of establishing job requirements, each with its own advantages and limitations. It is true that most of these (and other) schemes depend in one way or another on human judgments, which, as we all know, are fallible. But the use of systematic procedures—and frequently the use of the judgments of two or more people—tends to give reasonable assurance of the adequacy of such judgments.

References

Bouchard, T. J. *A Manual for Job Analysis.* Minneapolis: Minnesota Civil Service Department, 1972.

Christal, R. E. *The USAF Occupational Research Project.* USAF, AFSC, Occupational Research Division, AFHRL-TR-73-75. Brooks AFB, Texas: 1974.

Generic Skills: Keys to Job Performance. Occupational and Career Analysis and Development Branch, Advanced Development Division. Ottawa, Canada: Canada Employment and Immigration Commission, undated, but distributed in 1978.

Handbook for Analyzing Jobs. U.S. Department of Labor, Manpower Administration. Washington, D.C.: U.S. Government Printing Office, Stock no. 2900-0131, 1972.

Kawula, W. J., and Smith, A. D. W. *Handbook of Occupational Information.* Prince Albert, Saskatchewan, Canada: Manpower and Immigration, Training Research and Development Station, 1975.

McCormick, E. J.; DeNisi, A. S.; and Shaw, B. J. *Job-derived Selection: A Follow-up Report.* Department of Psychological Sciences, Report No. 4. West Lafayette, Ind.: Purdue University, 1977.

McCormick, E. J., and Tiffin, J. *Industrial Psychology,* 6th ed. Englewood Cliffs, N.J.: Prentice-Hall, 1974.

Marquardt, L. D., and McCormick, E. J. *The Utility of Job Dimensions Based on Form B of the Position Analysis Questionnaire (PAQ) in a Job Component Validity Model.* Department of Psychological Sciences, Report No. 5. West Lafayette, Ind.: Purdue University, 1974.

Mead, D. F., and Christal, R. E. *Development of a Constant Standard Weight Equation for Evaluating Job Difficulty.* USAF, AFSC, AFHRL-TR-70-44. Brooks AFB, Texas: 1970.

Mecham, R. C. Unpublished research report. Logan, Utah, PAQ Service, Box 3337, 1977.

Mecham, R. C., and McCormick, E. J. *The Use of Data Based on the Position Analysis Questionnaire in Developing Synthetically Derived Attribute Require-*

ments of Jobs. Department of Psychological Sciences, Occupational Research Center, Report No. 4. West Lafayette, Ind.: Purdue University, 1969.

Mullins, C. J., and Usdin, E. *Estimation of Validity in the Absence of a Criterion.* USAF, AFSC, Personnel Division, Lackland AFB, Texas: 1970.

Mussio, S. J., and Smith, M. K. *Content Validity: A Procedural Manual.* Chicago: International Personnel Management Association, undated.

Parry, M. E. "Ability of Psychologists to Estimate Validities of Personnel Tests." *Personnel Psychology* 21 (1968): 139–148.

Primoff, E. S. *Test Selection by Job Analysis: The J-Coefficient, What It Is, How It Works,* 2nd ed. Test Technical Series No. 20. Washington, D.C.: U.S. Civil Service Commission, 1955.

Primoff, E. S. *Preliminary Draft: The J-Coefficient Procedure.* Washington, D.C.: U.S. Civil Service Commission, 1972.

Primoff, E. S. *Introduction to J-Coefficient Analysis.* Washington, D.C.: U.S. Civil Service Commission, 1973.

Primoff, E. S. *How to Prepare and Conduct Job-element Examinations.* U.S. Civil Service Commission, Technical Study 75–1. Washington, D.C.: U.S. Government Printing Office, 1975.

Standards for Educational and Psychological Tests. Washington, D.C.: American Psychological Association, 1974.

Trattner, H. M.; Fine, S. A.; and Kubis, J. F. "A Comparison of Worker Requirement Ratings Made by Reading Job Descriptions and by Direct Observation." *Personnel Psychology* 8 (1955): 183–194.

"Uniform Guidelines on Employee Selection Procedures." *Federal Register* 43 (Aug. 25, 1978, No. 166): 38290–38309.

11

Job Design

INDIVIDUAL jobs do not exist in vacuums but within the framework of an organization, or a system, that is set up to fulfill some objective. In a general sense, any discussion of job design really should be viewed as an important aspect of system design, since individual jobs exist by reason of the functions they are intended to fulfill within systems of which they are a part.

Factors That Influence Job Design

The basic nature of individual jobs or positions is predetermined by the objectives or goals for which they are created within the system in which they are to function. Within the constraints imposed by such objectives or goals, however, their more specific nature or content can be the consequence of any of several factors, including: the state of relevant technology; custom and tradition; the influence of the physical equipment, facilities, and workspace and layout; supervisory and administrative decisions about what work activities should be combined to form a job or position; the results of systematic methods analysis; and in some instances, the effect of individual job incumbents on the activities they perform and how they perform them. These and other factors are in turn affected by the decisions of supervisors, administrators, methods analysts, equipment designers, and individual job incumbents. Such decisions, however, can be made with or without full recognition of the impact of the decision on the nature of the job in question and on the individuals who are to perform it. For example, the designer of a machine can design the machine with a primary focus on its strictly engineering features, or he can design it with the operator of the machine in mind. Each of these two frames of reference might have a very different effect on what the operator has to do, his efficiency in doing it, and even his physical welfare or job satisfaction. In the one instance the nature of the job is the fortuitous or unintentional consequence of the decisions that are made, whereas in the other instance the nature of the job is the intentional result of the decisions regarding it.

It is evident that over the years there has been increased attention to the intentional designing of jobs. Such attention is represented by at least three major approaches. The first of these consists of the *methods analysis techniques* as carried out by industrial engineers; this approach had its roots in the work of Frederick W. Taylor at the turn of the century, and by Frank and Lillian Gilbreth some years later. The second approach is that of *human factors engineering* (also referred to as *human factors, human engineering,* and, in European countries, *ergonomics*). The major thrust of the human factors approach is to design equipment and facilities so they are most suitable for human use, considering the physical, sensory, perceptual, psychomotor, cognitive, and other characteristics of people. This effort (sometimes referred to as *designing for human use*) received its major impetus during World War II as applied to military equipment, but has been extended to other areas since then. In a sense, the human factors approach represents a logical extension of the methods analysis approach, and today many methods analysts (usually industrial engineers) are, for practical purposes, also human factors practitioners. The third major approach to job design is variously referred to as *job enlargement* and *job enrichment.* This approach began receiving considerable attention during the 1950s and 1960s.

Job Design Objectives

Although there are probably very few who would now argue against the notion that jobs should be intentionally designed, there are questions as to the objectives to keep in mind in the job design process. Generally, it can be said that there are two types of objectives. The first type, *functional effectiveness,* has an emphasis on designing jobs in order to increase productivity and to enhance the efficiency with which work is performed. The second type of objective is focused more on the maintenance or enhancement of desirable *human values* (such as health, safety, and job satisfaction); this second objective is essentially one of human welfare.

The methods analysis and human factors approaches mentioned above tend to focus on the design of jobs in terms of functional effectiveness (with additional attention to such human values as safety and health). To a considerable extent the primary emphasis of the methods analysis and the human factors approaches has been on work simplification, that is, on designing the physical equipment and facilities people use in their work, and the methods involved, so the work activities are simplified and usually standardized. Such efforts in job design tend to create situations in which, given a particular stimulus, the responses of individuals usually are predetermined, and presumably maximally effective. By and large, job simplification results in jobs which require less skill, are more repetitious, and have less autonomy. The effects of job simplification have at times been referred to as *idiot proofing;* although this expression exaggerates the objective of methods analysis and human factors approaches, there are at least a few grains of truth in this label.

In contrast, the job enlargement approach to job design is predicated on the notion that jobs that are "enlarged" provide for greater levels of job satisfaction than jobs that are, so to speak "unenlarged." The central focus on job satisfaction as an objective in job design is generally justified on two grounds. First, it is argued that from the social point of view, the working life of workers should provide reasonable opportunity for people to gain at least some satisfaction from their work. Second, it is argued that people who achieve reasonable satisfaction in their jobs may also be better employees in terms of increased productivity, better quality of work, longer tenure, and the like.

Thus, these have been two somewhat opposing efforts over the past years, one tending toward job simplification, the other toward job enlargement, and both having some impact upon the nature of the jobs people perform. Although we have intentionally exaggerated the difference between these two approaches, the disparity between them does represent a dilemma for those who must make job design decisions. Before discussing some of the evidence and issues relating to this matter, we need to provide some background regarding human motivation and job satisfaction as these relate to the job enlargement movement.

Some Aspects of Motivation and Job Satisfaction

It is postulated that human behavior generally is directed toward the fulfillment of the needs that people have. To the extent that this is true, we can assume that the work behavior of people is influenced by their motivation to fulfill their needs. Although there are various theories about human motivation, we must guard against accepting any particular theory totally, since no single theory has been demonstrated to be universally suitable to explain the basis for why people behave as they do. However, we should be familiar with at least certain theories since each one may have at least some relevance to work behavior and therefore to our interest in job design.

Hierarchy of Needs

One of the best-known theories of motivation is that of the hierarchy of needs, as postulated by Maslow. Fully recognizing the complexity of human motivation, Maslow makes the point that as one need becomes fulfilled another one takes its place, and suggests that this is a loosely organized hierarchy of needs. Starting with the lowest one, these needs are:

Physiological needs (need for food, shelter, etc.)
Safety needs (need for security and protection from danger and the natural elements)
Social needs (need for association with others, affection, etc.)
Ego needs (needs relating to self-esteem and recognition)
Self-fulfillment needs (need for achievement or realizing one's potential)

According to the theory, if a person's physiological needs are not fulfilled, these needs dominate all others. As those needs become fulfilled, the dominant need then becomes that for safety, and so on up the ladder. Although this formulation undoubtedly has some general applicability, there are wide individual differences in motivation that are not explained by the theory, and the hierarchy should in any event not be viewed as rigid. In fact, Maslow himself (1965) expresses serious qualms about the applicability of the theory to work behavior:

But I of all people should know how shaky this foundation is as a final foundation. My work on motivations comes from the clinic, from a study of neurotic people. . . . I would like to see a lot more studies of this kind before feeling finally convinced that this carryover from the study of neurosis to the study of labor in factories is legitimate.

Expectancy Theories

The central theme of expectancy theories was crystallized by Vroom as being based on the three concepts of valence, expectancy, and force. In discussing his theory let us start with a given situation in which there are alternative possible courses of action (such as working hard at one's job, "goofing off," or even taking the day off). Each such alternative has one or more possible outcomes associated with it. *Valence* refers to the value to the individual of each such outcome such as the value of a raise, or of the enjoyment of a game of golf (if the person takes the day off). *Expectancy* is essentially the person's estimate of the probabilities, or odds, of any given outcome taking place (such as the judged probability of a raise, or that of being asked by one's spouse to mow the lawn). And *force* is the result of adding up the combinations of valences and expectancies associated with the various possible outcomes. Although a given outcome might have a high value, its judged expectancy (the probability) might be low, and its force might therefore be lower than that of an outcome with lower valence but a high expectancy. According to the theory, the person would choose the course of action associated with the outcome with the greatest force.

Expectancy theories are also referred to as *instrumentality theories* (since a course of action can be instrumental in bringing about an outcome), and as *VIE theories* (valence-instrumentability-expectancy). There have been variations and elaborations on the central theme of these theories, but we need not go into them here.

Herzberg's Two-factor Theory of Job Satisfaction

Of the various theories relating to job satisfaction, Herzberg's has stirred up more dust than any other. On the basis of his research he postulates the notion that job satisfaction and job dissatisfaction are not opposite ends of the same stick, but rather are separate factors. He argues that positive job satisfaction can be experienced by workers only when certain motivator features of the job exist, features which are *intrinsic* to the job (that is, are part of the job *content*), such as a sense of achievement, recognition for good performance, the nature of the work itself, responsibility, and opportunity for advancement. On the other hand, he believes that dissatisfaction is experienced when certain *hygiene* features of the job are inadequate. These are features *extrinsic* to the job (that is, are part of the job *context* or work situation), such as the working conditions, company policy, the technical supervision received, interpersonal relations with peers and supervisors, and so forth. His theory holds that if these hygiene features are inadequate, the worker experiences dissatisfaction; if they are adequate, however, the worker presumably avoids dissatisfaction but does not achieve position job satisfaction. Job satisfaction could be brought about only by the presence of the motivator features of the job.

This theory has led Herzberg to become a strong supporter of job design. In this regard, however, he differentiates between what he refers to as *horizontal* and *vertical loading* of jobs. Horizontal loading consists in increasing the variety or diversity of job activities (or tasks); these additional activities are of the same general type as the already existing activities of the job. On the other hand, what he calls vertical loading consists of such changes as increasing the level of responsibility, challenge, and meaningfulness of the job, providing for greater self-fulfillment, and the like; these changes are primarily motivator features. Herzberg argues very strongly for vertical loading of jobs (which is consistent with his emphasis on motivator features), and uses the term *job enrichment* to reflect this emphasis. (He disdains the term *job enlargement,* arguing that horizontal loading cannot contribute to positive job satisfaction.)

It should be added that his theory has generated much criticism, with the result that at least some professionals and practitioners have adopted opposing views regarding the theory. The writer views the theory as being overly simplistic and lacking in broad applicability, although it may have relevance in some specific circumstances. Regardless of one's views about the theory, however, it has had the salutary effect of crystallizing the distinctions between intrinsic job characteristics (those associated with the job content) and extrinsic characteristics (those associated with the job context or working situation).

Discussion

The traditional assumption regarding the relationship between job satisfaction and job performance has been that job satisfaction brings about effective job performance, referred to as a *happiness* orientation. According to Porter and Lawler, this is putting the satisfaction cart before the performance horse. They argue that job satisfaction should be viewed as something that results from effective job performance rather than being the cause of effective job performance. This point of view (*performance* orientation) would depend upon the availability of adequate rewards for effective performance, such as pay, recognition, esteem, and opportunity for growth.

The various theories and views about human work motivation leave one slightly confused and uneasy. Although one might not take the extreme view expressed by Imberman that "all the theories about motivation are full of metaphysical flummery," one hopes that there might be some well-confirmed theoretical formulation for designing jobs that would be optimum in terms of motivating people in their work.

One approach to such a formulation, set forth by Lawler, was predicated on expectancy theory as discussed above. He expresses the view that an employee's motivation to perform effectively is determined by two variables. The first of these is the concept of an effort-reward probability, that is, the individual's subjective probability that directing a given amount of effort toward performing effectively will result in his obtaining a known reward or positively valued outcome. (This probability, in turn, is based on the subjective probability that the expenditure of a given effort would result in an expected level of performance, and the probability that such performance would result in the desired reward.)

The second variable is the concept of reward value or valence as discussed above. For any given possible reward (outcome), value (valence) and the effort-reward probability combine multiplicatively to determine an individual's motivation (force) toward that reward. Considering the rewards associated with the various alternative courses of action, the individual is expected to choose the course of action whose expected reward has the highest motivational level.

A critical feature of Lawler's formulation from this point on relates to the nature of the rewards that may be considered of value by individuals. He emphasizes the opinion that intrinsic rewards (those associated with job content) are generally more potent than extrinsic rewards (those that are part of the job context or situation and are given by others). It therefore follows that if the probability of possible intrinsic rewards is judged to be high, workers would tend to put forth more effort in order to perform more effectively, which in sequence would tend to bring forth the expected rewards.

This emphasis on intrinsic rewards is of course reminiscent of

Herzberg's motivator (intrinsic or job content) features of jobs, which he claims serve as more important sources of job satisfaction then do the hygiene (extrinsic) features of jobs. In turn, the intrinsic features of jobs generally are more strongly associated with the so-called higher level needs (such as the ego and self-fulfillment needs) than the extrinsic features of jobs (which tend more to be associated with the lower level needs (such as the physiological and safety needs).

In reflecting about Lawler's explanation, there is probably at least reasonable support for the notion that work behavior is in part triggered by the expectation of possible outcomes of the work (including recognition, achievement, pay, as well as other outcomes), over and beyond whatever potential satisfaction there may be from the work itself.

Collectively, the various theories and speculations about motivation as related to work performance seem to argue for the design of jobs that have the potential for intrinsic motivation. Such an objective in job design is, of course, the basis of the job enlargement approach. Despite the logic of such an objective, however, we should guard against the temptation to assume that job enlargement is *the* solution to problems of poor motivation, job dissatisfaction, and ineffective job performance. Clearly, job enlargement has an important role in this regard, but we must recognize that there are no work motivational principles with universal applicability to the design of jobs. Individual differences in the values and needs of people make generalizations extremely treacherous. One person's meat is another person's poison.

The Pros and Cons of Job Enlargement

Having touched briefly on the admittedly thorny topic of motivation, let us take an overview of the pros and cons of job enlargement, including a review of some of the opinions and research evidence relating to it.

Definition of Job Enlargement

In discussing job enlargement, we should recognize that the terms *job enlargement* and *job enrichment* have been used as an umbrella for a wide variety of practices, actions, and policies that are related to human work and that have been adopted as strategies for enhancing worker motivation. These strategies include modifying jobs in such ways as having the worker determine his own work pace, set his own hours of work, serve as his own inspector and correct his own mistakes, make setup and repairs, and adopt his own methods of work; adding more, and more varied, job activities; increasing the scope of the job so that the worker can follow through a complete job process from beginning to end; providing greater autonomy or control (and less supervision) over a worker's job; assigning total responsibility for a particular operation to a work group who collectively make decisions about the operation; providing for greater worker autonomy and more democracy in the work place; providing appropriate work incentives and feedback to workers' job rotation; and improving communication channels. Some of these strategies represent management and supervisory practices (such as the setting of work schedules or establishing incentive systems). Others deal more directly with the nature of the jobs to be performed (such as adding responsibility for setup and repairs to equipment, or for quality control).

For our purposes, we will consider job enlargement in the second, narrower sense as applying to the modification of the activities and responsibilities of jobs, that is, to the modification of the nature of jobs themselves. We will also consider job enlargement to include both vertical and horizontal loading of jobs. (Good management and supervisory practices and strategies are, of course, important aspects of any work situation for enhancing worker satisfaction and efficient worker performance.)

Research Evidence about Job Enlargement

Katzell et al. point out that research studies dealing with job enlargement generally fall into two classes. In the first class are the *intervention* studies, which are experimental studies in which jobs are actually changed (enlarged) and in which the effects of the change are studied (such as the effects on job satisfaction or work performance) usually on a before-and-after basis. In the second class are the correlational studies, in which already existing jobs are investigated and analyses are made of the relationship between certain jobs or job characteristics on the one hand, and such criteria as job satisfaction, attitudes or opinions, or work performance of the job incumbents on the other hand.

Over the years many studies of job enlargement have been reported, studies of both an intervention and a correlational nature. A reading of these studies leaves one with a sense of the ambiguity of their collective import. However, Katzell et al. have carried out an intensive analysis of most such studies in order to summarize in some quantitative fashion their results. They first set forth certain guidelines for evaluating the individual studies in terms of the research and statistical methodologies used. Of the several dozen studies reviewed, not a single study fulfilled all the guidelines, and only 14 met a fairly modest set of guideline requirements. Of these, five were correlational studies and nine were intervention studies.

The summary of these 14 studies categorized the findings of each study according to these criteria: better attitudes (motivation and/or job satisfaction); better productivity; and less withdrawal (absenteeism, turnover, etc.). The results for each study, summarized below, were categorized by criterion and by whether they supported or failed to support the hypothesized criterion effects (note that the better productivity finding applied to only 12 of the 14 studies, and the withdrawal finding applied to only 6.)

Criterion	Supporting	Failing to Support	Total
Better attitudes	10	4	14
Better productivity	8	4	12
Less withdrawal	6	0	6

Clearly, the results of the studies represent something of a mixed bag. In any event, although the number of supporting studies was greater than the number of studies failing to support, there were a few studies whose results were not positive. The overall results as expressed by Katzell et al. are summarized below:

Most of the studies indicated that workers in expanded jobs had higher job satisfaction or job attitudes that were otherwise more favorable than in the case of more restricted jobs.

In about half the studies, aspects of productivity were found to be better, in addition to better attitudes. In six of the studies where job satisfaction was higher, manifestations of withdrawal (turnover or absenteeism) were typically less frequent.

In three instances, job redesign failed, on balance, to significantly improve either job attitudes or performance; admittedly, the job changes in these cases were relatively trivial.

In the studies in which there was the clearest support for the effects of job enlargement in terms of improved attitudes and performance, there had been extensive and pervasive changes in the jobs themselves, and also greater authority and responsibility for the workers.

Not all workers are equally responsive to job enlargement. Enlarged jobs seem to have more favorable effects on workers whose bread-and-butter needs for security have been met, those who have stronger needs for self-expression and growth; those who are younger; those coming from nonurban and work-oriented culture patterns; and those in higher-level jobs. Conversely, job enlargement tends to have negligible or even adverse effects in the case of some blue collar, lower-level jobs.

The most consistent evidence that the scope of job content reacts to worker motivation, job satisfaction, and job performance comes from correlation studies of workers whose jobs already differ in scope, thus possibly implicating other contaminating causes such as pay level, worker values, and technology. Interventional efforts to redesign jobs have not produced results that are generally persuasive, although there are tantalizing bits of evidence to suggest the potential value of such an approach to both the quality of working life and economic performance.

On the basis of other reviews of job enlargement research, Hulin (1968) and Hulin and Blood (1968) conclude that the research evidence does not support the hypothesis that either job size or job level is positively correlated in *general* with job satisfaction. On the basis of their reviews they conclude that the positive relationship between job size and job satisfaction cannot be assumed to be general, but rather depends to a great extent on the backgrounds of the workers in question. It should be added, however, that questions have been raised about the extent to which this relationship depends upon the backgrounds of the workers in question (Stone and Porter).

The research evidence certainly indicates not only that job characteristics have much to do with job satisfaction on the part of job incumbents, but also that job satisfaction is in part a function of the individuals in question. Some further information on the relevance of both job and personal (that is, individual) factors comes from a study by Calitz et al. In this study, 407 employees on 29 jobs in two telephone companies completed a job satisfaction questionnaire, the Job Description Index (JDI) (created by Smith et al., 1969), which measures satisfaction with work, as well as other aspects of people's jobs. In addition they completed the Job Activity Preference Questionnaire (JAPQ)* and certain other question-

---

*Copyright 1972 by R. C. Mecham, A. F. Harris, E. J. McCormick, and P. R. Jeanneret. PAQ Services, Inc., P. O. Box 3337, Logan, Utah 89321.

naires. The JAPQ measures the interests of individuals in terms of the job elements of the Position Analysis Questionnaire (PAQ), and can be scored in terms of the same job dimensions as those for which jobs are scored. Thus it is possible to match the interests of individuals with job dimensions of the PAQ.

In the Calitz study the following variables were correlated with the satisfaction with work (as measured by the Job Description Index): the PAQ job dimension scores of the jobs of the individuals; the interests of individuals as measured by the JAPQ job dimensions; and the degree of match between the PAQ and JAPQ scores (a measure of the degree to which each person's interests matched their job. The resulting correlations are given below:

Variable	Correlation with Job Satisfaction
PAQ	.61
JAPQ	.35
Degree of match	.15

These results show that certain combinations of job characteristics were indeed rather strongly related to job satisfaction (correlation .61). But we also see that the interests of people were moderately related to job satisfaction (correlation .35). However, it is significant to note that the direct correlation of a combination of interest dimensions was higher (.35) than that of the match between interests and job characteristics (.15). The most reasonable interpretation of this is that some people *generally* have more positive interests in job-related activities than other people. In other words, some people have a stronger disposition toward work activities *in general* than do other persons. And this frame of reference, or degree of predisposition toward work activities (positive or negative as the case may be) is in turn reflected somewhat in their expressed job satisfaction. (For persons with a negative predisposition toward, or interest in, job-related activities, it is probably doubtful if any but a very few jobs could make them happy in their work.)

Thus, we probably can expect appropriate job design to tend to enhance the work satisfaction of many if not most people, but not of all people in the work force.

Opinions About Job Enlargement

On the opinion side of the coin, there are those who view job enlargement as the panacea for all the ailments of human work, and—to exaggerate a bit—imply that if all jobs were to be enlarged, everyone would be happy in their work. This point of view is very strongly set forth in the book *Work in America* and is promoted by Herzberg as well as others.

On the other hand, there are those who take a somewhat more jaundiced view of this effort. For example, MacKinney et al. state: "The fact of individual differences . . . is a central factor of life in the behavioral sciences, and yet would-be reformers apparently believe that all people must react in exactly the same way to the same job. The observer says to himself, 'that job would drive me nuts in half an hour.' From this he somehow concludes that it must drive everyone else nuts as well. This simply is not so! (For that matter, it's highly probable that many of the workers interviewed by sympathetic social scientists privately regarded their questioner's activities as a pretty terrible way to earn a living too.)"

In connection with the reactions of people to job enlargement, Katzell et al. asked union members and members of management to indicate their judgments about various factors that might influence organizational productivity and employee attitudes and motivation. Following are their responses as related to job redesign and enlargement.

Statement	Union	Management
"Very important" to productivity	13%	12%
"Very useful" for improving attitudes and motivation	23	16

These responses seem strangely at odds with responses of the same individuals to a few specific related questions, as given below:

	Percent Who Said "Strongly Agree" or "Agree"	
Statement	Union	Management
Job enrichment is a promising strategy for improving productivity	78%	75%
Workers who have experienced job enrichment almost invariably indicate greater satisfaction with their work	74	73

Note that responses to the second statement were based on how the respondents felt *other* people would react, and were not their own reactions to enlarged jobs.

Discussion

The varying opinions and reactions of people to the potential effects of job enlargement, plus the somewhat ambivalent results of some of the job enlargement studies, seem to support a couple of inferences about job enlargement. In the first place, it is probably safe to say that, by and large, job enlargement should be viewed as falling on the positive side of the ledger—that the pros tend to be stronger than the cons. But granting this generalization, it also is rather obvious that job enlargement probably should not be viewed as a universal panacea for improving employee motivation and job satisfaction and bringing about better job performance, because of individual differences in motivation, values, and interests. In this regard, the writer has been very much disturbed by the tendency on the part of some individuals to attribute subjective values to jobs when in fact they are the attributes of the people on the jobs. For example, there is a reference in *Work in America* to "dull, repetitive, seemingly meaningless tasks, offering no challenge or economy." There is no job or task that is intrinsically dull or meaningless or lacking in challenge. These are reactions of the individuals to their jobs, and are not attributes of the jobs themselves. Incidentally, there probably are the seeds of the self-fulfilling prophecy in describing jobs as "dull, meaningless, and boring." If we keep telling people that their jobs are dull, boring, and meaningless, there may be a tendency for them to believe us!

To the extent that jobs can be modified in the indicated directions, one would expect that enlarged jobs would make life more worthwhile (or less unworthwhile) for many—but not necessarily all—people, and that this heightened satisfaction might be accompanied by improved work performance. But job enlargement probably is not for everybody, because of individual differences.

Job Characteristics That Contribute to Job Satisfaction

If one is going to design, or redesign, jobs so that they are enlarged, it is reasonable to wonder what job characteristics would most likely contribute to job satisfaction on the part of most workers. (If one could identify such characteristics, it would then presumably be possible to design at least some jobs so they would have such features.)

General Job and Task Characteristics

In various job enlargement studies, the jobs in question have been described (usually with questionnaires completed by the job incumbents) in terms of various characteristics. By and large, these characteristics tend to be associated with job content rather than job context (or the work situation). Katzell et al. suggest that those interested in the effects of redesigning job content per se would do well to focus on such ingredients as the following:

Sufficient difficulty to be challenging.

Sufficient diversity to be interesting.

Constructive interaction with others.

A work cycle long enough so work is not repetitive or monotonous.

Sufficient identity or wholeness of the task to represent a meaningful share of the product or service.

Regular and frequent feedback concerning the consequences of one's work.

Considerable self-control over one's own work.

Direct responsibility for the welfare of others outside one's immediate work group, especially customers or clients—a concept sometimes termed "stewardship."

They make the observation that in combination these comprise what may be regarded as job level or scope.

Still other sets of characteristics have been proposed. Dominant among these are the five characteristics proposed by Hackman and Oldham that are measured by the Job Diagnostic Survey (JDS). These are:

1. *Skill variety.* The degree to which a job requires a variety of different activities in carrying out the work, which involve the use of a number of different skills and talents of the employee.
2. *Task identity.* The degree to which the job requires completion of a "whole" and identifiable piece of work—i.e., doing a job from beginning to end with a visible outcome.
3. *Task significance.* The degree to which the job has a substantial impact on the lives or work of other people—whether in the immediate organization or in the external environment.
4. *Autonomy.* The degree to which the job provides substantial freedom, independence, and discretion of the employee in scheduling the work and in determining the procedures to be used in carrying it out.
5. *Feedback from the job itself.* The degree to which carrying out the work activities required by the job results in the employee obtaining direct and clear information about the effectiveness of his or her performance.

The JDS is a questionnaire that usually is completed by workers in describing their own jobs or some jobs with which they are familiar. The various questions are scored in terms of the above dimensions.

Still another set that has been proposed is that used by Ford in his studies at AT&T:

1. *Module.* The extent to which an individual has a "natural area of responsibility" of his own, or a "thing of my own," or a "piece of turf."
2. *Control.* Decision making over, and opportunities for, the exercise of worker judgment over the work within the module.
3. *Feedback.* Feedback that emanates from the work itself, rather than from some second source in the work situation.
4. *Skill and learning.* The opportunity to grow in the job through the acquisition of new skills that contribute to effective performance in the job and that are transferable, in whole or in part, to a job at a higher level in the organization.

As indicated in the review by Pierce and Dunham various types of job characteristics have been proposed as the ones which would contribute to job satisfaction, or have been used in various job enlargement studies. In these various reports a number of the same job characteristics keep surfacing, as revealed by the above listings by Katzell, Hackman and Oldham, and Ford, although there are some unique ones in certain listings. However, by and large, they have a common denominator, namely, that they deal with job content more than with job context, or what Katzell refers to as job scope.

Discussion

Although there is a fair amount of similarity among the various sets of job characteristics that presumably contribute to job satisfaction (and that therefore might be incorporated in job enlargement programs), the fact still remains that no single combination of characteristics has been identified as *the* answer to this problem. To illustrate this lack of generality, Dunham et al. carried out an extensive statistical analysis of the responses of 5,945 individuals to the Job Diagnostic Survey (JDS). The JDS provides for individuals to report their perceptions of jobs in terms of 15 items which, in turn, are used in scoring jobs in terms of the five a priori characteristics mentioned earlier.) In the responses of each of 20 subgroups of the total sample Dunham et al. found that the responses to the individual items of people in the various groups indicated

that the perceptions of the subjects about their jobs did not necessarily form the same statistically identified factors or dimensions as
the five presumably measured by the JDS. In only 2 of the 20 samples did the responses reflect clearly the five hypothesized characteristics as representing the perceptions of the subjects of the dimensionality of their jobs. The factor analyses of the responses of
subjects in the other 18 samples indicated that people tend to think
of their jobs in terms of somewhat different dimensions. In some
instances those correspond with some (but not all) of the five original characteristics; in other instances they represent combinations
of the original dimension; and in still other instances they are
rather different from the original dimensions.

The various job characteristics that have been postulated as
being conducive to job satisfaction, and the results of studies dealing with them, add up to a fairly ambiguous and confusing picture,
and it must be granted that (in the words of many experimenters)
more research is needed to clarify the presently clouded picture.
However, as we blow some of the chaff away, there are probably
still enough kernels left to be able to conclude that, to a fairly substantial degree, jobs that are larger in scope (that is, in job content
characteristics) tend to be more satisfying to many people than jobs
that are more restricted in scope. (Having said that, we should also
point out that characteristics other than job scope might also be
contributing variables, such as pay, or job prestige.)

Approaches to Job Enlargement

Job enlargement of existing jobs should be considered only if there
are adequate reasons for it, and not simply because it is " the thing
to do." Ford makes the point that a "work-itself project" (his term
for job enlargement) should be undertaken only when the following conditions exist: (1) performance of a specified job can be better; (2) the motivation of the workers is in question; and (3) certain
procedures may correct the situation. He adds the particular point
that unless motivation is in question, there is no need for job re-
shaping. His own approach to job enlargement, as carried out in
AT&T, depends very heavily on workshops with supervisors for the
purpose of obtaining their commitment to, and ideas for, job restructuring. (Ford's book elaborates on the operation of these workshops.)

There are no magic formulas for enlarging jobs, partly because
the uniqueness of many job situations would require job-specific de-

sign adaptations. However, Ford has set forth a scheme for thinking about improving the work itself that may serve as a frame of
reference or backdrop for those embarking on a job enlargement
effort. This scheme is diagrammed in Figure 11–1. As an aid to
crystallizing this frame of reference, Ford suggests that the following questions be asked:

1. What does the supervisor now do for this person that he could do
   for himself once we are sure he is competent?
2. What steps that now precede his work should be *part* of his work
   if he is to have a meaningful module?
3. What steps that are now done after his work would make his
   module more meaningful and responsible?
4. What tasks should be pushed down to a job at a lower level of
   classification?
5. What could be automated completely?
6. Was there once a way of handling this work that was more meaningful or satisfying in some respect?
7. What do we let an employee do in an emergency or in the absence of his supervisor that he might be allowed to do all the
   time?
8. Can accounts or customers be divided into meaningful classes (all
   TV or radio accounts, all department stores, all hotels, and so on)
   so that an employee might be given responsibility for a certain
   type of customer? [Pertains specifically to AT&T jobs.]
9. Are there any verifiers or checkers who might be dropped?
10. What training could employees give each other? What specialized
    knowledge might they be encouraged to build up? What new
    things could they learn to do that someone else does now?

Two critical ingredients for job enlargement are, first, support
and commitment from top management on down the line; and second, ideas for redesign that could result in enhanced motivation
and job satisfaction. In addition, Katzell et al. emphasize a couple
of points that they consider to be important for an effective job enlargement program: the workers should be psychologically ready
for it (which is most likely to be the case with young, affluent, and
better educated workers); and the technology involved must lend itself to such change.

Some Guidelines for Job Design

Granting that there are no simple rules for job enlargement, Emery
and Thorsrud have set forth certain general principles that may
have some value for those who have the practical problem of job

Figure 11-1. Diagram of a scheme for thinking about improving the work itself. (Source: Ford, p. 157)

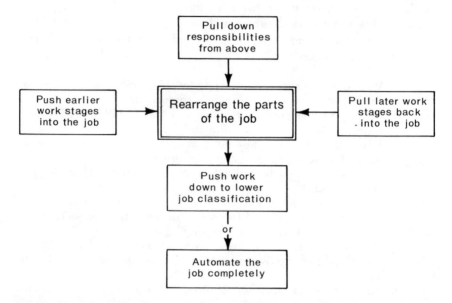

enlargement. These principles tend to focus on relatively specific actions that might be taken to enlarge jobs, and therefore they can perhaps serve to apply theoretical considerations to practical situations. These principles are:

(a) *Optimum variety of tasks within the job.* Too much variety can be inefficient for training and production as well as frustrating for the worker. However, too little can be conducive to boredom or fatigue. The optimum amount would be that which allows the operator to take a rest from the high level of attention or effort in a demanding activity while working at another and, conversely, allows him to stretch himself and his capacities after a period of routine activity.

(b) *A meaningful pattern of tasks that gives to each job the semblance of a single overall task.* The tasks should be such that, although involving different levels of attention, degrees of effort, or kinds of skill, they are interdependent. That is, carrying out one task makes it easier to get on with the next or gives a better end-result to the overall task. Given such a pattern, the worker can help to find a method of working suitable to his requirements and can more easily relate his job to those of others.

(c) *Optimum length of work cycle.* Too short a cycle means too much finishing and starting; too long a cycle makes it difficult to build up a rhythm of work.

(d) *Some scope for setting standards of quantity and quality of production and a suitable feedback of knowledge of results.* Minimum standards generally have to be set by management to determine whether a worker is sufficiently trained, skilled, or careful to hold the job. Workers are more likely to accept responsibility for higher standards if they have some freedom in setting them and are more likely to learn from the job if there is feedback. They can neither effectively set standards nor learn if there is not a quick enough feedback of knowledge of results.

(e) *The inclusion in the job of the auxiliary and preparatory tasks.* The worker cannot and will not accept responsibility for matters outside his control. In so far as the preceding criteria are met, the inclusion of such "boundary tasks" will extend the scope of the worker's responsibility for and involvement in the job.

(f) *The tasks included in the job should entail some degree of care, skill, knowledge, or effort that is worthy of respect in the community.*

(g) *The job should make some perceivable contribution to the utility of the product for the consumer.*

(h) *Provision for "interlocking" tasks, job rotation, or physical proximity where there is a necessary interdependence of jobs.* At a minimum this helps to sustain communication and to create mutual understanding between workers whose tasks are interdependent, and thus lessens friction, recriminations, and "scape-goating." At best this procedure will help to create work groups that enforce standards of cooperation and mutual help.

(i) *Provision for interlocking tasks, job rotation, or physical proximity where the individual jobs entail a relatively high degree of stress.*

(j) *Provision for interlocking tasks, job rotation, or physical proximity where the individual jobs do not make an obvious perceivable contribution to the utility of the end-product.*

(k) *Where a number of jobs are linked together by interlocking tasks or job rotation they should as a group:*
  (i) have some semblance of an overall task which makes a contribution to the utility of the product;
  (ii) have some scope for setting standards and receiving knowledge of results;
  (iii) have some control over the "boundary tasks."

(l) *Provision of channels of communication so that the minimum requirements of the workers can be fed into the design of new jobs at an early stage.*

(m) *Provision of channels of promotion to foreman rank, which are sanctioned by the workers.*

Examples of Job Enlargement Studies

There have been many studies dealing with job enlargement. It may be useful to describe a few of them very briefly by stating the nature of the changes made in the jobs in question. These cases do not necessarily represent ideal job enlargement cases, but rather are intended simply to illustrate some kinds of job changes that have been carried out. Other case studies are reported by Davis and Taylor and Davis and Cherns (1975).

□ Compilation of telephone directories at Indiana Bell Telephone Company (Ford). Individuals were given complete responsibility for performing 14 steps in the preparation of specific telephone directories (or sections of large directories).

□ Job "nesting" at Southwestern Bell Telephone Company (Ford). Various people involved in customer services (business office supervisors, service order reviewers, typists, and control center clerks) were formed into various groups. Each group was responsible for all types of service to customers in a specific geographical area. This system replaced specialized units that were organized by function and served all geographical areas.

□ Production teams of dogfood plant at General Foods (*National Observer*). Individuals were assigned to a team that is collectively responsible for virtually all aspects of production. Individuals learn all the jobs involved, and the team makes virtually all decisions regarding their activities.

□ Assembly of hotplates at Corning Glass Co. (*National Observer*). Assembly of hotplates changed from an assembly line (in which each person performed one step in the assembly) to a situation in which each person assembled the complete hotplate.

□ Assembly of radios at Philips Telecommunication of Australia, Ltd. (*Personnel Practices Bulletin*). Women who originally worked on the assembly line were given responsibility for the total assembly, from individual components to the final product.

□ Press setup and operation at R.G.T. Metal Parts Factory, Eindhoven (de Ligny). Originally, operators of automatic presses which stamped or pierced a large number of metal parts worked on only one machine, each of which was set up by specialized setters. The job redesign consisted in combining the operation and setup into the same job, with each person learning to set up and operate all machines.

□ Automobile assembly at Volvo assembly plant, Skoevde, Sweden (Karlsson). Production organization of automobile assemblies is based on autonomous groups, with provision for individuals to change their work places several times during the work shift (from simple assembly to inspection), and with group responsibility for inspection and materials handling.

□ Injection molding, fabricated plastics products (Miller). The original operator job was enlarged to include tending, finishing, and inspection tasks.

□ Distribution jobs at a chemicals company (Davis and Werling). The seven previously specialized jobs involved in the packaging and distribution of various chemical products were consolidated into two enlarged jobs, one for dry packaging to load dry products into containers, and the other for liquid-bulk loading to fill tank cars, gas cylinders, etc.

□ Maintenance jobs in a chemicals company (Davis and Werling). The job of maintenance repairman was enlarged to include general welding, layout and fabrication, pipe fitting, boiler making, equipment installation, and dynamic machine repair.

□ Bagmaking jobs (Davis and Cherns). Operators of bagmaking machines were given responsibility for quality checking (including authority to reject defective rolls of material and to discard bags that did not meet quality standards) for packing bags.

□ Technical representative job for office equipment (Davis and Cherns). Technical representatives in branch offices were given 14 additional responsibilities, such as: authority to utilize branch technical specialists and other personnel in management of their territory; authority to determine their own work hours; responsibility for determining need for overtime expenditures; involvement in screening and interviewing applicants for job of technical representative; some responsibility for training new technical representatives; and full responsibility for upkeep expenditures on assigned company car.

□ Keypunch operator (Davis and Cherns). Operators were given authority to schedule their own daily activities to meet delivery dates on both routine and special jobs, to correct obvious errors in data to be punched, and in some cases to send their own work to the computer room without verification.

Back to the Job Specialization Versus Enlargement Issue

Now that we have discussed the matter of job enlargement, let us return to a job design issue that was mentioned early in this chapter, the question of job specialization versus job enlargement. As indicated in that discussion, methods analysis and human factors approaches to job design by and large have tended to result in jobs that are more specialized, whereas job enlargement approaches have tended in the opposite direction. Thus, there may be something of a dilemma as to which way to jump in making such decisions.

Although there is no obvious, clear-cut resolution for this dilemma, there are two or three points that have some bearing on this matter. In the first place, as Ford points out, the simplification of jobs may lead to their complete automation, thereby eliminating the original job. In many circumstances, however, complete automation may not be technically feasible or economically practicable.

In addressing himself to this general problem, Davis (1961) points out that approaches to job design may be classified as (1) process-centered (or equipment-centered), which is the same as the methods analysis and human factors approach; (2) worker-centered, which is the job enlargement approach; and (3) the combination of these two. He goes on to say that the first two approaches are not really as incompatible as they might initially appear to be, and thus proposes the third approach, a combination of the two. He indicates that operations planning usually takes place at two levels, namely, *task design* (to accomplish elements of operations), and *task combination* (in which tasks are combined into jobs). In many circumstances, one could take a process-centered approach in *designing* tasks, and a worker-centered approach in *combining* tasks into jobs. It is primarily in the combining aspect that considerations of job motivation and satisfaction could be taken into account. To the extent that Davis's combined approach is feasible, one can then have his cake and eat it, too.

There are two dangling questions about such an approach. First, to what extent is it practical to take a process-centered approach in task design and a worker-centered approach in combining tasks into jobs? (The process-centered approach would involve taking advantage of available technology and of the potential contributions of methods analysis and human factors in equipment design. And the worker-centered approach would involve the combining of tasks into jobs in such a fashion as to achieve the objectives of job enlargement.) Although some of the experiments in job enlargement have indicated that the enlargement has resulted in improved work performance and improved job satisfaction, these results have by no means been universal. We probably do not yet have a good handle on the question of the extent to which both objectives can be achieved through appropriate job design.

The second question is, to what extent can those involved in the various aspects of job design be expected to pool their efforts toward creating jobs that might fulfill these two objectives? There are no hard answers available to this question, either. However, there are a few straws in the wind to suggest that at least some people are starting to worry about this. There are, first, the ardent proponents of job enlargement; although their primary focus is on motivation and job satisfaction they are also concerned with the possible enhancement of job performance from job enlargement. In addition, the industrial engineering profession (which has of course traditionally been involved in methods analysis and job simplification) has become increasingly concerned about the human aspects of work, including the possible use of job enlargement; at least a number of industrial engineers have been actively involved in job enlargement research and application. Further, some of the people interested in human factors as applied to the design of equipment and systems have in recent years also become more aware of the human implications of equipment design in terms of the motivation and satisfaction of the people who might use whatever they design. For example, Christensen, Chapanis, and McCormick have addressed themselves to this matter. A joint meeting of the International Ergonomics Association and the Ergonomics Society held in 1977 was devoted entirely to the subject of job satisfaction. As another indication of the shift in the wind, the International Organization for Standardization (ISO) has developed a draft of a set of proposed standards dealing with work systems from the ergonomic (that is, human factors) point of view that in part deals with the workers' control over the work process. The relevant section of the draft proposal is given here:

4.3 Design of the Work Process

The design of the work process shall safeguard the workers' wellbeing, health, safety, and performance, in particular by avoiding overloading and underloading.

Overloading and underloading will result from transgressing, respectively, the upper or lower limits of the operational range of physiological and/or psychological functions, for example:

Physical or psycho-sensory overloading produces fatigue.

Conversely, underloading or work sensed as monotonous diminishes vigilance.

The physical and psychological stresses exerted depend not only on factors considered in sections 4.1 and 4.2 but also on the content and repetitiveness of operations and on the workers' control over the work process.

Among the measures susceptible of influencing these characteristics of the work process, the following may be cited:

a. Having one operator perform several, successive operations belonging to the same work function, instead of having several operators (job enlargement).

b. Having one operator perform successive operations belonging to different work functions, instead of having several operators.

For instance, assembly operations followed by quality checks performed by the operator himself who also removes defects (job enrichment).

c. Change of activity as, for instance, voluntary job rotation among workers on an assembly line or in a team working within an autonomous group.

d. Breaks, organized or nonorganized.

In implementing the above measures, particular attention should be paid to the following:

e. Variations in vigilance and work capacity over day and night.

f. Variations in work capacity among operators.

g. Individual development.

These events seem to be at least the seeds of the integration to which Davis referred. Hopefully, in the not too distant future, increased attention will be devoted to the design of human work that on a broad scale would fulfill the two objectives of effective performance and improved quality of working life for those engaged in the production of our goods and services.

Special Aspects of Job Design

The traditional approaches of methods analysts to do job design were discussed briefly in Chapter 5, and are treated in various industrial engineering texts, and will not be covered in this text.* In addition, there are various sources of information relating to human factors that can provide guidance in the design of the physical equipment and facilities that people use in their jobs, and that can influence the nature of the jobs in question.†

Since it is not practical to reproduce here the substantial sources of material dealing with job design that are covered by industrial engineering and human factors texts and handbooks, we will here only touch on certain special aspects of job design. In particular, we will include reference to job restructuring and to job design for certain special groups of individuals.

*The reader is referred to Maynard, H. B. (ed.). *Industrial Engineering Handbook* (2nd ed.), New York: McGraw-Hill, 1963; Nadler, G. *Work Design*, Homewood, Ill.: Richard D. Irwin, 1963.

†The reader is referred to McCormick, E. J. *Human Factors in Engineering and Design* (4th ed.). New York: McGraw-Hill, 1976; Van Cott, H. P., and Kinkade, R. G. *Human Engineering Guide to Equipment Design* (rev. ed.). Washington, D.C.: U.S. Government Printing Office, 1972; and Woodson, W. E., and Conover, D. W. *Human Engineering Guide for Equipment Designers* (2nd ed.). Berkeley: University of California Press, 1964.

Job Restructuring

The restructuring of existing jobs may be desirable for any of various reasons, such as to take advantage of technological changes, to deal with difficulties in filling vacant positions, to create jobs that are more suitable for available personnel, to create enlarged jobs, and the like. It has been suggested that the immediate benefits of job restructuring are twofold *(A Handbook for Job Restructuring):*

> It frees experienced personnel to spend more time performing higher level tasks, and creates lower level jobs that can be filled by inexperienced persons or workers who now lack the ability to perform higher level tasks. A significant result is new employment opportunities for disadvantaged persons.

The Manpower Administration of the U.S. Department of Labor has prepared a handbook for use in the restructuring of jobs. Although this was prepared primarily for use by analysts of public employment services who might be working with organizations in job restructuring programs, the handbook should still be applicable for use by personnel within an organization that itself is interested in such a program. The procedures set forth in *A Handbook for Job Restructuring* are given below. These procedures refer to rating scales that are used by the United States Employment Service, most of which are given in Appendix B of this book.

Procedures for Job Restructuring

Job analysis as the basis of job restructuring should provide a more realistic and effective result in the job structure of an organization.

Objective information about the jobs to be restructured can be obtained in several ways — by observing the work situation; by interviewing workers, supervisors, and personnel specialists; or by referring to prepared company job descriptions or previously prepared job analysis materials. However, the most complete information can be obtained through a combination of the observation and the interview methods. The information gained during interviews should include estimates of the time spent on each task for use in step 3.

Step 1. Determine the relationship of the job(s) to the system of which they are a part. The first step in job restructuring is to determine exactly what the jobs and their limits are — where the jobs begin and where they end. For this purpose, the analyst should review the staffing schedule he has prepared. Once he has identified the jobs to be studied, he should proceed to analyze each in accordance with the remaining steps of this procedure.

Step 2. Describe in detail the tasks that comprise each job. Record them on worksheet. The effectiveness of restructuring may depend upon the analyst's ability to recognize the component tasks that comprise each of the jobs in the system.

The tasks should be recorded in outline form on the worksheet. [See Fig. 11–2.] A terse, direct writing style is preferable. If possible, each sentence should begin with an action verb and should be written in the present tense. Adjectives that reflect subjective judgment of the analyst should be avoided.

The tasks that comprise each job should be listed together on a separate worksheet. This will result in listings of tasks within the existing boundaries of the job at the time of the analysis.

Tasks should be listed, when possible, according to the sequence of operations to facilitate the subsequent grouping process. Note that process flow or plant layout may dictate a fixed sequence for certain tasks; such factors should be noted beside the affected tasks to prevent a meaningless grouping of tasks.

Step 3. Estimate the time required to perform each task during the average workday. Record the estimate on worksheet. During the task analysis the analyst determines the amount of time the worker spends in the performance of each task during the average workday. Estimates made by consulting either the worker whose job is being observed or the worker's supervisor usually will be sufficiently accurate for planning job restructuring.

Step 4. Rate each task in relation to worker functions. Record ratings on worksheet. Each task can be evaluated and rated in terms of how the worker functions in relation to data, people, and things. These relationships are defined in three worker function hierarchies. . . . Each task should be assigned the worker function in each hierarchy that most closely describes the activities listed in the task description. The result will be a three-part rating, expressing the estimated functional level of the task, such as the following:

DATA: Comparing (6)
PEOPLE: Speaking-signaling (6)
THINGS: Feeding-offbearing (6)

This functional level would be expressed on the worksheet as 666.

Step 5. Rate each task in terms of general educational development (GED). Record ratings on worksheet. Determine the level of GED required for a worker to acquire the background knowledge needed and follow the instructions for performing his job in a specific situation. Evaluate each task in terms of the three categories of the GED scale—reasoning, mathematical, and language development. . . . After determining the level required in each category, select the highest of these to express the GED rating for the task. Record the number of the selected level on the worksheet.

Figure 11-2. Worksheet for job restructuring used by the U.S. Department of Labor. (Source: *A Handbook for Job Restructuring*, p. 15)

JOB RESTRUCTURING WORKSHEET

Establishment Job Title_____ No. Employed_____ DOT Title and Code___ Date____

Department _____ Supervisor_____ Title _____ Analyst_____

Task Description	Time	Functions			GED	Important Aptitudes	Other Pertinent Worker Traits	Comments
		D	P	T				

Step 6. Rate each task in relation to important aptitudes. Record ratings on worksheet. Consider each task in relation to each of the 11 aptitudes [these are the aptitudes used by the U.S. Employment Service]. Decide which of these aptitudes are important to the performance of the task and estimate the level of the aptitude required for satisfactory (average) performance, according to criteria given. Record important aptitudes and their respective ratings on the worksheet.

Step 7. Evaluate each task in relation to other important worker traits and record ratings on worksheet. Although this method uses the concepts of worker functions, GED, and aptitudes as primary considerations in separating and grouping job tasks, other worker traits are sometimes important. For example, when restructuring to develop jobs for physically handicapped, physical demands and environmental conditions are basic considerations. When restructuring is for the mentally retarded or emotionally disturbed, temperaments are frequently pertinent, as they relate to the responsibilities placed on the worker and the interpersonal relationships in the work situation. . . . The analyst should be familiar with interests, temperaments, physical demands, and environmental conditions so that he can recognize the pertinency of these traits to specific tasks. Record pertinent factors on the worksheet.

Step 8. Group tasks according to worker functions, GED, aptitudes, and other pertinent worker traits. Consider worker function, GED, and aptitude ratings that have been assigned to the tasks, to determine where enough similarity exists to permit grouping of tasks on these bases. Specifically, those tasks that have been rated for similar or closely related levels of worker functions and, correspondingly, similar or closely related levels of GED and important aptitudes should be tentatively grouped for further inspection according to additional criteria. [See Fig. 11–2.]

Step 9. Record groupings of tasks on worksheets. Copy onto separate worksheets those tasks that seem most suitable for grouping into jobs according to the considerations listed in step 8. Each group should be on a separate worksheet.

Step 10. Evaluate groups by kind of work performed or technology. Determine if tasks grouped together involve the same or related technologies. It would be difficult to keep all jobs pure according to the type of work performed, but jobs should contain tasks as similar or related in this respect as possible.

Step 11. Review process flow, establishment layout, and machinery and equipment to determine if tentative groups are feasible. Review the process flow, establishment layout, and availability of machinery and equipment to determine if the tasks being considered for grouping can be performed without interrupting the sequence of operations. Adjust or rearrange tasks, if possible, to accomplish this purpose.

Step 12. Consider career lattice possibilities. Review the ratings of the tasks within the groups being considered as possible jobs to determine if these jobs would relate to each other and to other jobs in the establishment to permit the development of meaningful career lattices. Workers should be able to begin on less complex jobs and become qualified for promotion to more complex ones through work experience, on-the-job training, and/or classroom training. Promotional opportunities provided in the original job structure of the establishment should be considered in restructuring. They can be evaluated by studying the organization chart and staffing schedule and by discussing them with establishment officials.

Step 13. Determine if cumulative totals of estimates of workday time for tasks in tentative groups will justify full-time jobs. Determine if the cumulative totals of estimates of workday time for the tasks considered for grouping will justify full-time jobs. Remember that the number of persons performing the tasks in the original job can affect total time required. The employer may desire an increase or decrease in the amount of time spent on certain tasks in the restructured situation. If so, the analyst should determine the feasibility of doing this.

Step 14. Evaluate and adjust groups until most feasible and practical arrangements of tasks are developed. (1) If there are too many tasks for a job in one group, experiment with transferring tasks to another group. (2) Consider adding tasks at similar or related levels if there are not enough tasks in a group to form a meaningful job. (c) Consider increasing the time spent on certain tasks if it appears practical. (d) Review the ratings of the tasks within each group and determine how each group would be rated if considered as a job. This will help determine whether the proposed job is in keeping with the specific purpose(s) of restructuring and evaluate its position in the system of jobs being analyzed.

Step 15. Prepare detailed job descriptions. After all adjustments have been made in the groupings of tasks for restructured jobs, prepare final, detailed job descriptions. In addition to copying all tasks from the restructuring worksheet, the analyst may need to add transitional statements to make the descriptions read smoothly. These detailed job descriptions will be used by the employer in implementing the restructured job program.

Step 16. Prepare career lattices. Prepare charts to indicate the relationships among jobs in the establishment. These charts should indicate vertical, horizontal, and diagonal mobility among jobs (career lattices).

Step 17. Follow up after implementation of the job restructuring activity. The restructured jobs should be evaluated approximately 3 months after they have been implemented by the employer. This period should provide ample time for any problems that may arise to become evident. At this time changes should be made to correct such problems. It is assumed that the employer will correct obvious deficiencies as they appear while implementing the program, but a follow-up evaluation of the entire program will insure that corrective action is taken and, possibly, will help prevent any future problems.

Job Design for Special Groups

In the design (or redesign) of jobs there frequently are special groups of workers for whom special consideration needs to be given. Two such groups are those with handicaps of one sort or another and the aged. Although it is not feasible here to deal with the many individual job design considerations that would be relevant for such groups, a few examples will at least serve to illustrate the importance of giving special attention to such groups.

For persons who perform physical tasks, and especially persons with certain physical handicaps, the biomechanical features of the work space and of the work methods can influence—for better or for worse—the physical well-being of workers and the effectiveness with which workers perform their tasks. Biomechanics is the study of the living body as a structure, with particular reference to the anatomical functions of the body and body members. A thorough discussion of this is presented by Tichauer. As an example, Tichauer refers to the matter of posture in typing, which may be a particular problem with people who have arthritis of the spine. The posture of a typist can be affected not only by the design of the seat and physical location of the typewriter, but by the illumination that is provided. If the illumination requires a person to bend over a bit to see the paper in the typewriter, greater strain may be placed upon certain vertebrae, thereby aggravating any arthritic condition that may exist; and even with normal people this may cause physical strain and discomfort.

As for older persons, it is a well-documented fact that certain functions tend to go downhill with age. In his discussion of the effects of aging on the ability of persons to carry on work activities, Griew has prepared a list of job features that call for special attention. It is obvious that the kinds of items he lists for older workers are applicable to younger workers as well. Griew's list is:

A. THE WORKING ENVIRONMENT
1. Excessive heat or humidity.
2. Atmospheric pollution.
3. Inadequate lighting; source of glare.
4. Excessive noise.

B. THE DESIGN AND LAYOUT OF EQUIPMENT AND THE WORK PLACE
1. Design features causing prolonged stooping, bending, stretching, etc.
2. Weight of tool or part of body supported by operator without aid.
3. Close visual, or intense auditory activity.
4. Fine discriminatory activity.
5. Complex, ambiguous or "unnatural" informational displays.
6. Narrow tolerances of accuracy.
7. Hazards likely to cause tripping, stumbling, etc.

C. THE ORGANIZATION OF WORK
1. Speed of work not under operator's own control (pacing).
2. Short-term memory requirement.
3. Short bursts of extremely heavy work.
4. Continuous, heavy work.
5. Low distribution of rest-pauses.

D. COMBINATIONS OF FEATURES WHICH APPEAR TO CALL FOR REDESIGN
1. Continuous, heavy work in hot environments.
2. Close visual work or work requiring fine discriminations in badly lighted work places or in presence of glare.
3. Continuous, heavy work of a paced variety.
4. Complex informational displays which have to be read at speeds outside the operator's own control.
5. High levels of accuracy which have to be maintained during paced work.
6. Responding to auditory instructions or signals in excessively noisy conditions.

Discussion

It has not been the intent of this discourse on job design in this chapter to serve as a how-to-do-it book. Rather, it has been the intent to bring attention to some of the problems and issues relating to job design, and in some instances to bring in brief overviews of relevant research along with the opinions of at least a few individuals. The lack of pat answers to the problems of job design is admittedly unsatisfying. However, there seems to have emerged during the past couple of decades something of a consensus regarding objectives, if not regarding ways and means.

The emerging consensus seems to be a widening recognition of the desirability of creating work circumstances in which people are not only reasonably productive but also have the opportunity to achieve reasonable satisfaction from their work. This dual objective gets us beyond the mechanics of job analysis processes per se, but achieving it depends in part upon the data that are generated by job analysis.

References

Calitz, C. J.; Hillael, T. M.; McCormick, E. J.; and Peters, L. H. *Job Characteristics, Personal Interests, and Response Disposition of Incumbents as Related to Job Satisfaction.* Department of Psychological Sciences, Report No. 8. West Lafayette, Ind.: Purdue University, 1974.

Chapanis, A. "What Does Ergonomics Have to Do with Job Satisfaction?" Paper presented at international symposium on ergonomics, Bucharest: September 1974.

Christensen, J. M. "Limitless Man." Presidential address, annual meeting of the Division of Military Psychology, American Psychological Association. Montreal: September 1973.

Davis, L. E. "The Concept of Job Design and Its Status in Industrial Engineering." In *Symposium on Human Factors in Job Design.* Report SP-611. Santa Monica, Calif.: Systems Development Corporation, 1961.

Davis, L. E. "The Design of Jobs." *Industrial Relations* 6(1966): 21–45.

Davis, L. E., and Cherns, A. B. *The Quality of Working Life,* Vol. 2. New York: The Free Press, 1975.

Davis, L. E., and Taylor, J. C., eds. *Design of Jobs.* Harmondsworth, England: Penguin Books, 1972.

Davis, L. E., and Werling, R. "Job Design Factors." *Occupational Psychology* 34(1960): 109–132.

de Ligney, J. W. "Work structuring + 2: What Can Be Done." *Philips Personnel Management Review* (Eindhoven, Netherlands) 11(1964): 9–17.

Dunham, R. B. "The Measurement and Dimensionality of Job Characteristics." *Journal of Applied Psychology* 61(1976): 404–409.

Dunham, R. B.; Aldag, R. J.; and Brief, A. P. "Dimensionality of Task Design as Measured by the Job Diagnostic Survey." *Academy of Management Journal* 20(1977): 209–223.

Emery, F. E., and Thorsrud, E. *Form and Contrast in Industrial Democracy.* London: Tavistock Institute of Human Relations, 1969.

Ford, R. N. *Motivation Through the Work Itself.* New York: American Management Associations, 1969.

Ford, R. N. "Job Enrichment Lessons from AT&T." *Harvard Business Review* 51(1973): 96–106.

Griew, S. *Job Re-design.* Paris: Organization for Economic Cooperation and Development, 1964.

Hackman, J. R., and Oldham, G. R. "Development of the Job Diagnostic Survey." *Journal of Applied Psychology* 60(1975): 159–170.

A Handbook for Job Restructuring. U.S. Department of Labor, Manpower Administration. Washington, D.C.: U.S. Government Printing Office, 1970.

Herzberg, F. "One More Time: How Do You Motivate Employees?" *Harvard Business Review* 46(1968): 53–63.

Herzberg, F.; Mausner, B.; and Synderman, B. B. *The Motivation of Work.* New York: Wiley, 1959.

Hulin, C. L. "Effects of Changes in Job Satisfaction Levels on Employee Turnover." *Journal of Applied Psychology* 52(1968): 122–126.

Hulin, C. L., and Blood, M. R. "Job Enlargement, Individual Differences, and Worker Responses." *Psychological Bulletin* 68(1968): 41–55.

Imberman, A. A. "NLRB Election: Who Wins and for How Long?" *The Personnel Administrator,* September 1977, pp. 56–61.

International Organization for Standardization (ISO). ISO/TC *Ergonomic Principles of the Design of Work Systems* (draft proposal). Geneva, Switzerland: 159, 1977.

Joint IEA/ES (International Ergonomics Association/Ergonomics Society) International Conference: Job Satisfaction. *Ergonomics* 20(1977): 565–591.

Karlsson, A. H. *The Volvo Kolmar Plant.* Stockholm: Rationalization Council SAF-LO, 1976.

Katzell, R. A.; Yankelovich, D.; et al. *Work, Productivity, and Job Satisfaction.* New York: The Psychological Corporation, 1975.

Lawler, E. E., III. "Job Design and Employee Motivation." *Personnel Psychology* 22(1969): 426–435.

Locke, E.; Sirota, D.; and Wolfson, A. D. "An Experimental Case Study of the Successes and Failures of Job Enrichment in a Government Agency." *Journal of Applied Psychology* 61(1976): 701–711.

McCormick, E. J. "Ergonomics: Future Perspectives." *Perspectives in Industrial Psychology* (University of Stellenbosch, South Africa) 2(1967a): 1–27.

McGregor, D. M. "The Human Side of Enterprise." *Management Review* 40(1957): 22–29, 88–92.

MacKinney, A. C.; Wernimont, P. F.; and Galitz, W. O. "Has Specialization Reduced Job Satisfaction?" *Personnel* 39-11(1962): 8–17.

Maslow, A. H. *Eupsychian Management.* Homewood, Ill.: Richard D. Irwin, 1965.

Maslow, A. H. *Motivation and Personality,* 2nd ed. New York: Harper & Row, 1970.

Miller, W. "What Is Job Restructuring?" Madison: Wisconsin State Employment Service, undated.

National Observer. "Job-enrichment Plans Let Worker Shape His Own Job." March 17, 1973.

Nicholson, N.; Brown, C. A.; and Chadwick-Jones, J. K. "Absence from Work and Job Satisfaction." *Journal of Applied Psychology* 61(1976): 728–737.

Personnel Practices Bulletin. Eindhoven, Netherlands: Philips, (Sept. 1968).

Pierce, J. L., and Dunham, R. B. "Task Design: A Literature Review." *Academy of Management Review,* October 1976, pp. 83–97.

Porter, L. W., and Lawler, E. E. III. "What Job Attitudes Tell About Motivation." *Harvard Business Review* 46 (Jan.–Feb. 1968): 118–126.

Smith, P. C.; Kendall, L.; and Hulin, C. *The Measurement of Satisfaction in Work and Retirement: A Strategy for the Study of Attitudes.* Chicago: Rand-McNally, 1969.

Stone, E. F., and Porter, L. W. *Job Scope and Job Satisfaction: A Study of Urban Workers.* Graduate School of Business Administration, Technical Report No. 22. Irvine, Calif.: University of California, 1973.

Tichauer, E. R. *Occupational Biomechanics: An Introduction to the Anatomy of Function or Man at Work.* Institute of Rehabilitation Medicine, Rehabilitation Monograph No. 51. New York: New York University Medical Center, 1975.

Vroom, V. H. *Work and Motivation.* New York: Wiley, 1964.

Work in America. Cambridge, Mass.: The MIT Press, 1973.

12

Job
Evaluation

THE problem of establishing satisfactory wage and salary scales is
one that haunts the management of many organizations. Wage and
salary policies have an impact upon each and every employee of an
organization, and therefore are of concern to all employees.

The Concept of Equity in Compensation

In discussions of theories relating to compensation policies the notion of equity is perhaps the problem that comes up most often.
Without getting too deeply into the theoretical aspects, let us touch
briefly on a couple of formulations relating to equity in pay.

Adams' Equity Theory

Adams contends that an individual's perception of equity in pay is
based primarily on his comparison of his own situation with those
of others. His equity theory is predicated on the relationship between a person's perceived *outcomes* from his work involvement and

his perceived *inputs* into his job, compared with the outcomes and inputs of other so-called comparison persons. The outcomes include any aspect of the job situation that are viewed as having value, such as pay, fringe benefits, status, intrinsic interest in the job, and so on. The inputs, in turn, include any costs to the individual, such as his education, skill, personal qualifications, and effort. Adams hypothesizes that when an individual compares his outcomes and inputs with those of other persons, this comparison can be expressed as a pair of ratios:

$$\frac{\text{The individual's outcome}}{\text{input}} \quad \text{vs} \quad \frac{\text{The comparison person's outcome}}{\text{input}}$$

If we express the outcomes as simply high (H) or low (L), the following illustrate conditions of equity or inequity:

Equity: $\quad \frac{H}{H} \; \text{vs} \; \frac{H}{H} \qquad \frac{L}{H} \; \text{vs} \; \frac{L}{H} \qquad \frac{H}{H} \; \text{vs} \; \frac{L}{L}$

Inequity (over reward): $\quad \frac{H}{L} \; \text{vs} \; \frac{L}{L} \qquad \frac{L}{L} \; \text{vs} \; \frac{L}{H} \qquad \frac{H}{H} \; \text{vs} \; \frac{L}{H}$

Inequity (under reward): $\quad \frac{L}{L} \; \text{vs} \; \frac{H}{L} \qquad \frac{L}{H} \; \text{vs} \; \frac{L}{L} \qquad \frac{H}{H} \; \text{vs} \; \frac{H}{L}$

Adams's equity theory is based on what Festinger (1957) refers to as *cognitive dissonance*. In the realm of pay, a person presumably would experience some dissonance if the ratios are those of inequity, as those characterized above. Such dissonance, or inequity, can of course be in either direction, reflecting over reward or under reward (although it is probably only human to be more aware of under reward than of the reverse).

Jaques's Equitable Payment Concept

Another theoretical formulation relating to equity in pay is by Jaques in Great Britain who has postulated the notion that equitable pay for jobs is based primarily on what he calls the time-span of discretion (TSD). In his scheme he differentiates between the *prescribed* content of jobs (those elements of the work about which the person has no authorized choice), and the *discretionary* content (those elements about which a choice of how to do a job is left to the person doing it). The time-span of discretion is defined by Jaques (1964) as follows:

Time-span of Discretion (TSD): the longest period which can elapse in a role before the manager can be sure that his subordinate has not been exercising marginally substandard discretion continuously in balancing the pace and the quality of this work.

In effect, this is the maximum period during which the manager relies on the discretion of his subordinate, and the subordinate works on his own account. This conception, in turn, is very much dependent upon the review of discretion, which is defined as follows:

Review of Discretion: review by the immediate manager (or by someone acting on his behalf who is accountable for reporting to him) of the discretion exercised by a subordinate in carrying out a task, as shown in the completion time and the quality of the result.

The review of a person's work may be either direct (as by the manager), or indirect (as by an inspector, or by someone else in the organization, or by the complaints of a customer).

The time-span of discretion can be thought of as the time before a person's sins catch up with him. In the case of, say, a production job, the inspector can detect unsatisfactory work within a matter of hours, whereas in the case of, say, the president of a large corporation, it might be several years before his performance can be adequately reviewed (in this case by his superiors, the board of directors). The procedures for measuring the time-span of discretion are set forth by Jaques (1964, 1970, 1972) and will not be repeated here, but in general, the TSD is expressed in terms of minutes, hours, days, weeks, months, and years.

After defining the time-span of discretion of jobs, Jaques proceeds to make the point that such measures are highly correlated with the opinions of people regarding what are fair or equitable rates of pay for jobs. Jaques (1972, p. 45) reports that persons whose work carried the same maximum time-span of discretion, whatever their field of work, were found to state with only slight variation the same salary as being a fair return for the work they were doing. For example, eight persons with very different jobs, whose work was established by themselves and their managers to carry a maximum time-span of one month, all, quite independently, stated practically identical sums of money (about £12.10s) as fair salaries for their work.

Figure 12–1 shows the general pattern of the relationship between time-span of discretion values for over 1,000 jobs and what were judged by the individual workers as being fair pay for the jobs in question. For any given time-span value the deviations between individual statements of felt-fair pay range are of the order of ± 5 percent, with standard deviations of 2 to 3 percent. Jaques expresses the opinion that such data reflect the existence of an unrecognized system of norms of fair payment for any given level of work, and that unconscious knowledge of those norms is shared among the population engaged in employment work.

In the experimental use of the Jaques TSD concept within a single organization, Kvålseth and Crossman derived TSD values for 29 positions within the organization and converted these to "level of work" (LOW) values. (The LOW value is equal to the largest TSD among the tasks performed by the individual.) A few examples of these are as follows: superintendent, 8 months; supervisor (maintenance and staff), 4 months; foreman (warehouse and shipping), 3 months; layout draftsman, 2 weeks; mechanic, 4 days; storeroom keeper, 2 days; shipping clerk, 1 day; and loader, half day. These values, in turn, had a correlation with the actual wages and salaries of the positions of .96, which is very respectable.

Various criticisms have been leveled at Jaques's formulation, so

Figure 12-1. Relationship between time-span of discretion values of jobs and going rates of pay in £. (Adapted from Jaques, 1970, p. 147)

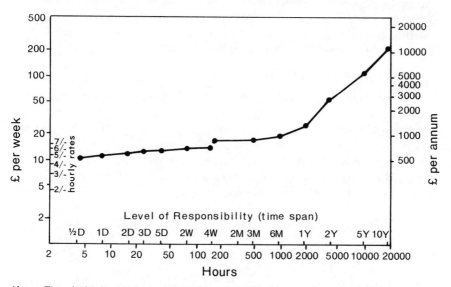

Note: The slight discontinuity at the four-week level has to do with whether people were paid for overtime or not, and can generally be disregarded.

there is a question of its usefulness as the basis for establishing compensation rates for jobs, at least at the present time, although it seems to have enough relevance to this problem to warrant further experimental use and possible refinement. In this regard, Kvålseth suggests that its validity might be increased by incorporating some measure of the effects of substandard discretion (presumably a measure of the criticalness of inadequate performance), and some indication of the time devoted to the various tasks that comprise the job.

Objectives of Compensation Policy

With this brief discussion of Adams's equity theory and Jaques's time-span of discretion, let us now return to the matter of job evaluation to crystallize the appropriate objectives of compensation policy. To begin with, it is probably in order to accept the notion that, to be successful, the compensation policy should provide rates of pay that are perceived as being reasonably equitable. In practical terms there are probably two aspects of equity related to the rates of pay established on the basis of a job evaluation system. One of these deals with relative differentials in earnings among the jobs *within* the organization. The other deals with relative differentials in earnings between jobs within the organization and corresponding jobs *outside* the organization. We can think of these as *internal* and *external* considerations; this distinction may help us to identify the two objectives of compensation policy.

Internal Compensation Objectives

For a compensation policy to be acceptable to those whose earnings are to be determined by it there must be some scheme whereby the *relative* differences in pay for various jobs are generally recognized by the employees at large as reasonably equitable. We might depict the relative pay of several jobs as falling along a line such as this, in which the letters represent different jobs, and the distances between the letters reflect relative difference in pay.

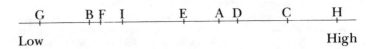

If one can order jobs along a scale in such a fashion that the employees generally recognize and accept the pay differentials, then the compensation policy can be said to have fulfilled one of the objectives. Such a scale must in turn reflect general recognition (within the organization) not only of the *order* of jobs along the scale, but also the relative *magnitude of the differences* between and among the jobs.

External Compensation Objectives

It is not enough that the employees recognize and accept the internal pay differentials of the job as equitable. The pay scales for the various jobs also usually need to have some reasonable relationship to those for corresponding jobs in the outside world, in particular to those in the labor market from which the employees come. Let us see what would happen if there were no such reasonable relationship. If the pay scales within an organization are appreciably *below* those of corresponding jobs elsewhere, one would expect the organization to have difficulty in hiring and keeping people for the jobs in question, since the people could generally earn more somewhere else. And if the pay scales within an organization were far above the prevailing pay scales for corresponding jobs elsewhere, the organization could well experience financial problems, and might not be able to compete in the market for the sale of its goods and services because of excessively high wage and salary costs. Although the pay for any given job within the organization need not be exactly the same as for the same job elsewhere in the labor market, it needs to be within some reasonable range.

Discussion

If we accept these two objectives of compensation policy as valid, we must, by implication, accept the notion that compensation rates for various types of jobs are primarily influenced by supply and demand factors in the labor market. There are obvious factors that at least in part undermine the supply and demand influence—such factors as union influences, temporary under- and oversupply, changes in cultural values, and so forth. But by and large, it seems reasonable to believe that the dominant factor that influences pay for various jobs is supply and demand.

Given this assumption, the typical problem for wage and salary administrators is to develop or adopt a procedure that would result in the establishment of pay scales for jobs that fulfill both of the objectives mentioned above. If an organization has only a few different jobs, and if those identical jobs exist in other organizations in the labor market, the organization might not need any system for setting its pay scales; it could just pay the going rate for the jobs in question. But if it has many different jobs, some systematic job evaluation system usually is desirable, particularly in the case of organizations that have some unique jobs that do not exist in their labor market. In such instances, an appropriate job evaluation system can provide for the establishment of pay scales for those unique jobs on the basis of job characteristics that do have their identical counterparts in the labor market in question. Thus, the pay for such jobs presumably would be perceived as reasonably equitable.

If an organization goes in for a job evaluation program, then the system that is used should result in evaluation of jobs in terms of job variables that collectively reproduce or predict the going rates for jobs that have their counterparts in the labor market. This point is illustrated in Figure 12–2, which shows, for two hypothetical job evaluation systems (A and B), differences in the degree to which the job evaluation point values for a sample of 15 jobs are related to going rates for those jobs. In the case of System B, the jobs are much farther from a "line of best fit" than in the case of System A. The vertical distance of any given job from the diagonal line illustrates how much the evaluation point value is off in predicting going rates, because it is either too high (if below the line) or too low (if above the line). The rate for any given job as based on either system A or B (that is, the predicted rate) would be on the diagonal line directly above or below the dot representing the job. The extent of over- and underprediction is illustrated in the case of System B for a couple of jobs.

In the case of these two hypothetical systems, it is clear that System A comes much closer to the prediction of going rates than does System B. The accuracy of prediction of going rates is essentially a function of the extent to which the system measures the various job variables that have been responsible for the establishment of the going rates in the labor market, or at least measures job characteristics that are correlated with those variables.

Thus, the going rates of pay of jobs in the labor market normally would serve as a standard or criterion against which to judge the adequacy (that is, the validity) of a job evaluation system. Although such rates would in most circumstances be the most appropriate criterion, it should be added that in certain circumstances the going rates within an organization can be used, since such rates usually have settled down at values that are reasonably in line with rates in the outside labor market. (The factor comparison systems to be described later involves the use of such a criterion.) The use of such a criterion of total job values as the basis for judging the

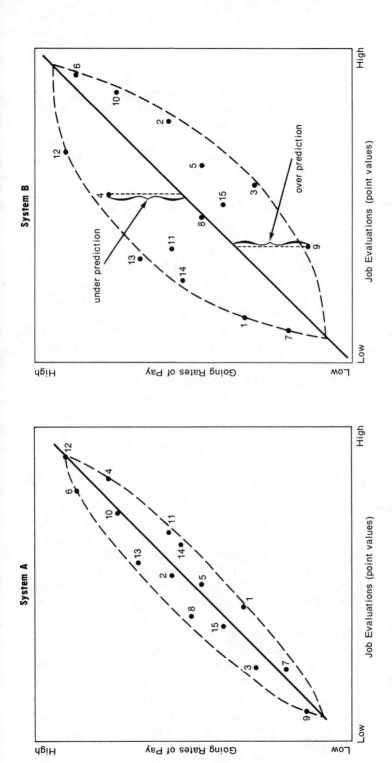

Figure 12-2. Two hypothetical job evaluation systems (A and B) of differences between the predictability of going rates of Pay and job evaluation point values based on those systems.

adequacy of a job evaluation system is essentially a "policy capturing" approach. A job evaluation system developed to reproduce such rates can be thought of as capturing the prevailing pay policy of the organization or the labor market in question.

In certain special circumstances, ratings by experts of overall job values have been used as the criterion against which job evaluation systems have been compared or judged.

Traditional Job Evaluation System*

Job evaluation systems generally provide methods for deriving indexes of relative job values within an organization; these indexes are usually based on the judgments of individuals—members of a job evaluation committee—about the jobs or certain job characteristics. In turn, these indexes are used as the basis for determining wage rates for the jobs covered by the system. Usually this conversion to wage rates is made on the basis of a wage survey to determine "going rates" of a sample of jobs. In effect, then, a job evaluation program provides a systematic basis for an organization to establish compensation rates for its jobs so that they are in reasonable alignment with going rates for corresponding jobs in the labor market.

The four traditional job evaluation methods are (1) ranking method, (2) classification method, (3) point method, and (4) factor comparison method.

Ranking Method

In the ranking method, jobs are compared with each other, usually on the basis of judged overall worth. Most typically, these judgments are obtained by a simple ranking of jobs—hence the name *ranking method*. However, because jobs can be judged relative to others by the use of other procedures, such as the paired comparison procedure, this method could more appropriately be called the *job comparison* method. The reliability of the evaluations usually is enhanced by having several individuals—preferably people who are already familiar with the jobs in question—serve as evaluators. When there are many jobs to be evaluated, however, it usually is impossible to find individuals who are familiar with all of them. Although there are ways of combining evaluations when each rater

---

*The rest of this chapter is largely based on material in the chapter on "Financial Incentives and Job Evaluation" in McCormick and Tiffin.

evaluates only some of the jobs, this method is usually most suitable in small organizations with limited numbers of jobs.

Classification Method

The classification method consists of the establishment of several categories of jobs along a hypothetical scale. Each such classification usually is defined and sometimes is illustrated. The Civil Service System of the federal government is essentially a classification system. In using this method, each job is assigned to a specific classification on the basis of its judged overall worth and its relation to the descriptions of the several classifications.

The classification method is a rather simple one to develop and use. However, unless special care is taken, it permits a tendency to perpetuate possible inequalities in existing rates of pay if it is used for evaluation of existing jobs that already have designated rates.

Point Method

The point method is without question the most commonly used procedure. It is characterized by the following features: (1) the use of several job evaluation factors; (2) the assignment of "points" to varying "degrees" or levels of each factor; (3) the evaluation of individual jobs in terms of their "degree" or level on each factor, and the assignment to each job of the number of points designated for the degree or level on the factor; and (4) the addition of the point values for the individual factors to derive the total point value for each job. This total point value then serves as the basis for conversion to the corresponding wage or salary rate. The following illustration, taken from the system of the National Electrical Manufacturers Association (NEMA), shows how one of the factors used in this system (experience) is converted into points for the various degrees of this factor.

Degree	Amount of Experience	Points
1	Up to three months	22
2	Over three months up to one year	44
3	Over one year up to three years	66
4	Over three years up to five years	88
5	Over five years	110

Similar "degree definitions" are included for the various degrees of the remaining factors, of which there are eleven in this particular system. The eleven factors and the point values assigned to the various degrees of those factors are given in Table 12–1. This particular system was designed for use with hourly-paid shop jobs. The system used by the National Metal Trades Affiliates is essentially the same. Different systems usually are used for different major types of jobs, such as hourly-paid jobs, salaried jobs, and so forth.

Factor Comparison Method

The factor comparison method has been described in detail by Benge, Burk, and Hay. In this method, 15 or 20 tentative "key jobs" are first selected. These are jobs that have present rates not subject to controversy and that are considered by the job evaluation committee to be neither underpaid nor overpaid. These jobs then are compared to others in terms of factors common to all jobs. The factors used in the Benge, Burk, and Hay system are:

Mental requirements
Skill requirements
Physical requirements
Responsibility
Working conditions

The "key jobs" are first *ranked* on each of the factors mentioned, with all of the jobs appearing on each of the factor lists. The rankings usually are made independently by several people, and usually three times by each rater, with approximately one week intervening between each ranking. Next, these jobs are subjected to a *rating* process in which the going rate (salary or hourly rate) is divided for each of the tentative key jobs into the amount being "paid" for each of the factors. From these two independent procedures, two rank orders of the tentative key jobs on each factor are determined. The first ranking results from the direct ranking of the jobs on the factors. The second comes from the rank order of the monetary values that result from the rating process. Any of the tentative key jobs that do not come out with essentially the same rank orders in the two independent ranking procedures are eliminated from the list of key jobs. The jobs remaining constitute the framework of the factor comparison system for the company making the installation. All other jobs are compared with these key jobs, and each is located in its appropriate place on each of the fac-

TABLE 12-1. Job characteristics and point values corresponding to various degrees of each used in the National Electrical Manufacturers Association Job Evaluation System. (Source: *NEMA Job Rating Plan — definitions of the factors used in evaluating hourly rated jobs*)

	Points Assigned to Factors and Key to Grades				
Factors	First Degree	Second Degree	Third Degree	Fourth Degree	Fifth Degree
SKILL					
1. Education	14	28	42	56	70
2. Experience	22	44	66	88	110
3. Initiative and ingenuity	14	28	42	56	70
EFFORT					
4. Physical demand	10	20	30	40	50
5. Mental or visual demand	5	10	15	20	25
RESPONSIBILITY					
6. Equipment or process	5	10	15	20	25
7. Material or product	5	10	15	20	25
8. Safety of others	5	10	15	20	25
9. Work of others	5		15		25
JOB CONDITIONS					
10. Working conditions	10	20	30	40	50
11. Unavoidable hazards	5	10	15	20	25

tors included in the system. The amounts to be paid the job for the various factors are then added, which gives the evaluated rate for the job.

Discussion

It should be noted that, among the four traditional methods of job evaluation (i.e., ranking, classification, point, and factor comparison), there are differences both in the *techniques* of evaluation and in the *bases* of evaluation. These differences are illustrated in Figure 12-3.

Job Component Method of Job Evaluation

The traditional methods of job evaluation involve judgments that usually are based on information contained in job descriptions and on the knowledge the evaluators may already have about the jobs in question. In recent years, however, certain procedures have been used either experimentally or operationally that provide for deriving job evaluations directly from structured job analysis question-

Figure 12-3. Differences among methods of job analysis.

Technique of Evaluation

		By comparison with other jobs	By evaluation against a standard
Basis of Evaluation	Whole job	Ranking method	Classification method
	Job factors	Factor-comparison method	Point method

naire data, thereby completely by-passing the need for evaluations based on judgments. Such procedures have been referred to as the *job component method of job evaluation*. (This term is a slight misnomer since no evaluation is called for, but we will use it because the process of establishing wage and salary rates is typically called job evaluation.)

The basic scheme involves the following processes:

1. The development or selection of an appropriate structured job analysis questionnaire that provides for the analysis of jobs in terms of various units (components) of job-related information. Such questionnaires can consist of job-oriented work elements (such as task inventories), or of worker-oriented elements (such as those in the Position Analysis Questionnaire).

2. The derivation of numerical weights for the various components that reflect the values of the individual components as contributors to a criterion of total job values. Such weights have in some instances been derived from the ratings of the individual job components, and in other instances by a statistical analysis of their importance as predictors of the criterion of total job values.

3. The analysis of the jobs in question using the structured job analysis questionnaire in question. Such an analysis typically results in a quantitative score for each job on each component, or at least an indication of its presence or absence in the job.

4. The use of an appropriate statistical procedure for building up an index of total job values from the combination of the weights of the individual components and of the scores for the individual components as related to the individual jobs.

Although there are variations on this central theme, such procedures result in *statistically derived* indexes of total job values from quantitative job data based on structured job analysis questionnaires. Thus the traditional process of evaluating jobs is entirely eliminated. Certain examples of this method will illustrate the potential application.

Clerical Task Inventory (CTI)

An early example of this approach was reported by Miles using a checklist of office operations that is now called the Clerical Task Inventory (CTI).* The CTI consists of a listing of 139 tasks performed in clerical and other office jobs. These tasks were rated by psychologists in terms of relative monetary worth. In using the CTI, the analyst rates the importance of each of the tasks to the job in question. The mean of these ratings for each task is used as an index of its worth.

In the case of the CTI for job evaluation purposes, each job in question is analyzed in terms of the importance of each CTI task. The importance rating for each task for each job is multiplied by the index of worth for the task. The products of these multiplications for the various tasks are then added together to derive a total weighted value for each job. In practice, it has been found that these total values for the five most important tasks result in the optimum correlation with a criterion of going rates for jobs.

The Position Analysis Questionnaire (PAQ)

In a more generalized application of the job-component method, McCormick *et al.* employed the Position Analysis Questionnaire (PAQ) with a sample of 340 jobs of various kinds in various industries in various parts of the country. As indicated in Chapter 6 the PAQ is a structured job analysis questionnaire that provides for analyzing jobs in terms of 187 worker-oriented job elements. In this particular study, job dimension scores were derived statistically for the 32 principal components that resulted from a previous principal components analysis of the PAQ. A statistically weighted combination of scores on nine of these job dimensions produced correlations of .83 to .90 with actual rates of pay for subsamples of 165 and 175 of the jobs as well as for the total sample of 340.

*The Clerical Task Inventory is copyrighted by C. H. Lawshe, and is distributed by the Village Book Cellar, 308 West State Street, West Lafayette, Indiana 47906.

With a larger sample of over 800 varied jobs, the correlation with the actual rates of pay was .85, as reported by Mecham. And for a sample of 79 jobs in an insurance company, Taylor reports a correlation of .93 between a weighted combination of job dimension scores and actual rates of pay.

In the use of the PAQ for job evaluation purposes, the scores of jobs on the various job dimensions are used in the derivation of total job evaluation points for individual jobs, along with statistically determined weights for the individual job dimensions. There are two alternate approaches that can be used in deriving the weights for the individual job dimensions. The first approach is based on data for a large number of varied jobs as described above; the result of the statistical analysis (technically, regression analysis) is an equation that incorporates weights for the dimensions that, collectively, best predict a criterion of going rates for the jobs in the large and varied sample.

The second approach is one in which the going rates of a sample of jobs within the organization are used as the criterion, rather than the going rates of a broad and varied sample as in the first approach. In this instance the statistical analysis results in the derivation of an equation that incorporates weights for the dimensions that, collectively, best predicts the rates for the sample of jobs within the organization. This unique equation approach is an example of the policy capturing approach mentioned earlier in that it captures, statistically, the prevailing pay policy of the organization.

A slight variation of this approach is represented by a study by Robinson et al. This study dealt with a sample of 19 jobs in a medium-size city. The variation consisted of obtaining data on the going rates for these 19 jobs from 21 cities of similar size, and using the median rates for the individual jobs as the rates to be captured in the statistical analysis. The correlation coefficient between the predicted point values based on the PAQ job dimensions and the median rates for the jobs (from the 21 other cities) was .945. In addition, the 19 sample jobs were evaluated by four other methods of deriving compensation rates. The intercorrelation coefficients between the various methods ranged from .82 to .95. The job component method of job evaluation in this instance resulted in values for the various jobs that were as highly correlated with the going rates of jobs as the values derived by any of the other traditional methods of job evaluation, and more highly correlated than some of the methods.

The PAQ has been used operationally for job evaluation by various private organizations, including those in public utilities, finance, insurance, service industries, manufacturing, and transportation. It has also been used by organizations in the public sector, especially in state and local government units.

Discussion

The job component method of establishing pay rates for jobs basically provides for deriving some index values for various individual components of jobs (such as tasks or job dimensions), thus making it possible to derive total job evaluation values by combining the values of the individual components of the job. In other words, it is based on the direct statistical use of quantitative job analysis data from a structured job analysis procedure. The bridge between job analysis data and job values is thus strictly statistical, eliminating the need for making judgments about jobs that is required by the traditional job evaluation methods.

Converting Job Evaluation Results to Pay Scales

In most job evaluation systems, jobs are placed along some hypothetical scale of job values. In the case of the point method and the job component method, the values are expressed in terms of points. The rank order and classification methods result in rankings or job categories. These values, in turn, need to be converted to actual money values in order to establish the rates of pay for the individual jobs. (The conventional use of the factor comparison method is the only exception to the need for such conversion, since it results in values that are actual money values.)

The conversion of job evaluation results to money values typically involves the establishment of a criterion of total job values, which usually is based on going rates in the labor market. In turn, a going rate curve usually is developed, showing the patterns of the relationship between job evaluations (such as point values) and the going rates for a sample of jobs. In addition, an organization-rate curve usually is prepared, showing the basic relationship between evaluations from the sample jobs and the rates for those jobs that are established by the organization as the basis for setting compensation rates for all jobs.

Developing a Going Rate Curve

At some stage of developing a wage or salary administration program it is necessary to determine the relationship between evaluations—usually of a sample of key jobs—and rates of pay for corresponding jobs in the labor market. In case data on the going rates of such jobs are not available, a wage or salary survey is carried out. For our present illustrative purposes, data on the median "going" rates of pay of a sample of jobs have been drawn from a survey by the Bureau of Labor Statistics. (We could consider these going rates as the median rates for a sample of companies in any given labor market.) These going rates along with illustrative evaluation points for the jobs are shown in Figure 12–4 to illustrate the establishment of a going wage curve. Although this particular relationship is linear, with some job evaluation systems the relationship is curvilinear.

Setting an Organization Rate Curve

The next stage is that of establishing a wage or salary curve for the specific organization. (In the case of private companies this is called the company wage or salary curve.) This curve, derived on the basis of the going wage curve, sets the general pattern of rates for the jobs covered by the job evaluation system. Although this curve is based on data for a sample of jobs that exist in other organizations in the labor market, it is, of course, used in establishing rates of pay for all of the jobs covered, including those that are unique to the organization. This assures that all the jobs covered will have their rates of pay established on the same basis.

Figure 12–5 shows an "organization" wage curve for the same jobs illustrated in Figure 12–4. In this case it is shown as slightly below the going rate curve of the labor market. Where this curve is actually set with respect to the going wage curve in any given case, however, is a function of various considerations, including economic conditions, contract negotiations, and fringe benefits. Thus, it can be at the *going* level of the going wage curve as such, or at various levels above or below.

There is, of course, the question as to how close the organization wage curve should be to the going rate curve. In this regard, Jaques (1970) indicates that individuals whose actual payment bracket remains within 3 percent of equity tend to express themselves as feeling that their role is being reasonably paid relative to others. In turn, those whose actual payment bracket falls 5 percent below equity tend to feel that they are being treated somewhat unfairly, and those whose earnings are 10 percent below equity definitely feel they are being treated unfairly. Persons whose earnings fall as far as 15 percent below equity would be expected to seek a

Figure 12-4. Relationship between job evaluation points and median monthly pay rates for 22 jobs. (Source: BLS Bulletin 1891, 1975)

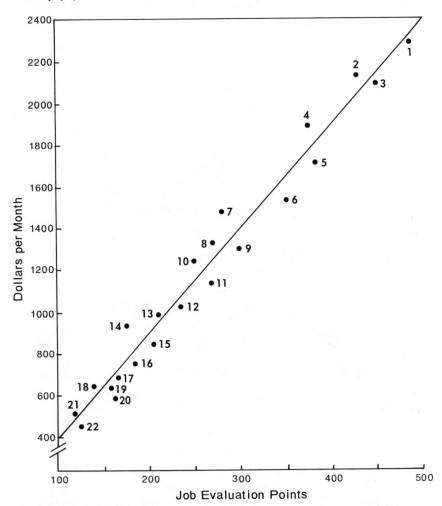

change in employment if opportunities exist. The implication of Jaques's interpretations is that pay scales generally should not fall much below about 5 percent of equity as he defines equity in terms of time-span of discretion. If we equate his concept of equity to the going rate, it would then seem that an organization wage curve should not fall much below 5 percent below the going rate curve.

In converting job evaluation points to actual rates of pay, different practices may be followed. It would be possible to take the

Figure 12-5. Illustration of an organization wage curve, and of one pattern of conversion of job evaluation points into rates of pay. (Adapted from McCormick and Tiffin, 1974, p. 417)

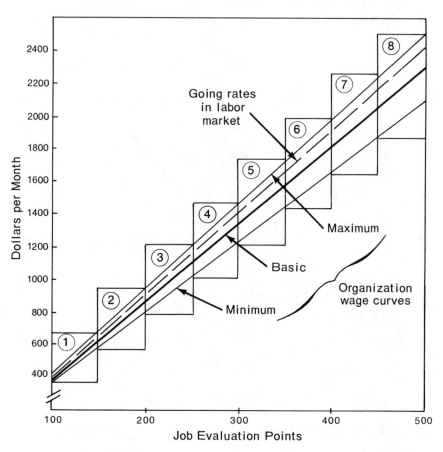

Note: In this example the point values are converted into pay grades, each of which has a range of rates.

evaluated points for a given job and derive the corresponding exact rate that would be applicable. Thus, every slight difference in points would result in some difference in hourly rate. In practice, most organizations (and unions) feel that the inherent lack of percent accuracy in the judgments that underlie a set of job evaluations makes it desirable to bracket together jobs of approximately the same point value and to consider these jobs as equal in setting up the wage structure. This bracketing results in so-called *labor grades.* The number of labor grades found in specific wage structures varies from around 8 or 10 to 20 to 25. The tendency of most current union demands in wage contract negotiations is to favor a relatively small number of labor grades.

When the jobs have been bracketed in labor grades, provision is usually made for wage increases within each labor grade, as illustrated in Figure 12–5. Various procedures have been used in granting wage increases within labor grades, as well as in upgrading employees to higher categories. Some organizations use an automatic acceleration schedule under which specified increases automatically become effective after a specified period of time on the job. This principle is employed most frequently in the lower labor grades and with new employees, but it is sometimes used at higher levels in the wage structure as well. A systematic employee evaluation program is also used by some organizations as a means of identifying employees who are eligible for a pay increase under the prevailing pay structure.

As mentioned above, there are various policies followed in converting points to rates of pay. Although these will not be discussed here, two or three variations will be mentioned. Figure 12–5 shows an increasing range of rates with higher pay grades; in actual practice the range may be constant, or may be greater or less than that illustrated. In some systems the width of the pay grades (in terms of job evaluation points) increases with higher rates; these increases may be systematic or adapted in some way to the concentration of jobs along the evaluation scale.

Features of a Desirable Job Evaluation System

Let us now crystallize a description of the features of a desirable or satisfactory job evaluation system.

Job Characteristics on Which the System is Based

In most circumstances a desirable job evaluation system would provide for the evaluation of jobs in terms of the job characteristics that, collectively, add up to total values that are reasonably correlated with a criterion of going rates in the labor market. In the point method (the most commonly used system) and in the factor comparison method, the characteristics used are job factors. In the job component method they are such components as tasks, job dimensions, and the like. For our discussion here let us think in terms of factors such as those used in the point method, although much of what might be said about factors would also be relevant in connection with other types of job characteristics.

To begin with, it can be said that most job evaluation systems tend to result in evaluations of various jobs that are relatively comparable. Years ago, for example, Chesler reported intercorrelations among the systems of six different companies ranging from .89 to .93. These were based on the evaluation of 35 jobs using various systems, two of which were based on the factor comparison method, three on the point method, and one on a combination classification and ranking method. Such intercorrelations probably imply that the various systems measure substantially the same aspects of jobs, either directly or indirectly.

Validity of the System

Granting the fact that most systems produce reasonably comparable job values, however, one preferably should select or develop a system that would be most valid in predicting the total job values represented by the criterion of job values that is considered to be most appropriate. In most instances this would be a criterion of going rates in the labor market. The validity of any given system is best reflected by the correlation for a sample of jobs between the job values that result from the system and the criterion values for the jobs in the sample. A system that produces a correlation, for example, of .90 is certainly better than one that produces a correlation of .85.

The point we are leading up to is that it is possible to determine statistically the effectiveness of any given system for producing job values that are correlated with going rates, or even to develop a system that would do so. This really involves the identification, by statistical procedures, of the factors and of their appropriate statistical weights that collectively result in the highest correlations with whatever criterion of total job worth is used (such as going rates in the labor market). The scheme, as applied to either an existing system or to an experimental system that has been developed, involves the following steps: (1) the selection of a representative sample of jobs in the organization; (2) the evaluation of the jobs using the factors of the system that has been selected or developed; (3) the derivation of criterion values of total job worth for the jobs in the sample (usually this is based on going rates in the labor market as determined by a wage or salary survey, but it may be some other criterion such as rates within the organization, or ratings by experts), and (4) the application of appropriate statistical procedures (specifically some form of regression analysis). The factors and their statistically determined weights could then be used in the organization with reasonable assurance that the rates of pay based on the system would have a reasonable relationship with rates in the labor market.

Job Evaluation Scales and Procedures

The results of a job evaluation system can to some degree be influenced by the nature of the scales that are used in making the evaluation, as well as certain other procedures that are involved. Some years ago the Personnel Research Laboratory of the U.S. Air Force carried out a series of studies dealing with various aspects of job evaluation systems. The implications of certain of these studies are discussed briefly below.

Use of benchmark jobs. The use of benchmark jobs to represent various scale values generally results in higher validity of resulting evaluations than the use of scales whose values are characterized by adjectives (Brokaw and Giorgia). (The use of scales with benchmark jobs also tends to result in somewhat lower—presumably less inflated—ratings.)

Context effects. The total group of jobs that are evaluated by individual evaluators seems to have some influence on the evaluation of individual jobs (Madden, 1960). This is sometimes referred to as *context effect*. The general implication of Madden's study is that the pool of jobs to be evaluated by individual evaluators should include jobs from the entire range of jobs. (If the pool contains largely high-level jobs the jobs tend to be evaluated lower than if the pool contains largely low-level jobs.)

Familiarity effects. The familiarity of the evaluators with the jobs tends to influence their ratings (Madden, 1961). If the familiarity derives from personal involvement in the job area in question, the evaluations tend to be a bit inflated, presumably because of ego involvement. However, familiarity derived from other sources (such as job descriptions, task inventories, technical manuals, and related materials) generally leads to obtaining adequate evaluations.

Reliability of Job Evaluations

Still another aspect of job evaluation systems that can influence its utility is the reliability of the evaluations. Reliability in this context refers to the degree of relationship between or among the evaluations of two or more independent evaluators, or between separate evaluations made at different times by the same evaluator. Reliability usually is measured by correlating pairs of independent evaluations for a sample of jobs, or by correlating separate (test-retest) evaluations made by the same evaluator at different times. The results of one study of the reliability of evaluations are reported by Scott (1963). The system used consisted of the following six factors: (1) general educational development; (2) specific job preparation; (3) physical demands; (4) working conditions; (5) job hazards; and (6) supervision. The evaluations were made independently by the members of several committees each consisting of five men. The average reliability coefficients ranged from .70 to .96 for the six factors, and was .96 for total point values based on all six factors. Reliability coefficients within these ranges can be considered as being quite respectable.

It might be added that the combination of the evaluations of several people tends to increase the composite evaluations as long as the evaluators in question are all good evaluators. Some indication of the increase in reliability that can be expected from the pooling of the evaluations of various numbers of individuals is given below. The reliability coefficients given are those estimated for various numbers of evaluators based on the assumption that the average test-retest reliability of the individual evaluators is .80.

Sample size:	1	2	4	6	8	16	20
Reliability:	.80	.89	.94	.96	.97	.98	.99

The pooled reliability of evaluations (or for that matter the reliability of other judgments) tends to increase appreciably with even three or four evaluators, and then increases more gradually with the addition of more evaluators, up to 10 or 15. Beyond such numbers there is virtually no increase in the pooled reliability of evaluations. Incidentally, there are hints that the pooled reliability of evaluations made *independently* by the several evaluators tends to be a bit higher than the reliability of evaluations made *collectively* by panels of three or five evaluators (Hoggatt and Hazel). This suggests that it may be preferable to obtain individual evaluation from two or more persons and average them, rather than obtaining group evaluations by consensus.

Discussion

Wage and salary administrators must feel that they are continuously walking a tightrope because of the conflicting pressures that impinge upon them. A wage and salary program simultaneously must provide positive work incentives for the employees, must be generally acceptable to employees, must be reasonably competitive with conditions in the labor market, and must keep the organization solvent. Obviously, there are no pat and simplistic resolutions to meet these various objectives. The note on which we would like to close this discussion is that insight and knowledge relevant to the problem, derived through research such as illustrated in this chapter, can aid the process of developing a satisfactory program. Further, attention should be called to the fact that the field of job evaluation has not yet taken full advantage of certain scaling procedures that could be applied to the processes of making judgments about jobs and their characteristics.

References

Adams, J. S. "Wage Inequities, Productivity and Work Quality." *Industrial Relations* 3(1963): 9–16.

Benge, E. J.; Burk, S. L.; and Hay, E. N. *Manual of Job Evaluation,* 4th ed. New York: Harper & Row, 1941.

Brokaw, L. D., and Giorgia, M. J. *Development of Benchmark Scales for Air Force Officer Position Evaluation.* USAF, AFSC, Personnel Research Laboratory, PRL-TR-66-9, 1966.

Bureau of Labor Statistics. *National Survey of Professional Administrative, Technical, and Clerical Pay.* Washington, D.C.: Bureau of Labor Statistics Bulletin 1891, 1975.

Chesler, D. J. "Reliability and Comparability of Different Job Evaluation Systems." *Journal of Applied Psychology* 32(1948): 465–475.

Festinger, L. *A Theory of Cognitive Dissonance.* Stanford, Calif.: Stanford University Press, 1957.

Hoggatt, R. S., and Hazel, J. T. *Reliability of Individual Versus Group Job Pay Ratings.* USAF, AFHRL, AFHRL-TR-70-10. Brooks AFB, Texas: 1970.

Jaques, E. *Time-span Handbook.* London: Heineman Educational Books Ltd., 1964.

Jaques, E. *Equitable Payment,* 2nd. ed. Carbondale, Ill.: Southern Illinois University Press, 1970.

Jaques, E. *Measurement of Responsibility.* New York: Wiley, 1972.

Kvålseth, T. O., and Crossman, E. R. F. W. "The Jaquesian Level-of-work Estimates: A Systematic Formulation." *Organizational Behavior and Human Performance* 11(1974): 303–315.

McCormick, E. J.; Jeanneret, P. R.; and Mecham, R. C. "A Study of Job Characteristics and Job Dimensions as Based on the Position Analysis Questionnaire (PAQ)." *Journal of Applied Psychology* 66(1972): 347–368.

McCormick, E. J., and Tiffin J. *Industrial Psychology*, 6th ed. Englewood Cliffs, N.J.: Prentice-Hall, 1974.

Madden, J. M. *Context Affects in Job Evaluation*. USAF, WADD, Personnel Laboratory, WADD-TN-60-220. Lackland AFB, Texas: 1960.

Madden, J. M. *A Further Note on the Familiarity Effect in Job Evaluation*. USAF, AFSC, Personnel Laboratory, ASD-TN-61-47. Lackland AFB, Texas: 1961.

Mecham, R. C. Personal communication, 1972.

Miles, M. C. "Studies in Job Evaluation: A: Validity of a Checklist for Evaluating Office Jobs." *Journal of Applied Psychology* 36(1952): 97–101.

Patchen, M. *The Choice of Wage Comparisons*. Englewood Cliffs, N.J.: Prentice-Hall, 1961.

Robinson, D. D.; Wahlstrom, O. W.; and Mecham, R. C. "Comparison of Job Evaluation Methods: A 'Policy-capturing' Approach Using the Position Analysis Questionnaire (PAQ)." *Journal of Applied Psychology* 59(1974): 633–637.

Scott, W. E., Jr. "The Reliability and Validity of a Six-factor Job Evaluation System." Ph.D. thesis, Purdue University, 1963.

Taylor, L. R. Personal communication, 1972.

APPENDIXES

A

Abbreviations
Used in this Book

Most of these abbreviations appear in the Reference sections at the ends of chapters.

AFB   Air Force Base
AFHRL   Air Force Human Resources Laboratory
AFSC   Air Force Systems Command
AMD   Aerospace Medical Division, Air Force Systems Command
AMRL   Aerospace Medical Research Laboratory, Aerospace Medical Division, Air Force Systems Command
DOT   Dictionary of Occupational Titles
OAI   Occupation Analysis Inventory
ONR   Office of Naval Research
PAQ   Position Analysis Questionnaire
PRL   Personnel Research Laboratory, USAF
TR   Technical Report
USAF   United States Air Force
USES   United States Employment Service
USN   United States Navy
WADC   Wright Air Development Center, USAF
WADD   Wright Air Development Division, USAF

B

Rating Scales
Used by United States
Employment Service

THIS appendix includes rating scales used by the USES in its job analysis
activities. These scales are given in full detail in the *Handbook for Analyzing
Jobs.** Certain of the scales are given in somewhat abbreviated form in *A
Handbook for Job Restructuring.†* Both of these publications give benchmarks
for use in rating jobs in terms of various worker traits. Because of space
considerations, the rating scales of worker traits that follow do not include
the benchmarks.

Worker Functions

Every task in a job requires the worker to function in relation to data,
people, and things in varying degrees. These relationships are expressed
in terms of worker functions and are arranged in a hierarchy for each

*U.S. Dept. of Labor, Manpower Administration, 1972. Available from the Su-
perintendent of Documents, Washington, D.C., 20402, Stock No. 2900-0131.
†U.S. Dept. of Labor, Manpower Administration, 1970.

relationship from the simple to the complex in such a manner, that, generally, each successive function can include those that are simpler and exclude those that are more complex. A combination of the highest functions which the worker performs in relation to data, people, and things expresses the total level of complexity for the task-worker situation.

Data (1st digit)	*People (2nd digit)*	*Things (3rd digit)*
0 Synthesizing	0 Mentoring	0 Setting-Up
1 Coordinating	1 Negotiating	1 Precision Working
2 Analyzing	2 Instructing	2 Operating-Controlling
3 Compiling	3 Supervising	3 Driving – Operating
4 Computing	4 Diverting	4 Manipulating
5 Copying	5 Persuading	5 Tending
6 Comparing	6 Speaking – Signaling	6 Feeding – Offbearing
	7 Serving	7 Handling
	8 Taking Instructions	
	– Helping	

DATA Information, knowledge, and conceptions related to data, people, or things, obtained by observation, investigation, interpretation, visualization, mental creation; incapable of being touched; written data take the form of numbers, words, symbols; other data are ideas, concepts, oral verbalization.

0 Synthesizing: Integrating analyses of data to discover facts and/or develop knowledge, concepts, or interpretations.

1 Coordinating: Determining time, place, and sequence of operations or action to be taken on the basis of analysis of data; executing determinations and/or reporting on events.

2 Analyzing: Examining and evaluating data. Presenting alternative actions in relation to the evaluation is frequently involved.

3 Compiling: Gathering, collating, or classifying information about data, people, or things. Reporting and/or carrying out a prescribed action in relation to the information is frequently involved.

4 Computing: Performing arithmetic operations and reporting on and/or carrying out a prescribed action in relation to them. Does not include counting.

5 Copying: Transcribing, entering, or posting data.

6 Comparing: Judging the readily observable functional, structural, or compositional characteristics (whether similar to or divergent from obvious standards) of data, people, or things.

PEOPLE Human beings; also animals dealt with on an individual basis as if they were human.

0 Mentoring: Dealing with individuals in terms of their total personality

in order to advise, counsel, and/or guide them with regard to problems that may be resolved by legal, scientific, clinical, spiritual, and/or other professional principles.

1   Negotiating: Exchanging ideas, information, and opinions with others to formulate policies and programs and/or arrive jointly at decisions, conclusions, or solutions.

2   Instructing: Teaching subject matter to others, or training others (including animals) through explanation, demonstration, and supervised practice; or making recommendations on the basis of technical disciplines.

3   Supervising: Determining or interpreting work procedures for a group of workers, assigning specific duties to them, maintaining harmonious relations among them, and promoting efficiency.

4   Diverting: Amusing others.

5   Persuading: Influencing others in favor of a product, service, or point of view.

6   Speaking-Signaling: Talking with and/or signaling people to convey or exchange information. Includes giving assignments and/or directions to helpers or assistants.

7   Serving: Attending to the needs or requests of people or animals or the expressed or implicit wishes of people. Immediate response is involved.

8   Taking Instructions-Helping: Attending to the work assignment instructions or orders of supervisor. (No immediate response required unless clarification of instructions or orders is needed.) Helping applies to "nonlearning" helpers.

THINGS Inanimate objects as distinguished from human beings, substances, or materials; machines, tools, equipment; products. A thing is tangible and has shape, form, and other physical characteristics.

0   Setting-Up: Adjusting machines or equipment by replacing or altering tools, jigs, fixtures, and attachments to prepare them to perform their functions, change their performance, or restore their proper functioning if they break down. Workers who set up and personally operate a variety of machines are included here.

1   Precision Working: Using body members and/or tools or work aids to work, move, guide, or place objects or materials in situations where ultimate responsibility for the attainment of standards occurs and selection of appropriate tools, objects, or materials, and the adjustment of the tool to the task require exercise of considerable judgment.

2   Operating-Controlling: Starting, stopping, controlling, and adjusting the progress of machines or equipment designed to fabricate and/or process objects or materials. Operating machines involves setting up the machine and adjusting the machine or material as the work progresses. Controlling equipment involves observing gages, dials, etc. and turning valves and other devices to control such factors as tem-

perature, pressure, flow of liquids, speed of pumps, and reactions of materials. Set up involves several variables and adjustment is more frequent than in tending.

3 Driving-Operating: Starting, stopping, and controlling the actions of machines or equipment for which a course must be steered, or which must be guided, in order to fabricate, process, and/or move things or people. Involves such activities as observing gages and dials; estimating distances and determining speed and direction of other objects; turning cranks and wheels; pushing clutches or brakes; and pushing or pulling gear lifts or levers. Includes such machines as cranes, conveyor systems, tractors, furnace charging machines, paving machines, and hoisting machines. Excludes manually powered machines, such as handtrucks and dollies, and power assisted machines, such as electric wheelbarrows and handtrucks.

4 Manipulating: Using body members, tools, or special devices to work, guide, or place objects or materials. Involves some latitude for judgment with regard to precision attained and selecting appropriate tool, object, or material, although this is readily manifest.

5 Tending: Starting, stopping, and observing the functioning of machines and equipment. Involves adjusting machines or controls of the machine, such as changing guides, adjusting timers and temperature gages, turning valves to allow flow of materials, and flipping switches in response to lights. Little judgment is involved in making these adjustments.

6 Feeding-Offbearing: Inserting, throwing, dumping, or placing materials in or removing them from machines or equipment which are automatic or tended or operated by other workers.

7 Handling: Using body members, handtools, and/or special devices to work, move, or carry objects or materials. Involves little or no latitude for judgment with regard to attainment of standards or in selecting appropriate tool, object, or material.

Worker Traits

For purposes of job analysis worker traits are defined by the following components: general educational development, aptitudes, interests, temperaments, physical capacities, and adaptability to environmental conditions. These are basic to the analysis of all job tasks and the requirements they make on the worker.

General Educational Development

General Educational Development (GED) embraces those aspects of education (formal and informal) which contribute to the worker's (a) reasoning development and ability to follow instructions, and (b) acquisition of "tool" knowledges, such as language and mathematical skills. It is education of a general nature which does not have a recognized, fairly specific, occupational objective. Ordinarily, such education is obtained in elementary school, high school, or college. It also derives from experience and individual study.

The GED scale which appears on the following pages is composed of three divisions: Reasoning Development; Mathematical Development; and Language Development. Each division contains six levels, and each should be considered independently of the others in evaluating individual tasks.

Aptitudes

Aptitudes are defined as the specific abilities required of an individual in order to facilitate the learning of some task or job duty. Eleven such aptitudes have been identified, through extensive research, to be important in assessing requirements of individuals to learn or adequately perform a job task. A list of these 11 aptitudes, their definitions, and guides for rating the individual aptitudes follow.

G INTELLIGENCE General learning ability. The ability to "catch on" or understand instructions and underlying principles; the ability to reason and make judgments. Closely related to doing well in school.

V VERBAL Ability to understand meanings of words and ideas associated with them, and to use them effectively. To comprehend language, to understand relationships between words, and to understand meanings of whole sentences and paragraphs. To present information or ideas clearly.

N NUMERICAL Ability to perform arithmetic operations quickly and accurately.

S SPATIAL Ability to comprehend forms in space and understand relationships of plane and solid objects. May be used in such tasks as blueprint reading and in solving geometry problems. Frequently described as the ability to "visualize" objects of two or three dimensions, or to think visually of geometric forms.

P FORM PERCEPTION Ability to perceive pertinent detail in objects or in pictorial or graphic material; to make visual comparisons and discriminations and see slight differences in shapes and shadings of figures and widths and lengths of lines.

Q CLERICAL PERCEPTION Ability to perceive pertinent detail in verbal or tabular material. To observe differences in copy, to proofread words and numbers, and to avoid perceptual errors in arithmetic computation.

K MOTOR COORDINATION Ability to coordinate eyes and hands or fingers rapidly and accurately in making precise movements with speed. Ability to make a movement response accurately and quickly.

F FINGER DEXTERITY Ability to move the fingers and manipulate small objects with the fingers rapidly or accurately.

M MANUAL DEXTERITY Ability to move the hands easily and skillfully. To work with the hands in placing and turning motions.

E EYE-HAND-FOOT COORDINATION Ability to move the hand and foot coordinately with each other in accordance with visual stimuli.

C COLOR DISCRIMINATION Ability to perceive or recognize similarities or differences in colors, or in shades or other values of the same color; to identify a particular color, or to recognize harmonious or contrasting color combinations, or to match colors accurately.

Scale of General Educational Development (GED)

Level	Reasoning Development	Mathematical Development	Language Development
6	Apply principles of logical or scientific thinking to a wide range of intellectual and practical problems. Deal with nonverbal symbolism (formulas, scientific equations, graphs, musical notes, etc.) in its most difficult phases. Deal with a variety of abstract and concrete variables. Apprehend the most abstruse classes of concepts.	**Advanced calculus:** Work with limits, continuity, real number system, mean value theorems, implicit function theorems. **Modern algebra:** Apply fundamental concepts of theories of groups, rings, and fields. Work with differential equations, linear algebra, infinite series, advanced operational methods, functions of real and complex variables. **Statistics:** Work with mathematical statistics, mathematical probability and applications, experimental design, statistical inference, econometrics.	**Reading:** Read literature, book and play reviews, scientific and technical journals, abstracts, financial reports, and legal documents. **Writing:** Write novels, plays, editorials, journals, speeches, manuals, critiques, poetry, and songs. **Speaking:** Conversant in the theory, principles, and methods of effective and persuasive speaking, voice and diction, phonetics, and discussion and debate.
5	Apply principles of logical or scientific thinking to define problems, collect data, establish facts, and draw valid conclusions. Interpret an extensive variety of technical instructions in books, manuals, and mathematical or diagrammatic form. Deal with several abstract and concrete variables.	**Algebra:** Work with exponents and logarithms, linear equations, quadratic equations, mathematical induction and binomial theorem, permutations. **Calculus:** Apply concepts of analytic geometry, differentiations and integration of algebraic functions with applications. **Statistics:** Apply mathematical operations to frequency distributions, reliability and validity of tests, normal curve, analysis of variance, correlation techniques, chi-square application and sampling theory, factor analysis.	Same as level 6

GED Scale *(continued)*

Level	Reasoning Development	Mathematical Development	Language Development
4	Apply principles of rational systems* to solve practical problems and deal with a variety of concrete variables in situations where only limited standardization exists. Interpret a variety of instructions furnished in written, oral, diagrammatic, or schedule form.	**Algebra:** Deal with system of real numbers; linear, quadratic, rational, exponential, logarithmic, angle and circular functions, inverse function; related algebraic solution of equations and inequalities; limits and continuity, probability and statistical inference. **Geometry:** Deductive axiomatic geometry, plane and solid, using properties of real numbers; use of rectangular coordinates. **Shopmath:** Practical application of fractions, percentages, ratio and proportion, measuration, logarithms, slide rule, algebra, geometric construction, essentials of trigonometry.	**Reading:** Read novels, poems, newspapers, periodicals, journals, manuals, dictionaries, thesauruses, and encyclopedias. **Writing:** Business letters, expositions, summaries, reports, using prescribed format and conforming to all rules of punctuation, grammar, diction, and style. **Speaking:** Participate in panel discussions, dramatizations, and debates. Speak extemporaneously on a variety of subjects.
3	Apply common sense understanding to carry out instructions furnished in written, oral, or diagrammatic form. Deal with problems involving several concrete variables in or from standardized situations.	Compute discount, interest, profit and loss, commission, markup, and selling price, ratio, and proportion, and percentage. Calculate surfaces, volumes, weights and measures. **Algebra:** Calculate variables and formulas, monomials and polynomials, ratio and proportion variables, square roots and radicals. **Geometry:** Calculate plane and solid figures, circumference and area, volume. Understand kinds of angles, and properties of pairs of angles.	**Reading:** Read a variety of novels, magazines, atlases, and encyclopedias. Read safety rules, instruction in the use and maintenance of shop tools and equipment, methods and procedures in mechanical drawing and layout work. **Writing:** Write reports and essays in proper format, punctuation, spelling, grammar, using all parts of speech. **Speaking:** Speak before an audience with poise, voice control, and confidence, using correct English and well-modulated voice.

*Examples of rational systems are: Bookkeeping, internal combustion engines, electric wiring systems, housebuilding, nursing, farm management.

GED Scale *(continued)*

Level	Reasoning Development	Mathematical Development	Language Development
2	Apply common sense understanding to carry out detailed but uninvolved written or oral instructions. Deal with problems involving a few concrete variables in or from standardized situations.	Add, subtract, multiply, and divide all units of measure. Perform the four operations with like common and decimal fractions. Draw and interpret bar graphs. Perform arithmetic operations involving all American monetary units.	**Reading:** Passive vocabulary of 5,000-6,000 words. Read at rate of 190-215 words per minute. Read adventure stories, comic books, looking up unfamiliar words in dictionary for meaning, spelling, and pronunciation. Read instructions for assembly of model cars and airplanes. **Writing:** Write compound and complex sentences, using cursive style, proper end punctuation, and employing adjectives and adverbs. **Speaking:** Speak clearly and distinctly with appropriate pauses and emphasis, correct pronunciation, variations in word order, and using present, perfect, and future tenses.
1	Apply common sense understanding to carry out simple one- or two-step instructions. Deal with standardized situations with occasional or no variables in or from these situations encountered on the job.	Add and subtract two-digit numbers. Multiply and divide 10's and 100's by 2, 3, 4, 5. Perform the four basic arithmetic operations with coins as part of a dollar. Perform operations with units such as cup, pint, quart; inch, foot, yard; ounce, pound.	**Reading:** Recognize meaning of 2,500 (two- or three-syllable) words. Read at rate of 95-120 words per minute. Compare similarities and differences between words and between series of numbers. **Writing:** Print simple sentences containing subject, verb, and object, and series of numbers, names, and addresses. **Speaking:** Speak simple sentences, using normal word order, and present and past tenses.

Interests

Interests are defined as preferences for certain types of work activities or experiences, with accompanying rejection of contrary types of activities or experiences. Five pairs of interest factors are provided so that a positive preference for one factor of a pair also implies rejection of the other factor of that pair.

1	Situations involving a preference for activities dealing with things and objects.	vs.	6	Situations involving a preference for activities concerned with people and the communication of ideas.
2	Situations involving a preference for activities involving business contact with people.	vs.	7	Situations involving a preference for activities of a scientific and technical nature.
3	Situations involving a preference for activities of a routine, concrete, organized nature.		8	Situations involving a preference for activities of an abstract and creative nature.
4	Situations involving a preference for working for people for their presumed good, as in the social welfare sense, or for dealing with people and language in social situations.	vs.	9	Situations involving a preference for activities that are nonsocial in nature, and are carried on in relation to processes, machines, and techniques.
5	Situations involving a preference for activities resulting in prestige or the esteem of others.	vs.	0	Situations involving a preference for activities resulting in tangible, productive satisfaction.

Temperaments

Temperaments are defined in terms of the different types of occupational situations to which workers must adjust.

1 Situations involving a variety of duties often characterized by frequent change.
2 Situations involving repetitive or short cycle operations carried out according to set procedures or sequences.
3 Situations involving doing things only under specific instruction, allowing little or no room for independent action or judgment in working out job problems.
4 Situations involving the direction, control, and planning of an entire activity or the activities of others.
5 Situations involving the necessity of dealing with people in actual job duties beyond giving and receiving instructions.

6   Situations involving working alone and apart in physical isolation from others, although the activity may be integrated with that of others.
7   Situations involving influencing people in their opinions, attitudes, or judgments about ideas or things.
8   Situations involving performing adequately under stress when confronted with the critical or unexpected or when taking risks.
9   Situations involving the evaluation (arriving at generalizations, judgments, or decision) of information against sensory or judgmental criteria.
0   Situations involving the evaluation (arriving at generalizations, judgments, or decisions) of information against measurable or verifiable criteria.
X   Situations involving the interpretation of feelings, ideas, or facts in terms of personal viewpoint.
Y   Situations involving the precise attainment of set limits, tolerances, or standards.

Physical Demands

Physical demands are those physical activities required of a worker in a job. The factors involved are:

1. STRENGTH   Following are the primary "strength" physical requirements, and generally speaking, a person who engages in one of these activities can engage in all. Specifically, each of these activities can be described as:

Lifting: Raising or lowering an object from one level to another (includes upward pulling).

Carrying: Transporting an object, usually holding it in the hands or arms or on the shoulder.

Pushing: Exerting force upon an object so that the object moves away from the force (includes slapping, striking, kicking, and treadle actions).

Pulling: Exerting force upon an object so that the object moves toward the force (includes jerking).

The five degrees of the physical demands STRENGTH factor are as follows:

S Sedentary Work

Lifting 10 pounds maximum and occasionally lifting and/or carrying such articles as dockets, ledgers, and small tools. Although a sedentary job is defined as one which involves sitting, a certain amount of walking and standing are often necessary in carrying out job duties. Jobs are sedentary if walking and standing are required only occasionally and other sedentary criteria are met.

L Light Work

Lifting 20 pounds maximum with frequent lifting and/or carrying of objects weighing up to 10 pounds. Even though the weight lifted may be only a negligible amount, a job is in this category when it requires walking or standing to a significant degree, or when it involves sitting most of the time with a degree of pushing and pulling of arm and/or leg controls.

M Medium Work

Lifting 50 pounds maximum with frequent lifting and/or carrying of objects weighing up to 25 pounds.

H Heavy Work

Lifting 100 pounds maximum with frequent lifting and/or carrying of objects weighing up to 50 pounds.

V Very Heavy Work

Lifting objects in excess of 100 pounds with frequent lifting and/or carrying of objects weighing 50 pounds or more.

2. CLIMBING AND/OR BALANCING

Climbing: Ascending or descending ladders, stairs, scaffolding, ramps, poles, ropes, and the like, using the feet and legs and/or hands and arms.

Balancing: Maintaining body equilibrium to prevent falling when walking, standing, crouching, or running on narrow, slippery, or erratically moving surfaces; or maintaining body equilibrium when performing gymnastic feats.

3. STOOPING, KNEELING, CROUCHING, AND/OR CRAWLING

Stooping: Bending the body downward and forward by bending the spine at the waist.

Kneeling: Bending the legs at the knees to come to rest on the knee or knees.

Crouching: Bending the body downward and forward by bending the legs and spine.

Crawling: Moving about on the hands and knees or hands and feet.

4. REACHING, HANDLING, FINGERING, AND/OR FEELING

Reaching: Extending the hands and arms in any direction.

Handling: Seizing, holding, grasping, turning, or otherwise working with the hand or hands (fingering not involved).

Fingering: Picking, pinching, or otherwise working with the fingers primarily (rather than with the hand or arm as in handling).

Feeling: Perceiving such attributes of objects and materials as size, shape, temperature, or texture, by means of receptors in the skin, particularly those of the finger tips.

5. TALKING AND/OR HEARING

Talking: Expressing or exchanging ideas by means of the spoken word.

Hearing: Perceiving the nature of sounds by the ear.

6. SEEING   Obtaining impressions through the eyes of the shape, size, distance, motion, color, or other characteristics of objects. The major visual functions are: acuity, far and near, depth perception, field of vision, accommodation, and color vision. The functions are defined as follows:

Acuity, far: Clarity of vision at 20 feet or more.

Acuity, near: Clarity of vision at 20 inches or less.

Depth perception: Three-dimensional vision. The ability to judge distance and space relationships so as to see objects where and as they actually are.

Field of vision: The area that can be seen up and down or to the right or left while the eyes are fixed on a given point.

Accommodation: Adjustment of the lens of the eye to bring an object into sharp focus. This item is especially important when doing near-point work at varying distances from the eye.

Color vision: The ability to identify and distinguish colors.

Environmental Conditions

Environmental conditions are the physical surroundings of a worker in a specific job.

1. WORK LOCATION

Inside: Protection from weather conditions but not necessarily temperature changes.

Outside: No effective protection from weather.

Both: Inside and outside.

A job is considered "inside" if the worker spends approximately 75 percent or more of his time inside, and "outside" if he spends approximately 75 percent or more of his time outside. A job is considered "both" if the activities occur inside or outside in approximately equal amounts.

2. EXTREMES OF COLD PLUS TEMPERATURE CHANGES

Extremes of cold: Temperature sufficiently low to cause marked bodily discomfort unless the worker is provided with exceptional protection.

Temperature changes: Variations in temperature which are sufficiently marked and abrupt to cause noticeable bodily reactions.

3. EXTREMES OF HEAT PLUS TEMPERATURE CHANGES

Extremes of heat: Temperature sufficiently high to cause marked bodily discomfort unless the worker is provided with exceptional protection.

Temperature changes: Variations in temperature which are sufficiently marked and abrupt to cause noticeable bodily reactions.

4. WET AND HUMID

Wet: Contact with water or other liquids.

Humid: Atmospheric condition with moisture content sufficiently high to cause marked bodily discomfort.

5. NOISE AND VIBRATION
Sufficient noise, either constant or intermittent, to cause marked distraction or possible injury to the sense of hearing and/or sufficient vibration (production of an oscillating movement or strain on the body or its extremities from repeated motion or shock) to cause bodily harm if endured day after day.

6. HAZARDS   Situations in which the individual is exposed to the definite risk of bodily injury.

7. FUMES, ODORS, TOXIC CONDITIONS, DUST, AND POOR VENTILATION

Fumes: Smoky or vaporous exhalations, usually odorous, thrown off as a result of combustion or chemical reaction.

Odors: Noxious smells, either toxic or nontoxic.

Toxic conditions: Exposure to toxic dust, fumes, gases, vapors, mists, or liquids which cause general or localized disabling conditions as a result of inhalation or action on the skin.

Dust: Air filled with small particles of any kind such as textile dust, flour, wood, leather, feathers, etc., and inorganic dust, including silica and asbestos, which make the workplace unpleasant or are the source of occupational diseases.

Poor ventilation: Insufficient movement of air causing a feeling of suffocation; or exposure to drafts.

C

Definitions of Fleishman's Human Abilities

Following are the definitions of the 37 human abilities identified by Fleishman.* This list represents what is probably the best available inventory of the most important human abilities.

1. VERBAL COMPREHENSION This is the ability to understand language. It is concerned with the understanding of individual words as well as words as they appear in context, i.e., in sentences, grammatical patterns and idiomatic phrases. In terms of communication, this ability is limited to the receiver of information; it does *not* apply to the sender or communicator.

2. VERBAL EXPRESSION This is the ability to utilize language (either oral or written) to communicate information or ideas to another person or persons. It requires the production and utilization of individual words or

*Theologus, G. C., T. Romashko, and E. A. Fleishman. *Development of a Taxonomy of Human Performance.* Technical Report No. 5. Washington, D.C.: American Institutes for Research, 1970.

of words in context (i.e., in phrases, sentences, etc.) to express ideas or factual information. Neither the actual production of the ideas nor questions relating to *the quality of an idea* are included under this ability. The ability is concerned *solely* with the *quality of the communication* of such ideas. Quality of communication can be thought of as depending upon factors such as (1) size of one's vocabulary, (2) knowledge of distinctions among words, and (3) knowledge of grammar and syntax.

3. IDEATIONAL FLUENCY This is the ability to produce a number of ideas concerning a given topic. It is only concerned with the *number* of ideas produced and does *not* extend to the quality of those ideas.

4. ORIGINALITY This is the ability to produce unusual or clever responses related to a given topic or situation. It is the ability to improvise solutions to problems or to develop procedures in situations where standard operating procedures do not apply. This ability is concerned with the *degree of creativity of responses* and does not deal with the number of responses made.

5. MEMORIZATION This is the ability to memorize and retain new information which occurs as a regular or routine part of the task. These new bits of information must be memorized to properly accomplish or carry out the task. This ability does not extend either to the memorization of the task procedures or to the recall of any information previously learned outside of the given task situation.

6. PROBLEM SENSITIVITY This is the ability to *recognize* or *identify* the *existence* of problems. It includes the specification of the problem as a whole as well as recognition of the elements of the problem. This ability encompasses all types of problems whether they be figural, symbolic, or semantic. However, the ability does *not* include any of the reasoning necessary for the solution of a problem.

7. MATHEMATICAL REASONING This is the ability to reason abstractly using quantitative concepts and symbols. It encompasses reasoning through mathematical problems in order to determine appropriate operations which can be performed to solve them. It also includes the *understanding or structuring* of mathematical problems. The actual manipulation of numbers is *not* included in this ability.

8. NUMBER FACILITY This is the ability to manipulate numbers in numerical operations; for example, add, subtract, multiply, divide, integrate, differentiate, etc. The ability involves both the speed and accuracy of computation.

9. DEDUCTIVE REASONING This is the ability to apply general concepts or rules to specific cases or to proceed from stated premises to their logical conclusions. This ability can also be termed syllogistic reasoning or analytic reasoning in that progression is from the *whole to the parts*.

10. INDUCTIVE REASONING This is the ability to find the most appropriate general concepts or rules which fit sets of data or which explain how a given series of individual items are related to each other. It involves the

ability to synthesize disparate facts; to logically proceed from *individual cases to general principles.* It also involves the ability to form hypotheses about relationships among items or data.

11. INFORMATION ORDERING   This is the ability to apply rules or objectives to given information in order to arrange that information into the best or most *appropriate sequence.* The types of information considered under this ability include numbers, letters, words, pictures, procedures, sentences, and mathematical or logical operations. Rules or objectives for ordering *must first be provided* to the operator or subject in the task.

12. CATEGORY FLEXIBILITY   This is the ability to produce alternative groupings or categorizations for a set of items, based upon rules or specifications produced by the individual who is carrying out the categorization. Each alternative group must contain at least two items from the initial list, but any specific set of alternative groups need not contain all of the items from the initial list.

13. SPATIAL ORIENTATION   This is the ability to *maintain one's orientation* with respect to objects in space or to *comprehend the position* of objects in space with respect to the observer's position. The question posed is often "If the environment looks like this, what is my position?"

14. VISUALIZATION   This is the ability to manipulate or transform the visual images of spatial patterns or objects into other spatial arrangements. It requires the formation of mental images of the patterns or objects as they would appear *after certain specified changes* such as unfolding, rotation, or movement of some type. The transformation or set of transformations the observer is asked to make may involve either entire spatial patterns or objects or parts of those patterns or objects. The observer predicts what an object, set of objects or pattern would look like after the specified changes were actually carried out.

15. SPEED OF CLOSURE   This ability involves the speed with which a set of apparently disparate sensory elements can be combined and organized into a single, meaningful pattern or configuration. The operator must combine *all* the elements presented from a single source of information into a meaningful configuration. He is *not told* what he is trying to identify; the elements appear to be disparate. This ability applies to all senses with the restriction that elements to be combined must be presented within the *same sensory modality.*

16. FLEXIBILITY OF CLOSURE   This is the ability to identify or detect a *previously specified* stimulus configuration which is embedded in a more complex sensory field. It is the ability to isolate the specified relevant stimulus from a field where distracting stimulation *is intentionally included* as part of the task to be performed. *Only one* information source is utilized. This ability applies to all senses with the restriction that both the relevant and distracting stimulation must occur *within the same sense modality.*

17. SELECTIVE ATTENTION   This is the ability to perform a task in the presence of distracting stimulation or under monotonous conditions with-

out significant loss in efficiency. When distracting stimulation is present in the task situation, it is not an integral part of the task being performed, but rather is extraneous to the task and imposed upon it. The task and the irrelevant stimulation can occur either within the same sense or across senses. Under conditions of distracting stimulation, the ability involves concentration on the task being performed and filtering out of the distracting stimulation. When the task is performed under monotonous conditions only concentration on the task being performed is involved.

18. TIME SHARING   This is the ability to utilize information obtained by shifting between two or more channels of information. The information obtained from these sources is either integrated and used as a whole or retained and used separately.

19. PERCEPTUAL SPEED   This ability involves the speed with which sensory patterns or configurations can be *compared* in order to determine identity or degree of similarity. Comparisons may be made either between successively or simultaneously presented patterns or configurations, or between *remembered* or standard configurations and *presented* configurations. The sensory patterns to be compared must occur *within the same sense* and not between senses.

20. STATIC STRENGTH   This ability involves the *degree* of muscular force exerted against a fairly immovable or heavy *external object* in order to lift, push, or pull that object. Force is exerted *continuously* up to the amount needed to move the object. This ability is general to different muscle groups (e.g., hand, arm, back, shoulder, leg). This ability does not extend to prolonged exertion of physical force over time and is not concerned with the number of times the act is repeated.

21. EXPLOSIVE STRENGTH   This is the ability to expend energy in one or a series of explosive muscular acts. The ability requires a mobilization of energy for a *burst* of muscular effort, rather than continuous strain, stress, or repeated exertion of muscles. The ability may be involved in propelling the body as in the activities of jumping or sprinting or in throwing objects for distance.

22. DYNAMIC STRENGTH   This ability involves the power of arm and trunk muscles to repeatedly, or continuously support or move the *body's own weight*. Emphasis is on resistance of the muscles to performance decrement when put under repeated or continuous stress.

23. STAMINA   This ability involves the capacity to maintain physical activity over *prolonged* periods of time. It is concerned with resistance of the *cardiovascular system* (heart and blood vessels) to breakdown.

24. EXTENT FLEXIBILITY   This is the ability to extend, flex, or stretch muscle groups. It concerns the *degree of flexibility* of muscle groups, but does *not* include repeated or speed flexing.

25. DYNAMIC FLEXIBILITY   This is the ability to make repeated trunk and/or limb flexing movements where both *speed* and *flexibility* of movement are required. It includes the ability of these muscles to recover from the strain and distortion of repeated flexing.

26. GROSS BODY EQUILIBRIUM   This is the ability to maintain the body in an upright position or to regain body balance especially in situations volve manipulation of objects (e.g., blocks, pencils), but does not extend to where equilibrium is threatened or temporarily lost. This ability involves only *body balance;* it does *not* extend to the balancing of objects.

27. CHOICE REACTION TIME   This is the ability to select and initiate the appropriate response relative to a given stimulus in the situation where *two or more stimuli* are possible and where the appropriate response is selected from *two or more* alternatives. The ability is concerned with the *speed* with which the appropriate response can be *initiated* and does not extend to the speed with which the response is carried out. This ability is independent of mode of stimulus presentation (auditory or visual) and also of type of response required.

28. REACTION TIME   This ability involves the *speed* with which a *single motor response* can be initiated after the onset of a *single stimulus.* It does *not* include the speed with which the response or movement is carried out. This ability is independent of the mode of stimulus presentation (auditory or visual) and also of the type of motor response required.

29. SPEED OF LIMB MOVEMENT   This ability involves the *speed* with which discrete movements of the arms or legs can be made. The ability deals with the speed with which the movement can be carried out after it has been initiated; it is not concerned with the speed of initiation of the movement. In addition, the precision, accuracy and coordination of the movement is not considered under this ability.

30. WRIST-FINGER SPEED   This ability is concerned with the speed with which discrete movements of the fingers, hands, and wrists can be made. The ability is not concerned with the speed of initiation of the movement. It is only concerned with the speed with which the movement is carried out. This ability does not consider the question of the accuracy of the movement; nor does it depend upon precise eye-hand coordination.

31. GROSS BODY COORDINATION   This is the ability to *coordinate* movements of the *trunk and limbs.* This ability is most commonly found in situations where the entire body is in motion or being propelled.

32. MULTILIMB COORDINATION   This is the ability to coordinate the movements of two or more limbs (e.g., two legs, two hands, one leg, and one hand). The ability does *not* apply to tasks in which trunk movements must be integrated with limb movements. It is most common to tasks where the body is at rest (e.g., seated or standing) while two or more limbs are in motion.

33. FINGER DEXTERITY   This is the ability to make skillful, coordinated movements of the fingers where manipulations of objects may or may not be involved. This ability does *not* extend to manipulation of machine or equipment control mechanisms. Speed of movement is *not* involved in this ability.

34. MANUAL DEXTERITY   This is the ability to make skillful, coordinated movements of a hand, or of a hand together with its arm. This abil-

ity is concerned with coordination of movement within the limb. It may involve manipulation of objects (e.g., blocks, pencils), but does not extend to machine or equipment controls (e.g., levers, dials).

35. ARM-HAND STEADINESS   This is the ability to make precise, steady arm-hand positioning movements where both strength and speed are minimized. It includes steadiness during movement as well as minimization of tremor and drift while maintaining a static arm position. This ability does *not* extend to the adjustment of equipment controls (e.g., levers, dials).

36. RATE CONTROL   This is the ability to make timed, anticipatory motor adjustments relative to *changes* in the speed and/or direction of a continuously moving object. The purpose of the motor adjustments is to intercept or follow a continuously moving stimulus whose speed and/or direction vary in an *unpredictable* fashion. This ability does not extend to situations in which both the speed and direction of the object are perfectly predictable.

37. CONTROL PRECISION   This is the ability to make controlled muscular movements necessary to adjust or position a machine or equipment control mechanism. The adjustments can be anticipatory motor movements in response to changes in the speed and/or direction of a moving object whose speed *and* direction are perfectly predictable.

Index